The Center Cannot Hold

Jenna N. Hanchey

The Center

DUKE UNIVERSITY PRESS   Durham and London   2023

Cannot Hold

Decolonial Possibility in the
Collapse of a Tanzanian NGO

© 2023 DUKE UNIVERSITY PRESS. ALL RIGHTS RESERVED.

Designed by Courtney Leigh Richardson
Typeset in Portrait and Fengardo Neue by Westchester Publishing Services

Library of Congress Cataloging-in-Publication Data
Names: Hanchey, Jenna N., [date] author.
Title: The center cannot hold : decolonial possibility in the collapse of a Tanzanian NGO / Jenna N. Hanchey.
Description: Durham : Duke University Press, 2023. | Includes bibliographical references and index.
Identifiers: LCCN 2022048900 (print)
LCCN 2022048901 (ebook)
ISBN 9781478020462 (paperback)
ISBN 9781478019978 (hardcover)
ISBN 9781478024569 (ebook)
Subjects: LCSH: Non-governmental organizations—Tanzania—History. | Decolonization—Tanzania. | Ethnology—Fieldwork—Moral and ethical aspects. | Tanzania—Politics and government—1964– | BISAC: HISTORY / Africa / East | SOCIAL SCIENCE / Ethnic Studies / African Studies
Classification: LCC DT448.2 .H36 2023 (print) | LCC DT448.2 (ebook) | DDC 361.7/709678—dc23/eng/20230208
LC record available at https://lccn.loc.gov/2022048900
LC ebook record available at https://lccn.loc.gov/2022048901

Cover art: *Gazing into Tomorrow*, 2019. Tanzania. Photo courtesy of the author.

To the people of the Little Community
and everyone who has been forced to act
around structures and push through cracks
in order to survive and thrive

In memory of Joseph Chow

Acknowledgments ix

INTRODUCTION
The Center Cannot Hold   1

1	Doctors with(out) Burdens	25	Part I
2	All of Us Phantasmic Saviors	58	
3	Haunted Reflexivity	88	

CONTENTS

Part II

4 Water in the Cracks 117

5 Fluid (Re)mapping 141

6 Things Fall Apart 163

CONCLUSION
Rivulets in the Ruins 185

Notes 195

Bibliography 217

Index 231

ACKNOWLEDGMENTS

The Center Cannot Hold only exists because of the many people who have graciously decided that I am worth the effort of befriending, loving, critiquing, and teaching. The relationships I have with communities, friends, and colleagues have molded me into the person able to write this book: someone willing to reflect over the ways I related to others in the past, examine how that affects me now, and labor to engage more justly with the world in the future. Many people who helped in forming the best parts of this manuscript are listed below, but many are not—those with whom I've had intellectual conversations over the years, whom I've only met through their works, whose names I don't know, or whose comments affected my thinking below my conscious ability to recognize it. I appreciate you all.

Foremost in my mind are the people at the nongovernmental organization (NGO) that, in this book, I've called Little Community (the name is a pseudonym). Nawashukuru kwa kila siku mliniruhusu kukaa nayi. Nilijifunza sana, na mlinionyesha mambo mengi kuhusu maisha na kazi kwenye NGO yenu, hasa ninyi mliozungumza nami. Asante sana kwa kuniamini na hadithi, maoni, mazungumzo, na mambo yenu. Natumaini niliyatumia vizuri ndani ya kitabu hiki. Nawataka kila la heri. (I am thankful every day that you allowed me to stay with you all. I learned so much, and you showed me many things about your lives and work in your NGO, especially those of you who had conversations with me. Thank you for trusting me with your stories, views, conversations, and other issues. I hope that I used them well in this book. I wish you every blessing.)

Beyond those at the NGO, there are many people in Tanzania whose friendships and guidance set me on the road to writing this book. To my Tanzanian family, Baba and Mama Wangwe, Toni, Patricia, Fani, and Priscilla, who helped teach me Swahili, how to live well, and always encouraged me to be free, I love and miss you all so much. To my students at Hagati Secondary School, I am so happy to see the amazing things you're doing now and honored to be a part of your lives.

The research trips to the NGO were made possible by multiple fellowships, grants, and releases. As a graduate student I was lucky to be granted a Jesse H. Jones Fellowship from the Moody College of Communication, as well as a three-year William C. Powers Graduate Fellowship, at the University of Texas at Austin (UT), which made two trips to the NGO possible. My research travel was also supported by a grant from the Organization for Research on Women and Communication. The first trip to the NGO was for fieldwork proper, but the second was just as important, as it allowed me to present my initial findings to the Tanzanian staff and receive their feedback and input. At my previous academic position at the University of Nevada, Reno, start-up teaching releases allowed for preliminary drafting of the manuscript. Finally, grant support from the Waterhouse Family Institute for the Study of Communication and Society at Villanova University provided the funding for returning to the Little Community a few years later, as well as the ability to help facilitate initial meetings of the project that grew out of it, Youth Leaders Tanzania.

From the inception of my research at UT, Dana Cloud and Joshua Gunn believed in this project and helped shepherd its development. Similarly, I was lucky enough to meet a cohort of people through Toyin Falola's course, "Subaltern Studies," to grow and learn with over those years: Abimbola Adelakun, Dotun Ayobade, Shery Chanis, Ogechukwu Ezekwem Williams, Cacee Hoyer, Daniel Jean-Jacques, Sheela Jane Menon, Hallie Ringle, and Mariana Sabino. I am grateful to have had the support of Teddy Albiniak, Lamiyah Bahrainwala, Robert Carroll, Diane Davis, Kristyn Goldberg, Tiara Na'puti, Erin O'Connor, Cynthia Peacock, Marnie Ritchie, Rae Rozman, Emily Scheinfeld, Beck Wise, and many others throughout my time in Austin and after. Simone Browne's brilliant teaching, scholarship, and mentorship has been integral to the development of my thought, and her guidance throughout the process of publishing has meant the world to me. Her support and advocacy made this book possible, from generously overseeing my independent study to connecting me to my editor at Duke University Press, Elizabeth Ault. I am so grateful to Elizabeth for challenging me to make this a better book than I could have imagined it to be while simultaneously giving me the tools and encouragement to make it happen. The anonymous readers also strengthened each part of the manuscript and spurred me to dig deeper in my critiques of whiteness and coloniality at every turn. I cannot express the depth of my appreciation for their careful readings and insightful comments.

I'm honored to have been supported by many friends and colleagues while drafting and revising the manuscript. Utmost thanks is due to Godfried Asante, who helped me work through frameworks and ideas and who provided comments on the entire manuscript when it was completed. Graham B. Slater also read through multiple versions of the manuscript, making it tighter and stronger every time. Much of the thought reflected here stems from the growing African intellectual community in communication studies, and particularly my collaborations with Godfried Asante, Joëlle M. Cruz, Nthemba C. Mutua-Mambo, and Gloria Pindi Nziba, as well as the mentorship of Eddah Mutua. The #ToneUpOrgComm Collective, comprising Joëlle M. Cruz, Elizabeth Eger, Angela Gist-Mackey, Kate Lockwood Harris, Peter R. Jensen, Sean Kenney, and Kathryn Joan Leslie, provided crucial support throughout the writing process. I'm particularly indebted to all those who provided feedback on chapters from the manuscript in progress: Nicole Allen, Lamiyah Bahrainwala, Jon Carter, Joëlle Cruz, Jamie Downing, Kate Lockwood Harris, Kristen Hoerl, Lydia Huerta, Peter R. Jensen, Lore/tta LeMaster, Anushka Peres, and Sohinee Roy. Kristen Hoerl and Casey Ryan Kelly are always there to help me through rejections and make me feel like a "real" rhetoric scholar, no matter what strange ideas I bring to the table. I'm inspired by those whose decolonial and anticolonial thought is transforming the shape of rhetoric, especially Roberta Chevrette, E Cram, Catalina de Onís, Michael Lechuga, Ashley Noel Mack, Tiara R. Na'puti, and Darrel Wanzer-Serrano. I hope that this book adds something meaningful to the impressive work already being done.

I appreciate all of the people who kept me going, even through the hardest parts of this process. Climbing and exploring with Caitlin Earley, Lydia Huerta, Ruthie Meadows, and Anushka Peres helped us all learn to "stand and reach." Writing dates with my advisees, Sam Gillespie, Michael Klajbor, and Ana Ortiz-Martinez, assisted with my process as much as theirs. The amazing friends I made through *not* getting a job—Nicole Allen, Chase Aunspach, Jon Carter, and Jamie Downing—kept me sane through silly memes and rounds of Dungeons & Dragons. Ross Haroldson, Laura Igarabuza, Leiha Lynn, Kate Scully-Ortega, and Andy Tompsett have seen me at my best and my worst and stuck with me through it all. The world is better because you all are in it. Reno would not have been the same without the friendship of Michael Ackermann, Nasia Anam, Sarah Blithe, Jared Bok, David Anthony Durham, Robert Gutierrez-Perez, Kjerstin Gruys, Gudrun Johnston, Ignacio Montoya, Laura Urban, Tennley Vik, and Ben Yust. At two points this manuscript needed a catalyst to get (re)started. Sarah Blithe provided the first through generously hosting a writing retreat at Lake Tahoe, and Tracy Van Epps convinced me to find the second by booking myself a hotel room when the pandemic had me spinning my wheels at home for weeks. Erika McAfee, Megan Sorensen, Tracy Van Epps—everyone needs a "woo crew" like you. When I went searching for decolonial futures in the realm of speculative fiction, Codex Writers' Forum became integral to the development of my imagination. I am so grateful for the magnitude and quality of support that the Codex community provides— they even won a Locus Award for it! My family also creates new avenues for imagination in their often delightful weirdness—especially Trent Craft, Alaina Hanchey, Nate Hanchey, Pippin Schroeder, and Claire Witcher. Dad and Mom, I'm thankful for your love and care, no matter what new project I've thrown myself into this time.

Parts of this manuscript expand on previously published work. Chapter 1 is derived in part from the article "Doctors without Burdens: The Neocolonial Ambivalence of White Masculinity in International Medical Aid," in *Women's Studies in Communication* 42, no. 1 (2019): 39-59, https://www.tandfonline.com/doi/abs/10.1080/07491409.2019.1576084. Chapter 2 builds on the article "All of Us Phantasmic Saviors," in *Communication and Critical/Cultural Studies* 15, no. 2 (2018): 144-49, https://www.tandfonline.com/doi/abs/10.1080/14791420.2018.1454969.

To all of you who gifted me with your intimacy, critique, thoughts, and stories, however small or fleeting, I appreciate you. I hope to look back on this book in the future and marvel at what you taught me, as well as how much I had yet to learn.

Introduction
The Center
Cannot Hold

Turning and turning in the widening gyre
The falcon cannot hear the falconer;
Things fall apart; the centre cannot hold;
Mere anarchy is loosed upon the world.
—W. B. Yeats, "The Second Coming," quoted
by Chinua Achebe in *Things Fall Apart*

Falling Apart

I spent the longest hours of my life sitting by a dying fire in a stranger's kitchen, watching as the coals slowly dimmed, leaving me alone in the dark. Hours passed as I sat, invisible, waiting. Waiting for the authorities to come, waiting for the past to undo itself, waiting to wake up from what had to be a dream. I was caught in a loop, repeating, "It's all my fault. It's all my fault," over and over and over again, rocking back and forth to accompany the rhythm of the words, replaying his fall like a scene from a film, over and over and over again. My phone was dead, my friend was dead, and I was falling apart.

I spent 2007–9 teaching Ordinary Level (O-Level) physics and mathematics in a rural government school in the Hagati Valley of the Ruvuma Region in the United Republic of Tanzania.[1] My friend Joe had come to visit, using some of his final time in-country as a Peace Corps volunteer to see beautiful sights before returning to the United States. I happened to live within hiking distance of Lake Nyasa, as well as what was colloquially rumored to be the second largest rock in East Africa, Mbuji. I had climbed it three times before. How had the danger not sunk in?

That night in 2009, falling apart felt like the end of the world. It has taken over a decade—multiple trips back and forth between Tanzania and the United States, and the writing of this book—for me to understand that it was the end of *a* world, of the ways I had been knowing the world.[2] And that from the end of a world can emerge something different. And that different worlds hold the potential to become more just. Better.

As I later reflected in field notes, I felt like I was falling apart because of the way my sense of self was dependent on African objectification: "Joe's death had shattered my volunteer image of Tanzania—as a time-out from 'real' life ... a dreamland, a place where you make things happen, but nothing happens to you. Because if it did, then it would not be the fantasy that you have created. It would be something tangible, something important, something agentic." The way Westerners understand ourselves is dependent, at least in part, on *not* recognizing, listening to, and learning from Africans.[3] We create and re-create ourselves through fantasies of Africa based on logics of whiteness and coloniality that disavow African agency and allow us to fashion ourselves saviors. We build on these notions of self to create nongovernmental organizations (NGOs), to offer aid. What, then, happens to Western selves and organizations when their (neo)colonial foundation is shaken? Or even when it cracks, breaks, falls apart?

Almost a decade after Joe's death, I assisted the North American managers of the Little Community, an NGO in the Mikoda village area where I had spent years doing ethnographic fieldwork,[4] in plotting what they termed "a coup" to overthrow the (neo)colonial white administrator of the organization. Sarah and Tim had long worked with the Tanzanian steering committee of the NGO, the Viongozi Wa Shirika, to run the organization in a way that moved toward a future of complete Tanzanian leadership. But after a decade of continual pushback from the British colonist who sat as chairman of the board, Mr. Giles, the NGO staff could no longer hold the organization together under the increasing tensions between their desired future and the neocolonial structures he enforced. And the Little Community fell apart.

In both of these cases, as things fell apart I began to understand exactly how little of these structures of self and organization had been solid in the first place. It took falling apart to recognize the flows of transformation that had been acting within and on us the whole time. At the Little Community, the

Viongozi Wa Shirika, with Sarah and Tim, had been slowly infiltrating the hierarchy and procedures emplaced by Mr. Giles, drops of water that had found holes in the solid order of the organization. The drops expanded those holes, slowly increasing in force to become streams, pushing, wearing away, until they cracked the walls. I, like Mr. Giles and other Westerners, had attempted to impose solidity by refusing to see myself as anything but coherent. In doing so I had missed the channels and disruptions that impacted my understanding of myself, as well as the opportunities they offered for transformation. Rather than reinforcing collapsing structures in vain, what happens if we follow the rivulets out of the ruins?

Situating the Study

The Center Cannot Hold argues that processes of ruination and collapse hold decolonial potential. I focus on two particular "centers" often assumed to be worth maintaining: first, the subjective coherence of Western volunteers and researchers, not least myself; and second, the operational structure of an internationally funded NGO in rural Tanzania. I argue that allowing such structures to fall apart, even when it may seem to bring nothing but destruction, is necessary to build decolonial futures. Part I focuses on Western subjectivities, building toward a theoretical argument for *haunted reflexivity*. Tired of seeing academics list identity categories (e.g., white, Western, woman) and then act as if the labor of reflexivity were complete,[5] I have developed the concept of haunted reflexivity, which stages how privileged subjects, who are trained not to see the violence of coloniality that we participate in and uphold every day, come to critical awareness through repeated encounters with our own complicity. Only by facing the ghosts of (neo)colonialism and our own hand in their creation, over and over again, can Western subjects transform into decolonial coconspirators. But we can never fully recognize all the ways that we have participated in or support (neo)colonial systems. Thus, haunted reflexivity is an unending process of (neo)colonial haunting, one that will never be finalized or complete.

Part II then shifts to the Little Community as an organization, using theories of liquid organizing and epistemological injustice to highlight what I term *liquid agency*. I define liquid agency as the ability to delink from and articulate opposition to the epistemologies of coloniality through emergent and contingent (re)actions based in relational and contextual connections. Liquid agency both precipitates and demonstrates the potential of the collapse of the NGO. I examine how the falling apart of the organizational structure produces the possibility for decolonial action. Moving around, against, and through solid structures, liquid agency opens paths to futures once deemed impossible. I conclude by describing how the creation of impossible futures depends on *decolonial dreamwork*. If the potential for decolonial futures arises when the center cannot hold, when things fall apart, then decolonial dreamwork is the labor required to imagine such futures and imbue them with the power to "draw us towards them, to command us to make them flesh."[6] Dreaming is important to this labor, as coloniality often circumscribes what is "possible" and "impossible" according to white, Western norms as well as neoliberal capitalist demands. By daring to dream outside these bounds, new worlds may be created: the impossible is turned into the possible.

This book draws together rhetoric, fugitive anthropology, critical development studies, and Women of Color feminisms to investigate how North American donors, volunteers, and workers in a Tanzanian NGO engage in communication with and about Tanzanian counterparts and aid recipients in ways that are both decolonial and neocolonial, and how the NGO acts as the locus of these contradictory approaches. At the same time, I investigate how US subjects who wish to engage critically with aid work and processes of development also embody a locus of (de)colonial contradiction, one that operates at the heart of subjectivity itself. In doing so, I thus connect the localized and tangible rhetorics used within aid work to those more disperse rhetorics of power and ideology used to sustain our understandings of ourselves.

I draw from these four particular fields of study for important reasons. The decolonial politics of my study resonate with critical development studies, which has long recognized that aid is not an unquestioned good and often acts to support neocolonial politics and imperialistic financial relations.[7] In large part, the West caused the exigencies seen as requiring developmental aid and is only in the position to "fix" such problems because of centuries spent stealing resources, destabilizing governmental forms, and colonizing and enslaving people.[8] Aid to Africa, in particular, traffics in representations of the continent that figure African circumstances as abject and African people as unable to act on their own behalf, thus requiring Western intervention.[9] These portrayals are also attached to material consequences, as the West derives financial gain from undermining African agency.[10]

Yet development scholars are often more focused on the big picture of global development than the details of lived experience. Erin Beck suggests that "while social scientists are generally interested in the fine-grained nature of people's lives, meanings, and motivations, this has not always been the case when it comes to those involved in NGOs or development projects."[11] To understand how people negotiate development politics in their particular contexts and lives, I couple the ideological critiques of critical development studies with the intimate insights of anthropological work. Anthropology points to the complexities of aid work in situated communities and how local actors play a fundamental role in the actualization of development plans. Notably, anthropology examines how Africans speak back to Western initiatives and have done so since the beginning of the colonial era, acting to reconfigure what development looks like.[12]

Yet, while critical and decolonial anthropologists have struggled for decades to reconcile contemporary anthropology with the discipline's colonial history, less attention has been paid to how issues of race and racialization are bound up with coloniality.[13] In order to examine how North American aid workers are caught up in logics of whiteness and patriarchy, as well as coloniality in Tanzania, I draw from the work of Women of Color feminists, who help us to think not only about how gender is imbricated in race and racialization but also how subjects themselves are the products of political relations.[14] As such, subjects become a locus of politics, carrying what would normally be considered the politics of the field around in their subjective experience and embodied presence. The home and the field, as with bodies and subjectivities, cannot be disentangled.[15] I carry the reverberations of my experiences with me wherever I go in ways that affect my understanding of and relations with people and places.

Rhetoric, then, ties all of these literatures together through a focus on how persuasive discourse mediates the divide between the macrolevel of ideological power structures and the microlevel of subjective statements and actions, as well as the divide between theoretical argument and subjective embodiment often upheld by disciplinary rifts. If "anthropology has downplayed ... the importance of theories of experience for understanding subjectivity,"[16] it is only responding in kind, as "crucial ethnographic and cross-cultural studies have even more rarely been taken up by philosophers, literary critics, feminist scholars, and other theorists writing about subjectivity."[17] Rhetoric can help to bridge this divide, bringing theories of subjectivity and embodied experiences into conversation to shed light on the suasive (dis)connections that support, in particular, US subjects' understandings of themselves as aid workers in relation to Tanzanians.

Rhetoric offers a means of tying the hyperlocal analyses of anthropology to global flows of racial and colonial power.[18] Particularly, I examine the ways that rampant neocolonial ideologies of white saviorism and North American exceptionalism are reconstructed, shifted, and challenged in the contact zone of a Western-funded but Tanzanian-implemented NGO.[19] And, perhaps more importantly, I am interested in what happens when an NGO becomes the center of that contact zone, when it attempts to hold together conflicting ideologies about aid and development—what happens when that center cannot hold and things fall apart.

Productive Ruination

When things break—whether they shatter immediately, scattering fragments that can never be reassembled into the shape they once were, or slowly dilapidate over time, losing chips, mechanisms, and boulders to corrosive forces—something is produced as ruination advances. Ann Laura Stoler defines *ruination* as "an active, ongoing process that allocates imperial debris differentially."[20] She draws from Derek Walcott's figuring of colonialism as "the 'rot' that remains" to examine how colonialism continues to act in dark corners and unexpected places, "eating away [at] bodies, environment, and possibilities,"[21] actively ruining lives of the colonized long after direct colonization has ended. Here I want to examine ruination in a slightly different manner. Can ruination emerge from not only the enduring forces of the colonizer but also the enduring resistance of the colonized? What might it look like to figure some processes of ruination as productive of possibilities for decolonization and justice?

The Center Cannot Hold examines how ruination may also affect structures emplaced by coloniality, as tensions between the colonial and decolonial act to tear them apart. Colonialism as rot affects not only the colonized but also the colonizer, albeit differentially. It poisons senses of ethics and politics, it leaves paternalism or hate where there should be care, it predicates development on domination.[22] If we are "to sharpen our senses and sense of how to track the tangibilities of empire as effective histories of the present,"[23] we should look to the ruination of neocolonial structures as well, and how their falling apart produces spaces out of which more just relations can emerge. Throughout the book I trace two processes of productive ruination: the dissolution of the NGO, unable to handle the contradictions between Tanzanian leadership and paternalistic relations; and the unstable subjectivity of Western volunteers—and myself as a researcher—unable to hold the contradictions between white savior and decolonial coconspirator, watching over and over as the self each of us thought we were continually falls apart. Tracing the concepts of haunted reflexivity and liquid agency through these processes, I argue that what waits on the other side of ruination is the possibility of decolonial justice.

Nongovernmental organizations are tenuous creatures, so often fighting for their own survival that they forget survival is not supposed to be the point.[24]

As Peace Corps volunteers we were often told that our mission was to work ourselves out of a job, but few development organizations can be said to substantively demonstrate this mission. Instead, Western-led international NGOs spend more of their time and energy catering to donors in whatever ways are necessary to secure funding than they do making sure that their services are what the people receiving them want, let alone providing services that guarantee lasting structural change.[25] In such NGOs, the emergent mission becomes ensuring financial stability rather than ensuring social justice. Erin Beck identifies this and similar tensions as generalizable throughout the NGO world, describing them as conflicts between developmental goals and organizational goals that arise from Westerners' "simplified views of the other."[26] It only makes sense, if they are generalizable to the structure of international NGOs, that sometimes these tensions must pull the entire organizational structure apart.

The Little Community grew into itself over the course of a decade, transitioning from a one-dormitory orphanage into a thriving mini-community containing a preschool, kindergarten, sewing school, medical clinic, and farm in addition to six homes where children lived. In these homes the children lived as families, with housemothers or -fathers from their tribe, and had regular contact with extended family or guardians in the nearby villages. Rather than providing a path to foster care or adoption, the Little Community worked to make sure that the young people would have a place in their home village when they reached a point where either their guardians were able to take them home to care for them or they were able to care for themselves. Projects stretched beyond the outskirts of Little Community as well, as its employees ran a Home-Based Care initiative for HIV/AIDS patients, planned events with local schools at the NGO's community hall in the nearby village center, and met with government officials to keep everything running smoothly and in line with community desires.

Over the past few years, however, the Little Community I knew has been slowly disintegrating. Gone are more than half of the employees that were there during my stay; after Sarah and Tim resigned, Mr. Giles took over the finances and slashed the budget, downsizing the staff considerably. Although he promoted a Tanzanian staff member to the position of manager, Mr. Giles retained control of all money, as well as hiring and firing decisions. Many women decided to leave the NGO to go back to school, studying to be hospitality managers. Sarah and Tim's plan to "stage a coup" did not come to fruition, but they partnered with two staff members, Musa and Faraji, to together begin a new NGO.

What is produced when an NGO falls apart, undergoes ruination, begins to rot, and particularly an NGO that was created by a British colonist whose colonial sensibilities were encased in the structuring logics that acted to filter interactions, relations, and projects? As I have suggested elsewhere, decolonizing aid work may require destroying its organizations.[27] In this case, it is in the ruins of the NGO that we may find the potential for an organization premised on delinking from coloniality, starting not from scratch but from the ruins that rot has left behind, building from both the desire for decoloniality and the negation of neocolonial domination.

This book describes both the US subject and the NGO as the epicenter of tensions and contradictions that each eventually is unable to continue to hold in place. I am not exempt from such contradictions as a white, US researcher.[28] The first part of the book thus culminates in my own subjective (de)colonial contradictions, with my own falling apart. In this book's titular twin, professor of law and psychoanalyst Elyn Saks writes of her struggles with schizophrenia. What she describes as the "disorganization" of schizophrenia is not unique to the disorder. The coherence of any subject is a fiction, a fantasy used to cover our structural inability to be whole and complete.[29] Though to a lesser degree than those dealing with schizophrenia, all subjects must continually labor to keep their subjective center together and keep things from falling apart. I will discuss this view of subjectivity further in chapters 2 and 3. Saks describes her personal experiences with the disorganization of losing her center in the following manner:

> Consciousness gradually loses it coherence. One's center gives way. The center cannot hold. The "me" becomes a haze, and the solid center from which one experiences reality breaks up like a bad radio signal. There is no longer a sturdy vantage point from which to look out, take things in, assess what's happening. No core holds things together, providing the lens through which to see the world, to make judgments and comprehend risk. Random moments of time follow one another. Sights, sounds, thoughts, and feelings don't go together. No organizing principle takes successive moments of time and puts them together in a coherent way from which sense can be made. And it's all taking place in slow motion.[30]

If all subjects do not experience such moments of intense destabilization, it is only because they are able to hold tightly to the organizing principles that social and cultural formations provide for them; but to do so, for any subject, is a constant form of labor because subjective consistency is a fantasy that can fall apart at any time. Coherence is a fiction—not only that, but an ideological fiction. All organizing principles, all means to solidify subjective coherence—however fictional and fleeting—are necessarily political. The ways that we organize reality are products of and productive of power. And for contemporary colonizers, in particular, it can be necessary for the center to dissolve in order to reframe our subjective realities in decolonial ways. As I will discuss in chapter 3, when subjects encounter parts of their own political structuring that have been foreclosed from conscious thought, falling apart is necessary to a reflexivity that aims toward justice.[31] Similarly, in chapter 6, I look to how the organization itself needs to dissolve for new organizing logics to take hold. Sometimes it is from the collapse of the center that decoloniality may emerge.

The Decolonial Potential of Liquidity

I contend that shattering not only fragments subjects and organizations but also offers a means to rebuild them in ways that epistemologically and ontologically break from coloniality. As such, my research at the Little Community was premised on a decolonial politics. I draw from this body of work, rather than alternative approaches, because decolonial theory necessarily moves us beyond critiques of neocolonialism into dismantling structures and recognizing alternative epistemologies. Yet as my research simultaneously examines what Western rhetorics and US subjective understandings produce in the contact zone of the NGO, I couple decolonial goals with critique.

Rather than maintain a typical anthropological focus on "the other,"[32] I turn the lens of critique onto North American subjects—though maintaining a relational understanding that attempts to avoid recentering domination—in order to search for destabilizing shifts that provide opportunities to decolonize NGO relations.[33] Ultimately I find that attempts from within to decolonize the NGO—or US subjectivities—can never be enough; the structures of the Western subject and international organization are so strongly moored in neocolonialism that it takes a shattering of the center to provide substantive decolonial transformation.

Darrel Wanzer defines coloniality as "a constitutive feature of Western modernity that structures exclusionary modes of power, knowledge, and being—it is the dark underside of modernity, which influences both first and third world people."[34] What Walter Mignolo terms "modernity/coloniality" undergirds the modern world system, differentially distributing ontologies and epistemologies in ways that secure Western hegemony. Decolonial theory then seeks to delink from modernity/coloniality by opening space for alternative rationalities and epistemic freedom, as well as ontological space for being human outside the delimitations of Man.[35]

I use the term *coloniality* throughout this work to refer to contemporary configurations of power, with neocolonialism and epistemic injustice being two of the primary forms coloniality takes within the Little Community and its relations. *Colonialism*, then, refers to the historical system of occupation, control, and subjugation that still has ramifications within contemporary coloniality. I will sometimes use the combination *(neo)colonial* to denote when relations demonstrate aspects of both colonialism and neocolonialism at the same time, such as settlements on land that reflect colonial logics of occupation simultaneous to neocolonial logics of use. Finally, I use *postcolonial* as a temporal marker to denote the shift from direct colonialism to the more disperse coloniality.

This book particularly looks to the ways that coloniality has led to African subjective and epistemological erasure and how the collapse of Western subjectivities and NGO structures based in such erasures can make way for decolonial possibility and epistemic justice.[36] Sabelo Ndlovu-Gatsheni argues that epistemic freedom forms the basis from which political and economic freedom can emerge in contemporary Africa. *The Center Cannot Hold* first examines Western subjectivities and how they uphold neocolonial relations, before turning to the way such unreflexive subjectivities then cause epistemological clashes with Tanzanian staff in the Little Community. As Ramón Grosfoguel asserts, "Decolonization of knowledge would require to take seriously the epistemic perspective/cosmologies/insights of critical thinkers from the Global South thinking *from* and *with* subalternized racial/ethnic/sexual spaces and bodies."[37] Part II of the book examines fluid epistemologies and liquid organizing practices that emerge from Tanzanian epistemologies and relations to marginalization, asking how taking such epistemologies and organizing seriously might transform the Little Community and other NGO contexts. This does not require an absolute abandonment of Western logics and rationalities, but rather an abandonment of their dominance or universality. Decolonial theory thus aims toward what Mignolo calls "a world in which many worlds can coexist," or what Ngũgĩ wa Thiong'o refers to as a "globalectic" view, where "any point is equally a center."[38]

Engaging with African epistemologies under conditions of coloniality is not as simple as it sounds, however. Joëlle Cruz and Chigozirim Utah Sodeke demonstrate this in regard to liquidity in particular. As African organizational scholars trained in the Western academy who returned to engage in fieldwork in Liberia and Nigeria, they found that their training made it difficult or even impossible to understand African means and epistemologies of organizing. As they write, "we were not prepared for the realities of researching organizing in motion due to our training that predisposed us to immobility."[39] They reflect over the ways that their Western training primed them to see "organizations" and "organizing" through a specific lens, one that was neither constructed for nor reflective of many African contexts.

Cruz and Sodeke put forth a theoretical lens capable of recognizing and understanding organizing as liquid, drawing from African epistemologies and contexts of marginality. They define liquid organizing as "so intertwined with political, economic, and cultural contexts at the margins . . . that it shape-shifts and moves like a liquid." Liquid organizing emerges from African epistemologies at the same time as it is forced on marginalized subjects by contexts of precarity. That is, Cruz and Sodeke note that "liquid organizing is normative in many non-Western contexts and anchored in alternative cultural logics," and yet, simultaneously, "globalization and neoliberalism push disenfranchised actors further into liquidity and in turn, actors use liquidity to circumvent survival threats and operate outside the realm of official actors."[40] Liquidity is thus both a means of surviving within economic disenfranchisement and global marginalization and of resisting their logics.

In part, liquidity breaks from the logics of coloniality by centering the importance of collectives and relations to the process of organizing. Whereas coloniality rests on assumptions of the liberal autonomous subject,[41] the ability to engage in liquid action depends on intimate relational networks. Elsewhere Cruz describes how African feminist organizing is "trust-based" and "integrated" into the community.[42] Similarly, liquid organizing only functions because of its "embeddedness . . . in context and local communities."[43] As fluid epistemologies reorient thinking and relationality, centering liquidity is one means of challenging the epistemic injustice that erases African ways of knowing.[44] This book engages in fluid epistemologies in a double sense: in the process of research itself, as an orientation to (inter)disciplinarity; and in the context of the Little Community, examining how liquid organizing and fluid epistemologies run into and work around the structures emplaced by coloniality. I detail both senses below.

Interdisciplinary Fluidity

Fluid thinking uses interdisciplinarity to level a critique of mainstream disciplinary structures from within. Rather than directly challenging disciplinary structures, fluid epistemologies channel disparate streams and flows, moving in and through solid disciplinary structures, often without their knowledge. Fluid epistemologies spill forth from disciplinary containers.[45] If decolonial work depends on undisciplining our thinking,[46] then a particularly salient undisciplining for decolonial work within the Little Community occurs at the intersection of rhetoric and anthropology. If anthropology is, on the one hand, obsessed with the exotic international other, and rhetoric is, on the other hand, girdled by the nation-state in its formulations of public and civic life, the meeting of the two produces a theoretical space where the NGO's messy intercultural relations and organizational strategies may be interrogated and reimagined in decolonial ways.[47] The fluidity of this work flows in ways that draws anthropology deeper into Western subjects' implication in interculturality and pushes rhetoric toward communal life as a global network.[48] Specifically, this book uses interdisciplinarity to stage an underground revolt against disciplinary limitations, refigure the subjective assumptions of Man, and organize through means different from those of typical activist scholarship.

The Center Cannot Hold will not resemble a typical anthropological or rhetorical text. As Aisha Beliso-De Jesús and Jemima Pierre state, "Mainstream anthropology continues to steer clear of analysis that centers race and processes of racialization," in addition to centering "the fetishization of a particular kind of ethnographic localization ... that tends to eschew broader structures of power."[49] Rhetoric can be said to have an opposing problem. Most critical rhetoricians locate their studies of coloniality, racialization, and gender within the construction and circulation of mediated discourse. This work critically examines representations of Africa and Africans, teases out the nuances of white saviorism and American exceptionalism, and investigates intersectional complexities.[50] Yet rhetoric is rarely connected to lived experience in the field.[51] Although rhetoricians have long assumed that hegemonic representations of and expectations regarding race, gender, and culture impact lived experience, they have only recently begun using fieldwork to investigate the relationship between mediated publicity and embodied interaction.[52] Many still do so, however, from a perspective that centers the nation-state, and particularly the United States, through citizenship logics of inclusion.[53] This book winds around such expectations, centering Western-Tanzanian intercultural relations on a global stage without reference to the state and eschewing logics of inclusion for the decolonial agency that arises from liquid maneuvers around and through such solid-seeming structures. Yet if "development interventions are ... interactive processes in which multiple dispositions, interests, and meanings conflict, interlock, and interpenetrate, and in which accommodation, reinterpretation, struggle, and adjustment are ongoing,"[54] then rhetorical scholarship still has something integral to offer in understanding how the politics of NGOs are negotiated on the ground, as well as the implications for global relations of power. But it must use alternative epistemologies to do so. As Tiara Na'puti argues, "Breaking from [its] history offers ways for Rhetorical Studies to become entirely different—constituted through non-Western perspectives and ways of knowing and being."[55]

Part of breaking from this history involves questioning the assumed white, masculine, Western liberal subject in which both anthropology and rhetoric are grounded. Maya Berry, Claudia Chávez Argüelles, Shanya Cordis, Sarah Ihmoud, and Elizabeth Velásquez Estrada "refuse the emblematic racially privileged male anthropologist" in a foreign land who grounds epistemologies of fieldwork in anthropology—even anthropology that claims activist goals.[56] Similarly, I have elsewhere written that when rhetorical scholars "absent bodies from discussions of theory, we implicitly ground our theories in somatic norms and tacitly accept their conditions—whiteness and coloniality—which circumscribe who the theories represent."[57] That is, even researchers who take an activist stance of partnering with participants to challenge dominant social structures often end up reifying the very racial, neocolonial, and heteropatriarchal dynamics they set out to critique. By examining how North American participants in intercultural communicative practices (re)construct racial, neocolonial, and gendered hegemonies derived from North American media and culture within a Tanzanian context, I am implicated as a researcher within the very rhetorics I analyze. Throughout *The Center Cannot Hold* I attempt to embrace my own complicity and interrogate what it means for theory and praxis. The concept of haunted reflexivity emerges from my struggle as a researcher to substantively theorize and put into practice what it means to do decolonial research as a colonizer, one whose very subjective bones are forged out of violence against others.

Even activist scholars often do not account for the violence out of which our subjectivities emerge, upholding instead "an implicit standard of whiteness and coloniality in our theorizing by starting from what Sylvia Wynter terms 'Man.'"[58] For one, the people that activist researchers are presumed to study are those who exist on the underside of modernity and do not hold any sort of hegemonic leverage, and the researcher is assumed to be in a position of relative dominance.[59] In this manner, activist research tends to mimic the politics of care that Miriam Ticktin describes, in which Western responsibility for the "wretched of the earth" places othered subjects outside context, obscures histories that placed them in marginalized positions, and produces only certain (raced, gendered, and sexualized) bodies as worth care.[60] At the same time, activist research also reinscribes the researcher as white savior.[61]

Thinking from a perspective that centers liquidity would make activism more dispersive, and also make the researcher who partners with a community an intimate part of the relational context required for emergent actions. Unlike typical activist research, there is no distinct and clear enemy to organize against. Rather, the struggle against structures of power in the postcolonial context is an ambivalent one. Godfried Asante describes ambivalence for queer Ghanaian subjects as a means of both engaging in and simultaneously undermining structures of power in ways that open possibilities for survival for marginalized subjects.[62] In the Little Community, the Tanzanian staff often must subvert Western donor desires without directly challenging them. As Damas put it, "We can't say we refuse, because we need the money." The Viongozi Wa Shirika had to find creative ways to resist in order to survive. As a researcher, then, I also have to think fluidly while recognizing that I am just as implicated within structures of whiteness and coloniality as the Western donors I would help the NGO leadership maneuver in different directions.

In the first draft of this manuscript, I tried to use the concept of fugitivity rather than fluidity to capture the resistance of Tanzanian NGO workers to neocolonial relations. This may not seem pertinent to the final work at first glance, but it reveals some of the more insidious ways that coloniality can affect research—even research that is explicitly attuned toward its implications. Through reviewer feedback and conversations with African friends and colleagues, I began to realize that though liquidity is related to fugitivity,[63] it does not figure quite the same relation to context. And to assume that fugitivity could be exported from diasporic theorizations into an African context is, in part, Western-centric.[64] Fugitivity emerges from the particular embedded histories of the African diaspora, drawing the primary concept of "flight" from the need to escape totalizing systems such as slavery and anti-Blackness and their inextricability from contemporary US life. For instance, fugitivity lays bare how diasporic subjects are encoded through lenses of criminality and madness when resisting the status quo.[65] But the neocolonial and racial formation of Tanzania is not nearly so totalizing as to make flight the only, or best, option for challenging systems of domination in-country. Certainly, NGOs in Africa participate in global contexts of neocolonialism.[66] And anti-Blackness still affects African subjects.[67] But in the postcolonial space of Tanzania, Indigenous relational structures, socialism and the fallout of villagization, and policies of non-racialism are just as formative to the contemporary context—if not more so—as are global structures of anti-Blackness and coloniality.

That is, the Little Community is situated within a historical context in which anti-Blackness and coloniality have important effects, but are not sedimented into the national structure in the way that they are in Western postslavery contexts. Ronald Aminzade describes how Tanzanian national development was based in "a common history of oppression by foreigners" rather than the ethnocentric nationalisms often seen in the West.[68] Tensions arose between desires for international legitimacy within the global economy and the ideological integrity of socialist principles within the nation. Tanzania's first president, Julius Nyerere, thus ingrained a focus on international class relations that sometimes obscured the importance of race in national and international dynamics. For instance, he saw "class struggle [as] less between the national bourgeoisie and the proletariat, than between the poor of the South and the rich of the North," leading to an inability to "accept that South Africans could have an exploitative relation with other African countries," even white South Africans.[69] Nyerere instead instituted policies of "non-racialism" in Tanzanian governance that failed to recognize whiteness and/or anti-Blackness as structuring forces.[70] After he stepped down as president in 1985, forthcoming leaders acceded to international pressures for neoliberal economic restructuring.[71] Tensions and contradictions between Tanzania's socialist history and the neoliberal present continue to have significant ramifications today. In short, the contemporary Tanzanian context emerges from struggles between socialism and capitalism, different ways of responding to neocolonialism after independence, and the racial histories of the nation that make it a context where "fugitivity" does not readily apply. Liquid maneuvers in and through tensions and contradictions better fit Tanzania's particular postcolonial context.

I still find the "fugitive anthropology" of Berry and colleagues to be useful to understanding a fluid approach to (inter)disciplinarity. They define it as "an anthropology that, grounded in black feminist analysis and praxis inspired by Indigenous decolonial thinking, centers an embodied feminist analysis while working within the contested space of the academy." Integrating fieldwork with issues of gender and sexuality, racialization, and coloniality, fugitive anthropology "critically examine[s] how dominant strands of activist anthropology replicate that which they critique, by silencing the racialized, gendered researcher's embodied experience or by inscribing it in new colonial narratives."[72] Like fugitive anthropology, interdisciplinary fluidity offers a means to decenter white, Western, masculine assumptions within normalized disciplinary frameworks of theory and praxis.

This study thus attempts to delink from the imperialist nostalgia that still insidiously acts to center even activist research back in coloniality.[73] I labor throughout this work to question my own role as a researcher, and to break through the white savior fantasies that hold my own fiction of subjective coherence in place, in order to see what decolonial potential arises from the act of falling apart. In part, "interdisciplinarity [is] the ideal orientation toward decoloniality,"⁷⁴ because flowing in and through walls weakens them, leaving channels and fissures, perhaps even causing collapse. At the same time, "interdisciplinarity is by no means an abandoning of one's discipline,"⁷⁵ but rather an opening of its constrained potential. I reach for the decolonial possibilities that emerge from the cracks as structures collapse, creating what Faye Harrison terms a "coalition of knowledges" that allows for the production of innovative theoretical claims and methodological approaches. Decolonial futures may just depend on interdisciplinary thought.⁷⁶

Liquid Agency in the Little Community

The Center Cannot Hold also examines how NGO workers in the Little Community display what I term liquid agency—that is, the agentic potential that emerges from alternative epistemologies disavowed under coloniality. It describes how the members of Viongozi Wa Shirika and other Tanzanian staff are able to work from within a neocolonial organization to destabilize and move around structures emplaced by coloniality, engendering alternative developmental paths and futures. When liquid flows enter solid structures, sooner or later they wear the structures away and things collapse. As the flows break through and the organization falls apart, opportunities to enact decoloniality emerge.

Even prior to the organization's collapse, the Tanzanian staff centered fluid epistemologies that allowed for liquid action and redirection depending on emergent conditions. When the NGO first began, it started out purely as an orphanage: one house on a hillside above a forest, where a number of children lived with a housemother. But everyone knew that orphaned children were a symptom of a larger problem: the devastating result of HIV/AIDS' sweep across the community. At one point, a survey commissioned by the Little Community found a 35 percent rate of positivity in the surrounding villages. The Little Community staff thus labored to emplace medical care for HIV-positive villagers: access to antiretroviral medications, a CD4 machine to track disease progression, and a Home-Based Care program to check in on those too ill to leave their houses. Eventually the tide of death began to ebb as access to medication and care enabled community survival.

At this point other problems began to emerge. Once emergency medicine for survival was secured, the need for more comprehensive day-to-day health care was clear. Once vulnerable children had guardianship, they now needed education. That required school uniforms. And what if some children failed out of school? Nongovernmental organization workers saw an emergent opportunity to connect two interrelated needs: to train those unable to continue in traditional schooling how to sew so that they would be able to supply the uniforms to those continuing to study. This is but one example of many. The Little Community grew and grew—not outward into other places or locations, like many NGOs tend to, but deeper into connection with its own community. Over the course of a decade, the single-facet NGO became a team of multiple interwoven departments supporting local community life and its evolving issues.

The departments emerged from liquid agencies that engaged organizing as "opportunistic, itinerant, and ebb[ing] or flow[ing] in space depending on the latest threats or opportunities."[77] Liquid agency depends on integration within the social fabric. The Little Community could not perceive the shifting circumstances, nor understand what might help address them, without deep and abiding relationships with people in the surrounding villages. Cruz and Sodeke identify liquidity as "normative in many non-Western contexts and anchored in alternative cultural logics,"[78] in part since it depends on non-Western understandings of collectivity and trust.

Yet such African understandings are erased or obscured under conditions of coloniality. As such, Ndlovu-Gatsheni argues that the fight for decolonial African futures must be an epistemological one.[79] In the context of the NGO we can find this struggle for epistemic justice staged between the liquid agencies employed by Tanzanian staff members and the solid solutions imposed by Western donors and leaders who often find liquid action unintelligible or nonsensical.

If liquid agency is enabled by a depth and intimacy of relation, then epistemological conflicts between Tanzanian staff and Western donors reveal a gap in intimate understanding, a context in which collectivity is elided by coloniality. Although Tanzanians and Westerners are intimately connected in the NGO in the way Lisa Lowe understands intimacy,[80] Western subjects do not share in the ways of knowing that would enable them to support liquid agency or organizing. That is, *The Center Cannot Hold* argues that systems of whiteness and coloniality produce Western subjects that inherently contribute to epistemic injustice by erasing African epistemologies and attendant liquid agencies unless they commit to a never-ending process of haunted reflexivity. As such, part I of the book details the ways that Western subjects are based in the foreclosure of their own coloniality, and part II then explores the problems this causes for Tanzanian staff at the NGO. To understand both how Western subjectivities become produced in these problematic ways and how they then are (un)able to relate to Tanzanian epistemologies, I offer a perspective attuned to relational politics.

Relationality against Man

I use the lens of *relationality* to lend definition to the political contours of being and becoming, but this is not the primary usage of the term in rhetoric. In examining how ontologies are not fixed, but rather brought into being through intimacy with objects, forces, and subjects, many rhetoricians tend to focus on the agency this view provides to things otherwise considered inanimate, nonhuman animals, and even the dead.[81] Decentering human agency can have important ramifications for perceptions of time, environmental justice, and economic circulation, providing alternatives to Western epistemological strongholds such as linearity, human supremacy, and capitalism.[82] Yet there is another implication to the relational constitution of ontologies, one that I find to be more important. If ontologies are constructed through relations with objects, forces, and subjects, then social and cultural forces impact the process of that construction. As I have argued elsewhere, it is imperative that rhetoricians attend to the *politics* of relationality if we want to decolonize theory and criticism.[83]

Decentering human agency only decolonizes understanding when it is explicitly decentering white, Western, heteronormative human agency. Without an approach to relationality that interrogates who is meant by "human" to begin with, relational ontologies serve only to reinforce the equation of human with Man, even as he is displaced as the focal point of analysis. I thereby draw my understanding of relationality from Women of Color feminist scholars and those who expand on their work. Particularly, I take up Aimee Carrillo Rowe's concept of *politics of relation*. Carrillo Rowe describes placing a politics of relation as the "aim to render palpable the political conditions and effects of our belonging to gesture toward deep reflection about the selves we are creating as a function of where we place our bodies, and with whom we build our affective ties."[84] Here subjectivity occupies analytic attention as the contact zone where myriad relational processes conjoin and disperse. This book thus conceptualizes subjects as products of relationality in order to analyze how political dynamics simultaneously undergird US subjectivities, assisting them with fantasies of coherence, and form cracks and crevices in these subjectivities, pulling them apart.

The Center Cannot Hold takes an expansive view of relationality, one that examines how these flows of power that momentarily cohere in subjects also produce the tensions that will eventually tear apart the Little Community as well. Relationality emphasizes that there is something to be gained in figuring the intercultural contact zone as center by interrogating the processes through which Tanzanian and Western subjects are produced in relation to each other.[85] Part II of the book thus examines the resultant tensions when Western donors, produced in and through neocolonial logics, attempt to emplace structures that conflict with Tanzanian needs and desires for their own community. Eventually these structures give way under the pressure of relational tensions. The center cannot hold; the NGO falls apart.

Unbinding the Future

When things fall apart, the strictures that coloniality places on possibility are loosened and futures that once seemed impossible enter the realm of potentiality. Yet, to be actualized, these futures must be fought for and built. Enabling decolonial futures is laborious. When things fall apart, the real work begins.

The Center Cannot Hold traces how the dissolution of coherent US subjects and the Little Community itself opens decolonial possibility, particularly through enactments of haunted reflexivity and liquid agency. I conclude with the invocation of decolonial dreamwork—the act of imagining impossible futures in order to bring them into being—as the work that continues in the aftermath.

Decolonial dreamwork is made possible by liquid agency and haunted reflexivity. On the one hand, the act of imagining beyond the limits that coloniality inscribes on possibility is a liquid act of epistemic freedom, of thinking in ways that are delinked from coloniality.[86] On the other hand, "(Im)possible futures where liberation is achieved require a reckoning with contemporary coloniality."[87] Decolonial dreamwork cannot be activated without first engaging in haunted reflexivity's continual attempts to engage one's own complicity in racial-colonial histories and relations.

The limits of our imaginations circumscribe what our futures have the potential to hold. Particularly in the context of Western NGO aid to Tanzania, "it takes the unthinkable to create a world where aid serves justice in Africa rather than Western capitalistic interests,"[88] as African life has long been posited by the West as antithetical to development. Decolonial dreamwork is only possible in the liminal space where things begin to fall apart—at the edges, where the system begins to unravel and new potentialities are revealed. But it takes the work of dreaming to seize hold of such potentialities and put the groundwork in place for them to flourish into actualities. I conclude with decolonial dreamwork, then, because decolonizing NGO aid in Tanzania ultimately requires the creation and amplification of Tanzanian visions of impossible developmental futures, fluid imaginings that are unintelligible within coloniality. Decolonial dreamwork makes the impossible possible.

Decolonial dreamwork emerges when structures are faced with their own contradictions and, as a result, weaken or fold. Each of the chapters in this book identifies a locus of tension between contradictory neocolonial and decolonial forces that the NGO attempts to contain within its metaphorical walls and discusses how some of the tensions with which the organization grapples are mirrored within Western subjectivities. As parts I and II progress, the walls begin to buckle, collapsing the tenuous center that both the US subject and the organization itself relied on.

Part I begins with chapter 1, "Doctors with(out) Burdens," which traces the difference between two groups of medical students who each spent a week at the Little Community NGO, providing free care and medicine in the surrounding villages. The group of second-year medical students acted in ways that aligned with hegemonic white masculinity and bled into neocolonial relations with the Tanzanian translators and patients, while the group of first-year students instead destabilized masculine medical norms by centering intersubjective care. I argue that medical missions provide an ambivalent space for the perceived crisis of white masculinity in the United States to be ameliorated—either by recentering masculine dominance through neocolonial relations or allowing for masculinity to accede to its fragility through relational understandings of subjectivity. Here I start to place the groundwork for haunted reflexivity.

Chapter 2, "All of Us Phantasmic Saviors," examines how US subjects maintain coherence as volunteers even while recognizing the neocolonialism that underwrites global volunteering itself. Drawing from psychoanalytic theories that pose subjectivity as grounded in the basis of foreclosure, the chapter demonstrates how US volunteers rely on denial and irony to avoid recognizing that they themselves embody the white saviors they love to hate. Both the NGO and the US volunteer subject rely on the contradiction between wanting to do decolonial work and the inability to avoid being a neocolonial subject. The chapter helps us to recognize ways in which haunted reflexivity and its potentials are refused and obscured in favor of the status quo.

Of course, as a researcher I also embody the same tension between decolonial coconspirator and neocolonial savior with which the volunteers struggle. Chapter 3, "Haunted Reflexivity," theorizes a type of reflexivity arising from relational politics that iteratively produces subjects and holds the potential to do so in ways that move toward decolonial justice. The chapter stages an encounter with ghosts, using my personal specter to unearth the colonial amnesia on which US subjectivities rely. I argue that haunted reflexivity allows Western subjects to be redone by repetitively facing their ghosts, listening and witnessing (to) what they have to say, and refusing the temptation to hold to a fiction of innocence. Witnessing (to) hauntings, to the "other" that demands response, fractures the fiction of Western subjective coherence: the center cannot hold. Part I ends by examining the decolonial potential in the undoing of Western subjectivities.

Part II then examines the implications of Western subjective coloniality on the organization itself, staging encounters between (neo)colonial and decolonial epistemologies. Chapter 4, "Water in the Cracks," demonstrates the ways that Mr. Giles and Western donors attempt to impose solid solutions on community issues that would better be served by emergent processes of liquid organizing. Using interviews with Viongozi Wa Shirika members, I argue that the inability for donors to think outside solid frameworks not only conflicted with Tanzanian liquid organizing approaches but also ironically reinforced the need for them, as liquid organizing becomes increasingly necessary under contexts of epistemic injustice and economic precarity.

Chapter 5, "Fluid (Re)mapping," locates another site of epistemological injustice: epistemologies of land usage in the NGO. When faced with (neo)colonial epistemologies emphasizing proprietary ownership and individual control over land, Tanzanian staff and Mikoda community members responded by engaging in what I term fluid (re)mapping. By discursively and materially redrawing relationships to land that combatted coloniality, Tanzanian actors countered epistemic injustice by centering use value and collectivity in relation to land.

If chapter 3 describes the productive dissolution of the Western subject, chapter 6, "Things Fall Apart," describes the productive dissolution of the NGO. Given the inherent tensions between coloniality and decoloniality in the organization, it was inevitable that things would, eventually, fall apart. The chapter follows the dissolution of the NGO as I knew it to search for the decolonial potential of collapse. I examine how liquid agency enabled the NGO staff to center Tanzanian leadership and desires as the organization fell apart.

The book's conclusion imagines what happens after the fall. When the center dies, what possibilities are born? What futures are enabled after contradictions between the colonial and decolonial have torn (neo)colonial structures and subjectivities apart? After all, falling apart allows things to be put together again, as the fragments can be assembled into something new: fragments of the NGO, of the subjects that worked and volunteered there, and of the community center that exists no more in the form that I witnessed.

The Center Cannot Hold suggests that, for NGO aid, falling apart should be embraced as a beginning that can lead to futures beyond imagining. In the conclusion I introduce the concept of decolonial dreamwork to describe how the liquid agency that emerges from falling apart may be utilized to draw impossible futures into being.

When the center cannot hold, when things fall apart, what is loosed upon the world?

It depends on what can be imagined.

Part I

Chapter One
Doctors with(out) Burdens

Language, any language, has a dual character: it is both a means of communication and a carrier of culture.—Ngũgĩ wa Thiong'o, *Decolonising the Mind*

The medical student volunteers arrived after dark. We had expected them to pull into the dirt lot of the Tanzanian village organization I call the Little Community around lunchtime. As they stepped out of the car, grinning and high-fiving each other, the more vocal students each fought to be the first one to tell us the story. Interrupting each other to add details, they described how there had been a miscommunication on the flight time from Dar es Salaam to the smaller city closest to Mikoda. The nongovernmental organization (NGO) had thought the plane would arrive at 10:30 a.m., and had planned transportation based on that. In reality, the plane left Dar es Salaam at that time. Because of this discrepancy, the vehicle meant for baggage transportation was unavailable when the group actually arrived. Instead of sending their luggage ahead of them in a different vehicle, the medical students held their luggage in their laps on the bumpy four-hour drive out to the village.

Notwithstanding the crowded discomfort of the car, this might have been unremarkable—if not for the events that followed. The delay put the medical students' vehicle on the only dirt road heading from town toward the NGO around the same time as much of the local transportation. Thus, when a small bus headed out to the village flipped over on the road, the medical students and their two attending physicians were there within minutes to help the people injured in the accident, and luckily happened to have all of their equipment and medicine on hand. The mood was exultant. As one of the students exclaimed about how "cool" it was to watch their trip leader, Dr. Greg, stitch up a wound, others declared that *this* is why they were here. That comment struck me: either they were here for miraculous occurrences to happen *to* them, or they were here to *be the miracle itself*.

The celebratory focus and jubilant descriptions obscure another side to this story. What does it mean to pose these Tanzanian villagers as *lucky* to have been attended to by second-year medical students? Rather than reflect on the inequalities that make a passing group of medical students these people's best hope at healing, or consider the ethics involved in treating people they are not legally qualified to treat in the United States, the students took up the mantle of heroes.

Although I was glad that injured people were able to receive immediate medical care, the narration of the event discomfited me. Two days later, I wrote in my field notes, "It might be partially because of this event that I started with a seminegative image of the medical student group. I read them as being arrogant, hegemonically masculine, and insensitive to the people and culture around them." Their behavior during the remainder of their time at the NGO only served to strengthen this read. Yet the medical students' performance of masculine heroism cannot be separated from its context, from the histories and cultural legacies bound up together when US medical students come to a Tanzanian village to treat patients for a week.

In this chapter, I investigate how masculinity relates to neocolonialism in intercultural relationships by examining the ways in which two different groups of medical student volunteers interacted with the Tanzanian translators, Tanzanian patients, and Western NGO staff. Drawing on research regarding white masculine victimhood and contemporary crises of masculinity,[1] I argue that medical aid to Tanzania provides a forum whereby hegemonic white masculinity can escape domestic crisis through a neocolonial fantasy of paternalism and control. And yet, at the same time, aid can also provide opportunities to decolonize international relationships by destabilizing hegemonic masculinities. In examining how a second group of volunteers behaved radically different from the first, I highlight the beginnings of a concept that will be further developed in chapter 3: haunted reflexivity. By iteratively questioning their own assumptions and behavior through the relationships they built with

Tanzanian translators, the second group of medical students started engaging in haunted reflexivity. They attended to the ghosts of their previous encounters, with the ways that coloniality structures their medical work and how that can be transformed. Haunted reflexivity thus provides a means for Westerners to support fluid agencies that refuse the epistemic injustice grounding white masculinity and its neocolonial relations in medical work.

Hegemonic Masculinity: Domestic Crisis and International Opportunity

In medicine, as in other US professions dominated by cisgender men, adherence to certain masculine norms is not explicitly taught but rather constituted as an expectation through rituals and cultural performances. Medical workers refer to this as the hidden curriculum, which is "used to describe the behaviors, attitudes, assumptions, and beliefs of medicine that are instilled in medical students beginning in the first year of training and becoming more salient throughout residency."[2] The hidden curriculum is modeled to students through the cultural context and performances of medical instruction—including attitudes, behaviors, expectations, rewards, and punishments—that become increasingly internalized as the students progress in their medical education.

Even within initial undergraduate medical training, scholars have found that students "move from being open-minded to being fact-surfeited, from being intellectually curious to being increasingly focused on just that set of knowledge and skills that must be acquired to pass examinations, from being open-hearted and empathetic to being emotionally well-defended, from idealistic to cynical about medicine, medical practice, and the life of medicine."[3] The hidden curriculum teaches medical students to value and perform a certain type of "white/collar" masculinity.[4] In particular, this version of masculinity centers mastery and professionalism, efficiency and time management, objectivity and detached concern.[5] Students report that as they progress in their medical studies, their increasing professionalism is accompanied concomitantly by increasing impatience and declining empathy.[6]

Yet these masculine medical values—as with all masculine values—are neither fixed nor imperative but constantly evolving through processes of reiteration. In addition, these values signify a standard for masculinity that can never be met or fully achieved. Given the contemporary US climate of white masculine victimhood,[7] it may come as no surprise that hegemonic medical masculinity is also imbued with anxiety and finds itself in a state of crisis. I argue that how the particular crisis of white US medical masculinity unfolds at the Little Community demonstrates an important aspect of hegemonic masculinity: its ability to recuperate itself through a neocolonial fantasy of dominance.

White Masculinity in Crisis

Hegemonic masculinity is conditioned by anxiety, as performances of mastery and control—such as those in medicine—are inextricably linked to anxiety and paranoia.[8] Anxieties are endemic to white masculinity, which must be constantly reconstituted in reaction to its context and is always rife with contradiction. The anxious compulsion to reenact white masculinity belies its claims to natural superiority.[9] In the contemporary US context, a sense of crisis imbues anxious reiterations of white masculinity. Casey Ryan Kelly describes crises in masculinity as "responses to the perceived loss of male privilege where, nonetheless, structural inequalities continue to disadvantage women."[10] That is, threats to the dominance of white masculine hegemony are felt as threats to men themselves, even as they retain material privilege.[11]

Medical masculinity has not escaped this contemporary moment. Kelly Underman and Laura Hirschfield detail many of the changes in medicine that underlie the sense of crisis. For one, what was once a bastion of white male authority now has an increasingly diverse pool of students in terms of both gender and race. In addition, patients no longer unquestioningly accept doctoral judgments, instead relying on their own research to help diagnose and treat their conditions. The rising demand for patient-centered care poses a threat to efficient time management. Finally, expectations for empathetic relation to one's patients challenge the value of detached objectivity. Doctors feel as if their (masculine) authority is under threat. Underman and Hirschfield sum up the medical masculinity crisis well: "A physician can no longer expect that his (and we do use a male pronoun deliberately) expertise alone dictates patient care."[12]

International Aid's Neocolonial Fantasies

In the United States, responses to the contemporary crisis of white masculinity often involve claims of white men's victimhood and fantasies of recuperating their lost—and fictive—whole, natural, masculine dominance.[13] Ameliorations of this perceived crisis depend on spaces and times where there can be a plausible "return," however false, to masculine dominance. Central to many forms of imperial expansion is a "'deep disquietude,' a feeling that 'something had gone wrong' at home."[14] Although medical missions are supposedly about filling a need for medical services in the Global South, they are also about fulfilling a desire for white masculine recuperation by seeking out "frontiers." US fantasies of white masculine wholeness seek to escape their contemporary fragmented state and seem complete by brokering distance, whether in space or time.[15] Such fantasies act to cover lack, or "an illusory sense that the male self, or subjectivity for that matter, was ever whole,"[16] by providing a narrative of possible wholeness that subjects may internalize as their own, which I will describe further in chapter 2.

International medical mission trips enable masculine recovery through a double distancing: first, geographically, and second, because the Global South functions in the US imaginary as developmentally backward in time.[17] As the distance between medical missions and contemporary US life draws one backward in time, it opens the possibility of reusing the "racial script" offered by the history of imperialism and its mediated portrayals as a means of engaging in a neocolonial context. Natalia Molina defines racial scripts as "the ways in which the lives of racial groups are linked across time and space and thereby affect one another, even when they do not directly cross paths." That is, "once attitudes, practices, customs, policies, and laws are directed at one group, they are more readily available and hence easily applied to other groups."[18] This is particularly true when the racial script has been codified in the US imaginary through repetition in the media.[19]

Imperial masculinity offers a particularly useful racial script for white medical masculinity to utilize as neocolonial fantasy. For one, the relationship between masculinity and imperialism leads to a gendering of physical space. In European colonial invasions, land was often feminized and sexualized, figured as virginal and "spread" for the taking.[20] At the same time, the virginal figuring could also double as an erasure of Indigenous peoples by painting the land as empty and clean. In this way, the feminizing of space is part of what allows for the violent acts of physical colonization and cultural imposition: the perceived weakness, lack, or nonexistence of the national "other" requires the guidance of white, Western man in order to initiate development. Today, international mission trips redeploy neocolonial relations in the form of medical assistance to those figured as unable to help themselves. As Stuart Hall describes, during the imperial period a sense of adventure accompanied international travels, which "became synonymous with the demonstration of the moral, social and physical mastery of the colonisers over the colonised."[21] Medical mission trips also recycle this sense of adventure as a neocolonial fantasy of mastery, albeit with less spectacularly violent outcomes.

Finally, imperial masculinity relies on a notion of masculine sovereignty, embodied in a figure who, Joshua Gunn notes, "has the power to transgress his own rules."²² Gunn deftly demonstrates how the figure of the father is tied to the figure of the nation, as the father takes on a masculine responsibility of operating outside and above the law as a vigilante in order to reinstate the order and control that the nation failed to maintain. The sovereign power to operate above the law—ostensibly for the good of all or with a heroic sense of responsibility—is a type of masculinity that is reused in contemporary neocolonial contexts through what Teju Cole has called "the white savior industrial complex." In this complex, white Westerners create the global economic systems and policies that pull resources out of African countries and then declare themselves solely responsible for fixing such "underdeveloped" nations.²³ Neocolonial masculinity conforms to ideas of the sovereign not only for the perceived benefits therein but also to avoid the detriments associated with being "a 'soft touch' for the nation," which includes "not only the risk of becoming feminine, but also of becoming 'less white.'" In order to remain globally dominant, masculinity requires performances of neocolonial sovereignty.²⁴ US fantasies of sovereign masculinity are thus notably raced and neocolonial in international aid relations, declaring sovereign control over African peoples, lands, and cultures.

Doing Aid Otherwise

Although international medical mission trips provide an opportunity for white masculinity to remake itself through fantasy, they do not necessitate such performances. Crises in masculinity reveal the fragility of masculine hegemony. Judith Butler claims that "the nonspace of cultural collision" opens the potential for reworking gendered performances and expectations.²⁵ Masculinity—and aid—can always be otherwise. The cultural complexities of international experiences provide a space where white medical masculinity may be either re-centered through neocolonial fantasies or challenged by relations with difference.

The crisis of white medical masculinity may yet also open opportunities for destabilizing the neocolonial relations that only recognize Tanzanian community members as "passive recipients" of health interventions who are "primitive and devoid of agency" and move instead toward culture-centered approaches to health that are based on dialogic relations.²⁶ Neocolonial white masculinity, in its sovereignty, rests on a notion of the subject as an autonomous individual. When this perspective is altered and the subject is seen as radically dependent on the systems and subjects around them for their being, a type of responsibility to the other opens up that is very different than the paternalism of sovereignty. The type of responsibility necessitated by relationality is one that no subject can ever fully meet. Subjects are radically indebted to those around them, predicated on the intimately political act of belonging to and with others.[27] When Westerners recognize their subjective indebtedness to cultural and/or racial others, potential arises for political transformation. The same crisis in masculinity that may act to restabilize masculine hegemony through neocolonial fantasies may also allow for a greater attunement to others.

In part, this greater attunement to others depends on the inability for relational responsibility to ever be fully met. Subjects can never escape from the ethical debt that they owe to the other—and I would add, the political debt that they owe to others more generally—for their very being. The cyclical nature of needing ever to be reexamining one's relationships as a subject forms the basis of what I call haunted reflexivity. Haunted reflexivity is a cycle of continual reengagement with the way coloniality and racism have structured our own understandings of ourselves and how we relate to the world. Here we see the beginnings of this mode of relation in that the second group of medical volunteers acted in ways that refused masculine hegemony and denied the white masculine imperative to reclaim stature out of crisis. The continual return to centering relationality as a political concern found in haunted reflexivity is precisely what allows for Western subjects to understand and support liquid agencies. Without dismantling the Western subject as we know it, tearing it down to its racial, masculine, colonial roots, we cannot hope to support the liquidities that avoid and escape (neo)colonial structures.

International aid trips may function as either/both an opportunity to recuperate white masculine dominance through neocolonial fantasies or/and a space where white masculine hegemony may be contested. The groups of medical student volunteers who came to work at the Little Community exemplify these two types of relations. The first group demonstrated how the distance between the medical mission field in Tanzania and the US cultural space of masculine crisis allowed for the medical students to resecure a fantasy of a white masculine dominance through interactions and attitudes of sovereignty, control, and denial of fragility. The second group, on the other hand, showed how the liminal "frontier" space of international medical missions can also disturb taken-for-granted power dynamics through enactments and behaviors of relationality, uncertainty, and care. Ultimately I argue that international medical mission trips display an ambivalent space, one that requires Western subjects to either take flight, or become inextricably caught up in both the recentering of white masculine dominance and its destabilization.

Medical Care at the Little Community

When the Little Community first came into being in 2009, orphan care and HIV/AIDS treatment were the foremost issues in the village area. The last measure put the rate of HIV infection at 35 percent of the local population.[28] Given this alarming need, the organization's health care projects focused almost exclusively on HIV/AIDS prevention and treatment. After securing consistent medication for HIV-positive adults in the village, lifespans in the village increased and other health issues became increasingly prevalent. The Little Community responded by building and supplying a clinic on-site. There was only one problem: They had no medical personnel with whom to staff it.

As luck would have it, in the spring of 2014, a medical student group at a public US university was looking for a new site for its annual summer medical mission trip. A friend of some of the students happened to know Sarah and Tim of the Little Community and put the two organizations in contact. In the summer of 2014, the first group of medical student volunteers came to hold clinics at and around Mikoda for a week. This group enjoyed the experience so much that it promised to come back the following year, in addition to the new team that would come then. As a researcher in the summer of 2015, I was able to interact with both the returning group of now second-year medical students and the new team of first-year medical students as they worked with translators to run clinics in the surrounding village area for a week each.

The relationship between the medical student volunteers and the translators with whom they worked played an integral role in how the clinics operated. The translators were trained by the NGO initially to work with research projects in the area. English is primarily taught and spoken in secondary school in Tanzania, so most of the translators had either recently completed their initial or advanced secondary studies or kept up English training since. Language use in the area tends to aggregate by age: older villagers primarily or only speak the tribal language; middle-age villagers speak both the local tribal language and Swahili, with perhaps a few additional English phrases; younger villagers will have learned some English in school, but speak mostly Swahili, and more rarely speak the tribal language.[29] The work of the translators, then, is imperative to ensuring quality care for those who attend the clinics. Yet this importance was not registered equally by both of the medical groups.

The first medical group comprised the second-year students, who swept in on a heroic high of having saved a vehicle-full of lives and carried that attitude through the week with them. Two men led this group: Dr. Greg, considered an expert in medical mission trips, and a student named Hunter. The remainder of the group included five men and two women medical students, as well as two women nurses and a supporting physician, Dr. Baker—a woman who would then be the leading doctor for the second group. All of the participants were white, except for one Indian American man. Most of the members of this group had come to the NGO the previous year and were further along in their medical studies than the second group. The group's two years of exposure to the hidden curriculum, along with the fact that most of the students had just taken the first part of the United States Medical Licensing Examination and were awaiting their results, provided a context whereby the crisis in medical masculinity was deeply felt and conditioned their experience at the Little Community. The group's previous experience at the NGO may also have contributed to how it re-centered medical masculinity through neocolonial fantasies; since the second-year students had been there before, they did not participate in any cultural awareness training or reflection over cultural dynamics. The evening debriefing sessions, which often started late, as the medical students worked until dark in the village clinics, focused entirely on the medical cases they had seen that day. The Tanzanian translators did not attend these sessions because they had already worked overtime and needed to get home to their families.

The second medical student group differed from the first in significant ways. These students had just completed their first year of medical school and were not as assimilated into the expectations of medicine's masculine hidden curriculum. For many people in the group, this was their first volunteer trip abroad. Everyone in the group was white; the leaders were two women physicians, and the medical students were mostly women. Significantly, because the leader of this group, Dr. Baker, arrived with the second-year students and stayed for three weeks in between the two medical trips, the context of the second group was altered in many ways. First, Dr. Baker and I held a debriefing meeting with the Tanzanian translators and incorporated many of their concerns and suggestions into the planning for the second group. In addition, she wrote a short handbook of Tanzanian culture and the NGO context, to which I added Swahili keywords, and sent it to the first-year medical students before their arrival. The evening debriefing sessions with this group were open to any questions or reflections the students had about the day, including medical case questions, cultural inquiries, and explanations of feelings. Additionally, the students ended work in the village on time each day so that the Tanzanian translators could also attend the meetings.

For this chapter, I analyzed my field notes and my transcriptions of interviews and conversations. The interviews included four with individual medical volunteers and four with individual translators. The conversations then include multiple group debriefings with each full medical student team, casual conversations with smaller groups of medical volunteers, and a formal meeting with the translators in between the departure of the first group and the arrival of the second. In the following pages, I weave these texts together to demonstrate how international aid both offers the opportunity to resecure masculinity through neocolonial relationships and the ability to challenge masculine dominance by embracing subjective instability.

Masculinity and Neocolonialism: Two Cases of Medical Volunteers

In the two cases in this section, I explore the contextual dynamics, attitudes, behaviors, and values that the two different groups of medical students displayed through their interactions with Tanzanian translators, Tanzanian patients, and NGO staff. The first case demonstrates how the medical students were able to restabilize a fantasy of masculine dominance through neocolonial relationships and interactions of sovereignty, control, and the denial of fragility. The second case, on the other hand, highlights the potential for subjective fragmentation to challenge neocolonial masculinity through relationality, uncertainty, and care.

Recuperating White Masculinity

RECLAIMING SOVEREIGNTY

At 8:00 a.m. on Sunday mornings, the sun is just beginning to crest the hills to the east of the Little Community. Sarah had boiled water, and was letting the French-press coffee brew while breathing deeply the chilly June air and enjoying the quiet. Workweeks in the village area are six days long, with a day off for most people on Sunday—Saturday for the Seventh Day Adventists. Living on the NGO grounds, Sarah often had people coming to her home with work requests at odd hours; Sunday offered a much-needed chance to relax. And with infant twins in the home, peaceful time alone was difficult to get.

A knock at the door shattered her reverie. Dr. Greg and four medical student men had decided that they did not want to do the activity planned for the group that morning, which was going to church with their translators, and had come to ask Sarah to arrange a fishing outing for them instead. The British colonist who started the NGO and ran an expatriate retreat lodge nearby, Mr. Giles, kept a lake stocked with fish on his land. I was staying with Sarah and Tim, and was quite shocked to find guests at the door so early on a Sunday morning. Later that day, I wrote in my field notes that Dr. Greg and the medical students seemed "to not take into account the people around them, and how their 'needs' and requests might greatly inconvenience other people."

As I have noted, masculine sovereignty functions as above or outside the laws that constrain other people.[30] Here Dr. Greg and his compatriots not only considered themselves able to shirk the plans that had been made by the NGO for them that morning but also deemed themselves and their leisure activity important enough that those around them should forgo relaxation in order to provide last-minute arrangements for them. I use this event as an exemplar for attitudes, comments, and interactions displayed by the majority of the group throughout the week, but there are a myriad of other examples. For instance, the students often complained that their transportation did not take them straight to the clinics where they were working each day, but stopped along the way to pick up patients who could not walk or pay for transportation themselves. Although it is common in Tanzania for transportation to never be fully private and ride-sharing is expected, the medical students seemed to feel this was demeaning, and they grumbled about being "a shuttle service."

The masculine sovereignty embedded in this assumption that the medical group is or should be the main priority revealed itself in two particularly salient types of interaction with other people: either a paternalistic responsibility for others who ostensibly need saving or a dismissive treatment of others and their work as less important or even unimportant. When performed in this context—where the host country has a history of colonization, where predominantly white bodies are laboring to save or fix Black bodies, and where the visiting peoples come from a nation centered on an ideology of exceptionalism[31]—masculine sovereignty catalyzes and constitutes neocolonialism through paternalism toward and relegation of Tanzanian others.

The paternalistic responsibility for others was clearest in the treatment of patients. Take, for example, a young woman who came to the clinic with her father. Dr. Baker described her in a daily debriefing as "doing a two-week freak-out on her family," where her behavior had suddenly changed such that at times she wouldn't speak and would "sometimes go into fits of rage." She then noted that it was important to find out "what has happened to her, who has hurt her" in order to solve this young woman's strange condition. After finding out that her family had stopped paying her school fees, one medical student exclaimed, "If we only had some cash on us right now!" Others replied "Right?" and "Yeah!" To the medical team, this seemed like an easily identifiable problem that one often hears about in connection with the developing world: young women being denied schooling by their parents, whether by dint of conservatism or poverty. The simple solution, then, is for the medical team to pay the school fees, since they are surely not very expensive in US middle-class terms, and by doing so this young woman's future can be secured.

Yet Sarah immediately interrupted this train of thought by forcefully requesting, "Please *don't* give cash." She explained that though this sudden behavioral shift in a teenage girl might seem out of place to the medical team, it is actually quite common in the area. When young women are found out to have a boyfriend, parents cut off school fees out of concern the young woman will get pregnant and their money will have gone to waste, leading to the drastic behavioral changes and displays of anger.[32] With the quick option of saving the young woman removed, the medical team did not seem interested in continuing the conversation. Instead, Dr. Greg quickly said, "I'll just kind of follow up," before moving into praise for the care and concern shown by the nurses and women doctors that day. The paternalistic attitude toward the situation led to jumping to quick conclusions in order to save the day. Yet when the students were forced to think beyond immediate assumptions and easy solutions into more complex territory, the project was abandoned. As I will describe in more detail, there is a sense of fragility to these masculine savior displays.

A sense of responsibility toward Tanzanian others was also continuously emphasized through declarations about the group's purpose. The medical volunteers repeated comments such as, "I mean, that's why we're here. To give back and to help people"; "I'm here to treat, more than to build relationships, really"; and "I'm here for one purpose, you know, like I'm trying to work one hundred percent of the time, like, as much as possible." Their words were accompanied by actions such as working through lunch and past sunset in order to see as many patients as possible, ignoring my requests for interviews out of a sense that it would be a waste of their time, and skipping over greetings in patient interactions in order to move quickly through to diagnoses. Their intense focus on a perceived responsibility to treat patients may seem laudable, but it functioned as a neocolonial paternalism and excluded any other foci as interruptions to that work.

The most palpable example of this phenomenon is the way this group handled translator assignments. Rather than each individual medical worker having a single translator that they worked with throughout the week, translators were constantly picked up and discarded for one task or another; they were related to as tools that enabled the medical students to do their work rather than as subjective partners who actively assisted in the work being done. The Tanzanians struggled with the constant change of partners. One translator, Denis, described how being traded between medical students (who were often called doctors in the Little Community) was difficult: "Because, like, I met with the doctor the first day. And I need to study what he likes and what he doesn't like. So I know that this is my doctor. And we know each other, so it will be easy for me to process with this doctor. But when the time comes to change, to go to the new doctor, you're—you need to study, to start again studying each other. So that is . . . a challenge." Other translators such as Happy and Idda explained that they had trouble understanding people who were talking too fast at first, but if they were able to get used to the style of a single speaker, they could better understand what they were saying at a fast pace. Innocent and Damas added that spending time with one medical student was not only important to understand them but also to know how to communicate with them, as certain medical students prized brevity in answers and others desired as much detailed explanation as possible. The translators explained that they had to take care in explanations in order not to annoy the medical workers.

The medical students did not notice the burden placed on the translators by the shifting assignments. Translators were sometimes detained by lunch, breaks, or patient requests for a translator of a particular gender. Because the medical students' attention was consumed by the primary goal of seeing as many patients as possible, they considered these delays a waste of time and would simply grab the nearest translator to continue their work. Some even saw the interchangeability of translators as fun, allowing them to meet new people. In this manner, the masculine imperative of time management and efficiency was reinscribed through neocolonial relationships with the Tanzanian translators, who were treated like interchangeable objects.

Since the translators were seen as tools to be utilized for the medical students to do *their* work, translator knowledge about culture and context were often dismissed as extraneous. The construct of what "the job" is was constituted by the US medical workers and constrained how they thought it should be approached. For instance, Mustafa, the medical officer at the NGO, interrupted one of the medical student debriefing meetings to talk to Sarah. She then asked for his opinion on a question about birth control that had been raised by one of the nurses. As he began to speak in Swahili, with Sarah translating, about birth control options in the village and the systemic issues with family planning, many of the men tuned out and began their own whispered conversations. One of the first to do so was the student leader of the team. This is not only demonstrative of a masculinist notion that birth control is a women's issue, but also a US-centric belief that the work that they do in the village is not affected by cultural constraints or systemic issues, and that as workers who are only here for a week, they do not need to understand the Tanzanian village context in order to do their work well. It is telling that Mustafa had not been asked to participate in the meeting in the first place. As the person in charge of village medical outreach, as well as the NGO clinic, his knowledge of medicine in the area could be seen as integral to the project. Yet when US masculine sovereignty defines US medical workers and their understanding of the job as primary, Tanzanian knowledge and concerns are pushed to the background.

GRASPING CONTROL

Walking into the community hall on the day of the first clinic, I noticed first the lace and flowers draped around the edge of the stage. As the largest meeting place in the village, this building held most important community events—including nearly all weddings in the area. Kept to the side, the decorations would not affect the tables placed on the stage to act as a pharmacy. All the work of diagnoses would happen in the three small rooms behind the stage, as well as makeshift "private" areas within the folds of the curtains, secluded enough to see patients who had minor wounds and injuries. In front of the stage, the majority of the hall was filled with rows and rows of brightly colored plastic chairs. At 8:00 a.m. the first few rows were already filled; by noon the room would hold hundreds of patients from miles around.

The first task when met with a large number of patients to be seen in a relatively short period of time is to triage, or determine the urgency of each patient's medical situation. At the very least, this requires that someone take down the basic information of the patient and their primary complaint. In addition to making sure that the more serious wounds are attended to in a timely manner, recording patient information prior to admission to the limited examination space saves time so that patients can be diagnosed more quickly. On the first day of clinic, the medical workers had not started triaging immediately; they did not realize they needed to until midday. Later that evening, during the debriefing, one of the nurses described why she started triage: "Well, it's like, I know one thing is you've got to spell out, like, names, and I'm like, oh my gosh! I can't imagine! That takes, like, five minutes for somebody to just—for the translator to give you every letter of their name. I have no clue how to spell their names or even what they're saying." Although the medical students all lauded her work and the time that she saved them, I wondered why no one thought to simply hand a notebook to the translator and let them write the name down. Looking back, I cannot remember if I spoke up in the meeting or not. Many times I did not make suggestions to this group because they did not seem to take me seriously.

For example, later in the meeting, the doctors were planning how to communicate with each other when the team split into four groups the following day to do clinics and home visits in two different village areas. They were concerned that they only had two phones, and were discussing how they could get access to a third, when I interrupted and asked if they had considered that the translators also had phones. The idea that the translators could also call or text each other, or the medical group's phones, had not occurred to them. After nodding to acknowledge my comment, they continued their discussion as if I had not spoken at all.

In both of these examples, the medical workers have a need to maintain control of operations, even when the Tanzanian translators would be better able to perform the task at hand. In part, this need is connected to the sovereign aspect of masculinity and its centering of white US individuals at the expense of Tanzanian knowledge; that the translators could possibly have something to offer to their work, other than the singular act of translation, threatens the masculine mastery of the medical students. The neocolonial fantasy of white masculinity requires holding on to control and not ceding it to cultural or racial others.

To the translators this registered as a feeling that they were not really considered part of the team, leading to frustration at not being allowed to help to the fullest extent. For instance, when I asked Innocent what he had learned from his experience translating, he said he learned that "cooperation is the best thing in solving anything." He went on to describe how the medical team worked together so well, even though "some of them are doctors, some of them are school of medicine [meaning medical students].... Asking questions to each other—even the doctors, like Dr. Greg, Dr. Baker, Shelley, Becky, Tiffany, and others—they are cooperating so well." Painting a picture of cooperation as something that only occurred between the medical workers, Innocent seemed to imply that Tanzanians were not a part of the team. In a different interview, Happy made this view explicit. When waiting for the transportation to arrive in the mornings, and while traveling to the clinics, Happy was frustrated that the medical workers did not talk with the translators. She said, "Sometimes I feel a little angry, thinking, why are they speaking just to each other when we're here as a team?" She went on to narrate how each morning, when preparing to leave for clinic, the US medical workers would load the bags of supplies and medicines into the cars themselves without asking the Tanzanian translators for help. She was upset because she felt that if they were really working as a team, the medical students should include the translators in this task.

Insidiously, the performances of mastery and control at some points made the Tanzanian translators question their ability to help in areas other than the singular skill the medical group seemed to allow them. For instance, when I asked Innocent if there were ways for cooperation to be improved in the group, the means that he gave was to prepare better translators. He then emphasized the importance of the translator: "He or she makes sure a good connection between patient and doctor." In other words, the task of the translator was to work as a conduit, a tool that allowed for the connection of patient and doctor. Even Innocent seemed to accept the premise that the translators were tools that allowed the medical students to do *their* work. Happy also described how sometimes the patient, after the medical student had gone to check his diagnosis with either Dr. Greg or Dr. Baker, would suddenly tell her something else that was wrong that the patient had been holding back from the medical student. Happy said that this put her in an uncomfortable position, because when she told the medical student they would often be frustrated and annoyed at the further use of time, and she felt that annoyance to be taken out on her. Happy felt like she was bothering the medical students by bringing up issues that required further attention, and because of this sometimes she simply would not tell them.

The attempts to control time and keep everything moving efficiently also made the translators uncomfortable in other circumstances. When asked what they had learned about US medical workers from this experience, nearly every translator first noted, "They care a lot about time."[33] The focus on schedules and efficiency was not as important to the translators as it was to the medical students. The translators instead saw food, rest, and taking time to understand each patient's needs as more important to providing comprehensive care than maintaining a schedule. Yet, under contexts of epistemic injustice,[34] it was the translators who were required to shift their norms of interaction rather than the medical students. As we will see further in chapters 4 and 5, Westerners are often unable to register Tanzanian epistemologies of organizing, space, and time, causing problems for the Tanzanians with whom they work. The translators still labored to operate in a way that suited the visitors, but they had a difficult time predicting in advance how the Western care for time would appear in context.

For instance, every day the medical workers and Tanzanian translators would drive out to a different village area and hold a clinic. The US medical workers were given sack lunches with peanut butter and jelly sandwiches, hard-boiled eggs, carrots, and cookies. The translators, not caring for such Western food, were given money to find a café in the village area. This required driving ten or so minutes up the road at the designated lunchtime, ordering the food, waiting while it was prepared, eating, and returning. The translators were often gone for an hour. They were unprepared for the animosity it bred with the medical students. As one student put it, "The Tanzanians were kinda dicking around and stuff, and I would be a little frustrated." Although the translators recognized the problem and felt uncomfortable that the medical students were so upset by waiting for them, they did not value efficiency in the same way as the medical students. As Happy put it, "Us Tanzanians, we don't know time! . . . We don't know! We eat, we sit a while, we rest, but our friends [the medical workers] go by time." Idda, unwilling to cope with the discomfort of the situation, started cooking her own lunch at night after finishing work, and bringing it with her the following day.

Control was not something the medical workers *had* but was instead a performance that masculinity demands in order to secure an unstable sovereignty. Perhaps this is why the inability to control the Tanzanian translators' use of time frustrated the medical students: the inability to control their timeliness highlighted the instability of neocolonial sovereignty.

I next look at examples of where the medical students met with, and denied, the fragility of masculinity, as well as how the medical students attempted to address their anxieties stemming from the inability to perform imperial masculinity perfectly or finally.

DENYING FRAGILITY

The morning after the medical group arrived, I trudged up the hill from where the leaders of the group and I were staying to a guesthouse where the students and nurses roomed. Although I had helped the housemothers to plan meals the previous week based on the separate housing locations, Dr. Greg insisted the group eat together at all meals. I, unable to get breakfast in the new configuration at the house where I was staying, figured that meant I should also eat with them at their guesthouse. In the courtyard of the house, I greeted the housemothers, and then entered to find the medical workers split between two tables: one of younger students, and one including the older people—two doctors, two nurses, and some nontraditional students. I hovered around the older table sipping coffee, since there was no room for me to sit. From the other side of the room, I caught the end of someone's complaint: "Yeah, and there's just, like, this roll with some butter and a tiny bit of jam on it, an egg, and a couple carrots, and that's it!" I realized that they were talking about their packed lunches. Insulted on behalf of the housemothers, whom I had assisted with their work and knew its magnitude, I bristled.

Since I was then listening more closely to the conversation at the other table, I overheard a student who had not come the year before asking a man from the young table where she should put used coffee grounds. He said confidently, "Oh, just throw them over the fence." Turning, I caught her eye, and suggested she should ask the housemothers what they usually do with coffee grounds. She asked and found that there is a compost system, to which the coffee grounds are a useful addition.

Masculinity requires maintenance to stay in place, meaning it is fragile and imminently susceptible to failure. To maintain the fiction of masculine dominance, such fragility cannot be recognized or admitted. The comments I heard at that first breakfast both point to this fragility: one functions as a demonstration of masculine toughness—having to do long hours of exhausting work while eating such terrible food—and the other as a response to anxiety that sovereignty may not be as complete as it seems through a need to provide answers even if one does not have them. The medical students' behavior illustrates how the performance of hegemonic masculinity involves the refusal to admit to limitations and failure.

The fragility of US masculinity was often displayed through discomfort at times where the medical group felt out of control or that its sovereignty was threatened. For instance, Happy noticed the medical students' discomfort when the translators would be talking together in Swahili and laughing. She said, "Yes, we are translators, but aren't we also Tanzanian?" Her meaning was that Tanzanians are friendly people who love to talk and laugh. She also mentioned that in the car rides to the various clinic sites, the US medical workers often sat silently, so she would end up talking with other Tanzanians. Happy identified this as a "challenge" in the work, since she could see that it caused tension, but she did not know how to make the relationships between the Tanzanians and the US medical students better.

A more consequential example of masculinity's fragility lies in the way the medical students dealt with diseases that they did not have the means to treat. One evening during the debriefing session, a student described "an interesting case" of testicular cancer he had seen that day. He said, "It was kinda sad to see it," as there was "just kinda nothing that we could do about it" and since the untreated tumor had progressed far enough that one testicle was the size of a softball. The conversation centered on the disease as a case one might find in a textbook, abstracting it to the point where the Tanzanian man whose life and body were being spoken of faded into the background. Sarah interjected by asking the student directly, "Did you tell him that he has cancer?" He responded, "I told him that we thought he had a tumor and that we are planning on bringing a surgeon back next year, and that we would like to take a picture so we can show the surgeon so that when we come back next year we could hopefully take care of it." He later quietly added, "He won't make it a year." Even though the student knew that the patient could not last a year, he denied the fragility of his masculine power to save by extending it into the (fictive) future—it *will* happen, next year. At the same time, the medical student paternalistically made a decision on behalf of this Tanzanian man about what knowledge he should or should not have about his own body. By not telling the man that he had cancer, the medical student presumed that the Tanzanian man would not be equipped to handle his diagnosis and thus should be protected from it.

This example is one case of many over the week where the medical students were afraid or unwilling to tell patients that they had untreatable diseases. They voiced concern to a US college student volunteer that the Tanzanian patients would be angry, or might blame the medical workers for their condition, concluding it was better not to tell them. Neocolonial paternalism underlies these attitudes; withholding information from Tanzanians about their own bodies necessitates an assumption of cultural superiority to make those decisions on their behalf. Yet *why* the medical students feel the need to do so is not initially clear. Even supposing that the Tanzanians did blame the medical workers for their disease, or were angry at the diagnosis, why should this be a problem? What are the US medical workers afraid of? To start, withholding that someone is terminally ill can only be "for his own good" if there is first a grounding assumption of the medical worker's superiority over the Tanzanian patient, which allows the worker to make those decisions. Neocolonial masculinity certainly works in this fashion, but the sovereignty of this identity also calls for control, answers: an ability to save. The reason the medical workers did not want to disclose that patients had terminal diseases, I suggest, is that they could not face the corresponding threat to their sovereign masculinity. Without an ability to save or fix the patients, their sovereignty faltered.

Encounters with fragility often lead to excessive demonstrations of masculinity as a means to combat attendant anxieties. Among the medical workers themselves, this entailed conversations about how "cool" and "awesome" it is to be seeing patients they wouldn't be allowed to treat unsupervised in the United States. As I have written elsewhere, US aid workers have a tendency to use such logic, suggesting that they should be lauded for doing work *precisely because* they do not know what they are doing, or do not have the proper training. Passion, ingenuity, and persistence are presented as viable alternatives to skill and preparation.[35] In medicine, this tendency is particularly detrimental.[36] Consider the following interchange with Ken:

JENNA: So what do you see as your role in coming here?
KEN: Providing health care. . . . I'm here, like, I'm a doctor—I mean, I want to be a doctor. That's what I want to do. Go and see as many people as possible.

Ken, and many of the other medical workers, slipped into the habit of referring to themselves as *doctors* throughout the week, in part because it was easier to translate than the term *medical student*. But assuming the title of doctor before it is earned can be seen as another type of excessive performance of masculinity, one that is reliant on being in a so-called underdeveloped country, treating patients who are considered too uneducated or poor to complain about being treated by underskilled workers.

Such excessive performances of masculine skill to hide fragility can also help explain the treatment of Mustafa. As a nurse-midwife, Mustafa was the only person with medical experience in the Little Community, and was the second most highly trained person in the village area. Although his education paled in comparison to that of the doctors, he often seemed to be treated as a threat by the medical group. As I have noted, he was not invited to debriefing meetings, and his opinions were not only rarely regarded but also actively talked over. Mustafa posed a threat to the medical workers because of the fragility of white US masculinity. His cultural knowledge and position at the NGO served as reminders that he would be working in the area with these very same patients long after the US medical workers had gone. Mustafa threatened the masculine performance of control over the medical operations in the village: people are not simply saved, and the job is not simply done when the medical workers board the plane to return to the United States. Mustafa could not be included as a helpful cultural liaison without the medical workers facing their inability to save people in the village, as well as facing their dependence on others.

On the final evening of their stay, the medical workers, along with Sarah, Tim, and I, and the other US volunteers currently staying at the NGO, put on very dressy Tanzanian clothing and rode up the hill to the Gileses' lodge for drinks and dinner, a tradition for the end of Western volunteer trips to the Little Community. After dining, we gathered by the fireplace so the medical students could discuss which patients would be receiving referrals for advanced treatment in a city hospital or, in dire cases, transport to the capital of Dar es Salaam. The medical students had worked throughout the school year raising funds to distribute, but there was not enough of this funding for everyone who needed help. Decisions would have to be made. To the chagrin of the medical students, some patients who had already been given money for treatment the previous year needed referrals again. They learned that many patients had arrived at hospitals, only to be turned away; others discovered the requisite surgeon had moved; and more had been unable to leave their families for so long a time. The medical students were deflated; ostensibly, they had failed to fully enact their roles as white saviors the year before. Yet, tonight, the air was again jovial. They had more money to give and another chance to leave with a clean slate—returning to the United States under the illusion that this time their masculinity was final and secure; this time the patients would be saved. By placing their masculine security in a future to come, they not only denied its fragility but also reinforced a perpetual neocolonial cycle of Tanzanian dependence on Western medical aid.

Divesting from White Masculinity

RELATIONALITY: CHALLENGING SOVEREIGNTY

Stepping out of the small airport, invariably each person in the newly arrived medical group looked around them, taking in the rolling hills and dry, dusty roads. I did not need to signal them to walk toward me; our van was the only one in the parking lot. I introduced myself, and helped them load their luggage into the vehicle. Unlike the first group, these students responded with interest to the description of my research and asked me questions to gather more detail.

We stopped in town to buy some comfort food supplies for the week, and then headed out on the main road that we would eventually leave to turn toward the NGO. First, however, Sarah had requested that we stop by a farm run by a Zimbabwean couple, as it was the only place in the area where she could purchase produce such as lettuce and beets. We exited the main road at the proper place, but after driving around dirt roads for about half an hour we realized we were lost. The driver stopped to ask directions, but we were still confused about how to tell the dirt road that led to the farm from all the others in the unchanging landscape of ankle-height grass peppered with trees. Finally, we talked with the farmer on the phone, and he agreed to meet us at the main road with the boxes of produce. After an hourlong journey that seemed like a fool's errand, we were back on our way to the NGO.

I was surprised to find that, after an hour of driving out of the way to buy food for someone else, the medical students were pleasant and uncomplaining. They did not express annoyance at being a "shuttle service," but rather were pleased to be able to do a favor for someone they had not yet met. The second group of medical workers seemed particularly attuned to relationality in their encounters, and how work such as theirs could only be successful as a collective endeavor.

Consider, for instance, the way they related to the translators. In between the two medical groups' visits, Sarah and I had held a meeting with the translators to gauge what worked well in the first week, and what we could change to make things better for the translators with the second group. The translators all agreed that it would be far easier for them if they were each able to work with one medical student for the whole week. This had originally been the plan for the first medical group as well; however, trading translators like so many available tools had quickly become the norm. Happy registered this use of translators as tools by differentiating between when the first medical group treated her as a *translator* from when they treated her as a *person*. Singling out Dr. Baker from the first group, Happy explained how she would provide explanations of medical issues, saying she "didn't just treat me like a translator" but took time to build a relationship with her.

Dr. Baker stayed for two weeks in the Little Community when the first group left and remained to lead the second group. On the evening after the first day of the second group's clinic, she facilitated a debriefing session including all of the medical students *and* translators, Sarah and Tim, Mustafa, and myself. Each of the medical students sat next to their translator. Rather than asking what "interesting cases" the medical workers had seen that day, Dr. Baker asked, quite simply, "Does anyone have something they want to share?" Although some students asked medical questions, many of the students shared their feelings, celebrated their translators' hard work, and asked Mustafa about cultural issues. These responses portrayed the day's work as a partnership utilizing the skills of the medical students, translators, and NGO staff.

Kelly, the first medical student to speak, described how she was surprised by "how uncomfortable I could be while helping at the same time." She had performed her first vaginal exam on a patient that morning, and described the connection she experienced with her patient: "But I also—the same lady—got to talk to about getting HIV testing. And I feel like after that, like, intimate moment we *shared* something. So we were in a weird way bonded, and we had a long talk. It was terrifying and wonderful at the same time." Whereas the first medical group had seen any extra time used talking as wasteful, or distracting from the "real" work, Kelly located herself in the thick of relational complexity.

In a second reflection time later in the week, another medical student echoed this approach. Carrie, detailing her challenge of the day, explained, "I had this lady who had HIV and there wasn't really much wrong with her, but she was just very sad at the test [results]. And she just wanted to sit there and talk to me." Carrie took the time to talk with the patient, even though there was nothing she could do for her, because she recognized that medical work is not simply about healing physical ailments.

The second medical group wove this assumption throughout their experiences, treating language and cultural concerns as an important part of the work being done and thereby relying heavily on the translators for advice and assistance. In the following exchange at the first debriefing, the medical students professed their dependence on the translators and Mustafa in order to provide ethical and quality care to patients:

> DR. BAKER: Was everyone okay with the level of independence we gave you today? Was it surprising, was it scary?
> SAMANTHA: I was surprised by it. Um, I thought that . . . it was a lot more independence than that—than we would have. I just, I don't know. I didn't expect to . . . sit and do the whole history and my physical, everything by myself, and then come check with an attending [physician]. I thought we would be kind of surveilled the whole time.
> DR. LEWIS: Do you wish you had more supervision during it? Did you feel uncomfortable with it?
> SAMANTHA: Um, no. I felt good about it. Because I felt like I had kind of a built-in supervisor in my translator. You know? Like, somebody's there to help.
> DR. BAKER: Not their first rodeo!
> SAMANTHA: Yeah! They know what's going on too, and then I felt like you guys were pretty approachable.
> KELLY: I was really worried that our inexperience would give lower-level care. But it ended up being our input, and you guys' input, and the translators, sometimes Dr. Mustafa. I felt like we were working more together and had more ideas than most patients would ever get. Like having different perspectives on the problem.

For this group of students, the translators were more than simply tools; they were partners in providing quality care. The input of the translators allowed the students to feel comfortable, ethically, with treating patients even though they had only had two years of medical school. It is also worth noting that this group consistently referred to Mustafa as Dr. Mustafa. Instead of seeing Mustafa as a threat, they saw him as a valuable resource for cultural knowledge and asked him questions throughout the debriefing, listening carefully to his translated answers.

Each of the debriefing sessions ended in a short Swahili or tribal language lesson. The translators emphasized the importance of this in their meeting before the second group's arrival. By the first debriefing, Dr. Baker was already able to ask, "Translators, did the students use greetings today?" Francis hurriedly assure her, "Of course!" and the other translators laughed and chorused, "Yes!" She then turned to Sarah, coaxing, "You promised us you would teach us a little bit more everyday." The students exclaimed "Yeah!" The group was excited to learn Swahili and the tribal language, as they understood the importance of relationship building to medical treatment. Learning Swahili was not considered a waste of time but a way to build the connection necessary to having Tanzanian patients talk to them about their ailments and trust them with their health care. To these workers, medicine was about relationality: no treatment could be given without their Tanzanian counterparts.

UNCERTAINTY: LOSING CONTROL

Musa and Idda gathered everyone into a circle on the stage in the community hall that would be used for the first day of clinic. Musa clapped his hands and spread his arms wide to call for attention. "So we're going to sing a song called 'Songa Mbele,'" he said, elaborating on how *songa mbele* means to keep moving forward and never despair. The medical workers repeated the words slowly after him: *son-ga, m-be-le*. Many of them could not say the words correctly. He and Idda began to slap rhythmically, singing for everyone. As the verse repeated, they aimed it toward an individual, pulling them into the middle of the circle and having them dance until the chorus. The students and translators sang and danced unabashedly, even as patients began to filter into the community hall and wait for the clinic to start. The Americans were uncertain of the words, but that did not keep them from singing their gibberish attempts as loud as they could. As the song continued, energy would build and build until the entire group was clapping and stomping in rhythm, rocking the stage and causing the beat to reverberate through bodies and objects. When Musa ended the song, everyone clapped and cheered—including some of the patients. *Now* it was time for the clinic to begin.

Although both groups of medical workers were led in an opening song on the first day of the clinics, only the second allowed themselves to be carried away by the pulse in the Tanzanian music and relinquish control of their language and behavior. The first group had barely participated, perhaps because they were concerned with the time used up in singing, perhaps because they were embarrassed to sing when they were uncertain of the words. For whatever reason, their song had faded quietly into an ending. The second group's song went out with explosive energy. By embracing a relational perspective on medical care, the second group was also more willing to relinquish some control over its circumstances. Facing uncertainty head-on allowed the second group to create more equitable partnerships with its Tanzanian translators.

One implication of ceding control was immediately obvious that day in clinic: the medical students were able to triage much more quickly and efficiently. They immediately realized that they were hopeless at writing unfamiliar Tanzanian names, so Francis was assigned triage duty. He handled it with aplomb—instructing patients where to sit, letting them know when they would be seen, and taking down their introductory information. That evening in the debriefing time, Musa congratulated his fellow translator on a job well done, saying "Francis was very good today at, like, the management of patients. . . . Last time we met this challenge that, in the reception part, people would come, then they [the medical workers] would use, like, Western—they used Western writing style. *Long* time there. And, you know, arranging everybody . . . I have to give my big ups to Mr. Francis for always doing it!" Everyone seconded Musa's praise, and many clapped Francis on the back. The medical students were not only unperturbed to have a Tanzanian doing a job other than direct translation but were also thankful for the help and appreciative of his skill.

Throughout the week, the US medical workers praised the Tanzanian translators' abilities. In one debriefing, Amy expressed her adoration of Musa:

> I just wanted to say, like, I mean—I think my experience with Musa as a translator has been amazing. He also seems like he's doing more of crowd control, and just keeping people happy, and, I don't know, he's just amazing. And so, I think he makes my job a lot easier. He—he's very good. Like, a lot of people were saying they've had trouble having people want to talk about their [HIV] status, but he seems to make people very comfortable. So I guess my experience has been pretty good because I think he just makes people very comfortable.

Referencing how the other medical students had trouble finding out a patient's HIV status, Amy explained that a lot of the success of her work over the week was due to her translator's ability to connect with patients and make them feel at ease in her presence. Ceding control allowed her to do a better job at helping. She recognized that Tanzanian knowledge and skill is integral, and that their medical work could only be done as a team.

The students were also willing to admit that they were uncertain about some of the medical issues their patients faced. They often met with situations that they found frustrating or even inconceivable when viewed through a Western frame, but they were open to listening to other cultural interpretations. During one debriefing session the students were asked to present a highlight, a challenge, and a learning moment from the day. James related that his challenge was dealing with HIV-positive patients who did not have the proper medical record information with them. "They just didn't seem to care!" he said. Dr. Baker reframed the situation by noting the large divide between HIV care and regular medical care in Tanzania: "They don't connect that those two things are put together, because they're treated totally differently by the health care system." I offered a third interpretation, mentioning that often the machine testing the progression of the disease is out of order at the local treatment center and that their shipments of medicine do not always arrive on time: "It might be that they're lackadaisical because sometimes their medicine just doesn't come in when it's supposed to." James sat thoughtfully for a moment before deciding that his "learning moment" of the day was this very exchange, as it made him face the fact that he was "not really thinking about the extenuating circumstances for all the people."

Later in the same session, Samantha voiced her concern for people having to relate their HIV status to her. "I had a lot of people look super ashamed," she said. "They look down, they get quiet, they barely whisper." I suggested we explore the possibility that the emotion she sees might not be shame but sadness or an expression of a burden. Samantha acted reticent to jettison her interpretation, but Dr. Baker then added, "I do think the entire diagnosis introduces fifty ways to get yelled at by health care providers, you know?" This was a reference to the fact that Tanzanian doctors are typically accustomed to chastising patients for their unhealthy behaviors. People in the room nodded in agreement, and Samantha seemed to consider the new perspective.

In both of the previous examples, although the medical students were quick to proffer explanations for the feelings of their Tanzanian patients, they were also open to challenges and reinterpretations. By the end of the session, the medical students were leading the reframing themselves and reflexively engaging with their own thought processes. Samantha brought up another frustrating occurrence, one of having an old woman ask for her help: "There are some things though that are not—I just don't understand. That people are like, 'I'm eighty-four, and my chest is tight when I'm walking up hill and carrying fifty pounds.' Like, I know that you *have* to know this is part of life! I don't understand why that's such a surprise. And that's really frustrating for me sometimes." One person suggested that they might not have biological education in schools, and another added that perhaps that woman is the oldest person in her village and doesn't have other older people to look to for similar experiences. Samantha realized, "I guess it's frustrating for me, because my answer is just, 'You're old,'" and later added, "I guess I'm just disappointed that I don't have a solution, and I project that on them." By the end of the debriefing session, the medical students had moved from assuming certain interpretations of Tanzanian emotions to realizing that their interpretations spoke more about themselves. This second group of medical students allowed for their own uncertainty and recognized that they could be wrong. Their willingness to embrace the realization that they might not be able to fully understand their patients broke from neocolonial masculine logics that assume US dominance over Tanzanian culture.

CARE: EMBRACING FRAGILITY

The second group of medical students demonstrated an ethic of care in engaging with their Tanzanian patients, taking care to investigate how their work fit into complex circumstances. The question of whether or not they should tell a patient that they have a terminal or debilitating disease never arose in this group. The medical team instead centered on Tanzanian cultural meanings in order to displace their own interpretations—and thus, discomfort—from the focal point. For example, James reflected in one debriefing session:

> I was really kind of surprised that even though I felt like ... it was all ... it was all very new to me, and maybe I felt like I wasn't doing that much to help, but still the people that I was working with still felt like I had done a lot for them. And that was, um, that was really nice. Because I guess in the [United] States, people feel like you've *never* done enough for them. So there's a complete one hundred eighty here, where even the littlest thing is greatly appreciated. So it was really cool.

James, like members of the first group, was concerned by his lack of ability to do "that much to help." But instead of letting this perceived failure consume him, he turned his gaze toward his patients' perspectives. The cultural meaning of his interactions with patients outweighed his own feelings of inadequacy or discomfort and was read as positively valued against what happens in the United States. Of course, glossing over how an entire nation deals with medicine is also problematic, but in this case the comment acted as a step toward recognizing that the US medical student's feelings and perspectives should not necessarily be held as primary or correct.

In order to be attentive to the feelings and perspectives of their patients, the second group had a number of discussions about how to avoid dismissing a patient too quickly because their symptoms look—on the surface—like things they knew to be common problems in the area. In the first day's debriefing session, Dr. Lewis challenged the medical students, saying, "You're going to see a lot of swelling, the arthritis, but don't . . . say, 'Oh, another leg pain!' and say "Motrin.' Take a look at the toenail, and say, 'Oh, we can remove the toenail, it's not just leg pain.' And don't become complacent. And I'm not saying that you will, but it can be easy: 'Oh, they've got back pain, let's do some Motrin and send them home.' These people are very sick sometimes, and there are things we want to make sure we can treat if we can." Dr. Lewis wanted to make sure that the medical students put patient care in front of expediency or efficiency. When dealing with over a hundred patients in a day, the medical workers could easily resort to a quantity over quality means of valuing their work. Instead this group labored under the assumption that even though they might not be able to see all the patients, the Tanzanians who came to the clinic deserved the best care that they could give them. In an interview, Amy described it as a balancing act: "I think everyday . . . like, I've seen more patients, got more efficient, and that way you kind of like develop those patterns. . . . But at the same time, like, being—being able to tailor it to individual people and then, like. . . . I think that has been the most rewarding for me. Just being a little better with patient care each time." In her view, both the pattern recognition that allowed her to spot diseases more quickly and the ability to recognize individual symptoms and quirks helped her to tailor her work to the patients' needs. By making care for patients the primary motivating force behind their daily work, the medical students in the second group tempered the drive toward efficiency, quantity, and easy solutions that might salvage wounded masculine pride.

The move away from easy or quick solutions also registered in the groups' questions regarding systemic concerns. The second medical group was acutely interested in how its treatment was situated in the complex circumstances of Tanzanian village life in the area. James, in the first debriefing, registered keen curiosity. His brow was furrowed as he waited for an opportunity to speak. When an opening appeared, he looked directly at Mustafa, and said, "We worked together on one patient who needed to go to the hospital, and I was just kinda curious—you got his number, and I think you gave him yours; I'm just curious where things go from there." Mustafa began by querying whether it was all right that he speak in Swahili. Following a chorus of yeses, Mustafa told a story. Tanzanians often speak in more detail than people from the United States expect, bringing up aspects of circumstances that may seem beside the point. But as Mustafa wove the tale, even though it was in a language that they could not understand, all the medical workers were attentive and focused on him. Sarah and I took turns translating, telling the students in English about how this patient's AIDS was quite advanced, and that Mustafa discovered that he was not taking his medicine regularly. He represented a common problem in the area, Mustafa explained through Sarah, where those who do not want their communities to find out they are HIV-positive go to the hospital under a fake name or go to a variety of different, far-away hospitals in order not to be found out. The flip side of this is that they do not get medication regularly, or may be prescribed different treatment regimens at different hospitals, leading to increased drug resistance. The students—even though they were only at the Little Community for a week and were unable to affect the problems of stigma and access to treatment—listened intently. Whether or not they could fix the problem did not matter; they cared about understanding the circumstances of the patients they were seeing each day.

Their attentiveness to context helped these medical workers engage with problems that could not be solved with a simple solution. Facing matters head-on, they asked the translators for advice on how best to relate thorny issues to their patients. In the first debriefing, Dr. Baker quizzed the medical students on all the possible problems that could cause leg pain, since they often see it in the patients. After wading through the different causes, she then turned to the translators:

> So, translators, tell me if this is good or not. When people have osteoarthritis, so it's usually because of age, and just wear and tear, use of the joints and the leg. So, when we explain it, it's something we can treat with ibuprofen, but will always be there and will probably get worse as they get older and older. I've been saying, "Your legs are tired from all the work you've done in your life." To try to explain, uh, it's not something that happened [like an accident] . . . and, unfortunately, it's not something I can fix forever. Is—is there a better way to explain that?

Damas was the first translator to answer, explaining that some patients will understand, and others will not, but that saying "It's medicine for pain, and not to fix" helped them to know their legs would not get better. Sarah pressed him to answer the specific question asked, to which he responded, "I think we can just tell them that their legs are hurting because you are *old!*" The room broke out in giggles and chatter, but Denis protested that even old people do not see themselves as old. They should be told, "You are suffering because you're exercising too much, carrying all these things." Francis fired back that if you tell them the pain comes from hard work, someone might think, "Maybe you can *do something* that makes you to be fine again."

The translators' discussion provided a window for the medical students to see that even something as simple as explaining leg pain can be quite complicated in an area with little access to medical expertise or resources. When this route to figuring out how best to care for the patients did not seem to be leading anywhere helpful, the discussion switched directions toward alternative solutions. Dr. Baker asked the translators what feasible lifestyle changes they could encourage to help ease the pain. The group continued discussing the availability of shoes with good arch support, if women might be able to get assistance in carrying water, and if carrying a pile of logs in two trips instead of one might work. This second medical team focused on the details in order to find better avenues for patient care. They could only do so in partnership with the Tanzanian translators, without whom the US medical workers could not have the necessary knowledge to understand their patients' lives.

The US medical group embraced their reliance on their Tanzanian partners and their inability to know everything. In this way, rather than treating their lack of proper training as a tender point of fragility, they treated it as an ethical dilemma, something to be carefully worked out with their patients. James described his approach to patients as "treading lightly" and making sure to ask, "Is it okay if I do this?" before attempting any tests or procedures. His surprise that the patients were continually obliging did not alter his approach; he continued to treat each one with care. James saw his solicitous approach as mitigating the possibility that he might be giving them substandard treatment.

Amy, on the other hand, found that the question of whether or not the treatment given was ethical could not be decisively settled. She reflected, "I feel like everyone [in the group] has this . . . idea of 'I want to help people.' But at the same time, like, I probably think this experience is more valuable for us—our learning and development, more than we're actually helping people. But . . . it's a conflicting—moral conundrum. Whether what we're doing is actually helpful or [not]." Amy never came to a conclusion; she allowed herself to be uncomfortable with the service she was providing in the village. Later in our interview, she added, "I think this is a good thing to experience now as, like, an eye-opening experience, and then, like, with more knowledge and more ability, I think it would be better to come back in a few years, once that is there." As Amy's comment indicates, the second medical group did not consider their interactions with the Tanzanian villagers as isolated interactions during a particular week. Thinking relationally, they recognized that the relationships they formed would continue to have reverberating effects. This perspective allowed Amy to think beyond her immediate trip and to recognize that the ethicality of her work hinged on a future return when she could give back from the wealth of cultural learning gained in this initial experience.

The Ambivalence of Medical Mission Trips

The preceding analysis illustrates how two groups of medical aid workers hailing from the same US university demonstrated vastly different ways of conceptualizing medical aid work and interacting with their Tanzanian counterparts and patients. For the first group, more heavily conditioned by the hidden curriculum of medical expectations of masculine authority, the international aid trip presented an opportunity to recapture a fictive past where white medical masculinity could be whole and unchallenged. This group re-centered white masculine dominance through neocolonial relations to their translators and patients. For the second group, only recently introduced to both medical school and international experience, the medical mission trip offered a means to better understand their interrelatedness to and dependence on others. Yet even though I have presented these two international responses to the contemporary crisis in US white masculinity as distinct, they cannot ever be fully disentangled, for white masculinity can never secure "permanent answers to the recurring crisis of the male self,"[37] much as it tries, and thus there can be no masculine subjectivity that is fully sovereign or individual; even the most overt masculinity is reliant on the otherness it ostensibly seeks to eject.[38]

For example, there were moments in the first group's visit that balked masculine standards and expectations. Consider Ken, who told me in an interview, "I'm here to treat, more than to build relationships, really." Later he admitted, "Like I said, I came here not really with the intention of building relationships, but it just kind of is what happens over time, and I guess maybe I should have been trying harder from day one to do that." As he continued talking about the relationships he had been building with the translators, he expressed frustration with how he had seen them "dicking around" and returns to the premise that he is here "to work one hundred percent of the time, like, as much as possible." Ken's attempt to consider a relational perspective toward his work was commandeered by the masculine imperative toward efficiency and expediency, curtailed before it could have much impact.

Abed also illustrates how the first group's behavior was not monolithic. In his side project, he partnered with NGO workers to train them how to treat a particular disease endemic to the area. Abed's project was dependent on the NGO workers' ability to implement the treatment plans once the medical group had left. Notably, he was the only Person of Color in the first group. He was also the only one who consistently represented his work as a partnership with Tanzanians. Describing how the partnerships came together, he exclaimed, "It's so many cogs in the wheel coming together to form something incredible!" Abed suggested that he had a different perspective than the rest of the group because his project allowed him to relate to the translators and staff in a more intimate way than those students who only saw patients at the clinic.

Abed and Ken demonstrate that there is a latent ambivalence in medical mission trips. The response of medical workers to the contemporary crisis of US white masculinity functions as an entangled *both/and*; neither groups nor individuals can perform medical masculinity perfectly, no matter their neocolonial fantasies, but they cannot completely disentangle from it either. The second group still expressed impulses to think of the Tanzanian patients as remarkably ignorant or even nonsensical. The neocolonial paternalism built into US identity over the course of centuries cannot be easily overcome, and neither can medical imperatives of masculine mastery and control. What makes the second group notable is that even when these students began to center masculine dominance or neocolonial views, they were still open to alternative interpretations and reframings of their experiences.

The relational ethic of the second group demonstrates the decolonial tactic that Sabelo Ndlovu-Gatsheni describes as "learning to unlearn in order to relearn."[39] Aimee Carrillo Rowe tells us that "deep connections across lines of difference are a transformative source."[40] In this case, relations that connect Western medical volunteers and Tanzanian patients and translators through a sense of subjective dependence on and belonging to and with each other hold the potential to transform the power relations underlying medical aid.

The potential to transform ultimately comes to fruition in what I call haunted reflexivity. In chapter 3, I describe how haunted reflexivity "stages an encounter, over and over again, with our own perpetuation of trauma and complicity in power relations that cannot yet be understood or taken in." The second group of medical students departed from white, neocolonial masculine norms by recognizing their subjective dependence on others—the first step toward engaging in haunted reflexivity. Haunted reflexivity is important in this instance not only because it stages a continual political encounter with the ghosts of (neo)colonial violence in everyday life but also because it offers the only escape from the ambivalence of masculinity in medical aid work. It is an escape that is not an escape; only by repetitively and continually engaging with the way our own subjectivities have been conditioned by racial, (neo)colonial, and gendered violences can privileged subjects avoid remaining mired in the ambivalence of white masculine crisis. In this way, haunted reflexivity opens relatively dominant subjects to the possibilities of attuning to fluid epistemologies.

As this chapter demonstrates, the liminal space of the "frontier" functions as a space where white masculine dominance can be rescued *and simultaneously* as a space where it can be challenged—or even dismantled. To focus on one of these aspects while relegating the other to obscurity does a theoretical and political disservice. Frontier space may indeed be feminized as eminently conquerable, recentering both white masculine dominance and neocolonial relations.[41] But the distance the so-called frontier provides from US gender relations also opens space for a refiguring of gender norms within this liminal cultural space. On the frontier, "material structures are open to restructuration and reinterpretation,"[42] affording agency to institute alternative genderings and decolonial relations.

But the frontier is as much a construction as masculinity itself. To those who live in the Little Community, it is no frontier, but the center of their relations. The NGO becomes the locus wherein others' masculine ambivalence is expressed, over which their battle between engaging in sovereign power and/or relational care is waged. For the NGO, the ambivalence of medical volunteer masculinity provides a consistent push and pull on relations, a repetitive tension between belongings and behaviors premised on coloniality and those that attempt to delink. Each specific volunteer group may only stay for a week, but group after group, week after week, they construct and replicate certain ways of relating with the Tanzanians at the organization and in the community. And the NGO is caught up in the fray.

For Western subjects, this repetitive tension must be met with a repetitive reflexivity, one that questions emergent relations of power and the subject's ever-evolving complicity with and in them. Only by keeping one's finger to the political pulse, the way historical forces have converged on this particular moment, can one conceptualize the emergent need and potentials for liquid responses. The ability of privileged subjects to engage in decolonial action depends on this reflexive connection to surrounding collectivities and alternative epistemologies.

What, then, of those who deny that they are haunted, cannot recognize their complicity in coloniality? Chapter 2 continues looking at how the Little Community is caught up in Western volunteer relations, but turns its gaze to how haunted reflexivity is stymied before it gets started, obscuring potentials for liquid action.

Chapter
Two
All of Us
Phantasmic
Saviors

One can only face in others what one can face in oneself.
—James Baldwin, *Nobody Knows My Name*

Sitting at Sarah and Tim's kitchen table with my coffee one morning, after the children had all left for school, I took advantage of the relative peace and quiet during breakfast to write my field notes from the day before. I was typing away as Tiffany, a medical student volunteer who had come with the first group but stayed for three weeks after they left, came into the house and sat down. Sarah and Tim's house was the only place at the Little Community with Wi-Fi, and it attracted all of the volunteers and donors in the early hours of the morning and late hours of the night—the times when the generator was running and the electricity was on.[1]

Looking back as I write this chapter, I do not remember exactly what took place between us, but I do know that my field note narrative of events and reflections from the day before was suddenly interrupted:

> (Sidenote: I'm typing this sitting at the kitchen table with Tiffany. I asked her if she was going to the CTC [HIV/AIDS Care and Treatment Center] today, and she gave me a 10-minute complaining answer about

how they don't give them any work to do there other than filling out forms. All I was trying to do was be polite! I tried to go back to my work, typing up the stories of what was going on yesterday, but she kept trying to get me to respond to her admonitions that their time is wasted at the CTC. I was not asking for a defense of their schedule; I was just asking, quickly, what they would be doing today. I kept trying to say, "Okay," or "That's fine," to stop the wave of desire that I acknowledge that they can be bitchy about not wanting to go to the CTC. What I wanted to say was that they were only there once, and it was a day that the clinical officer was left alone and overwhelmed with work. You cannot make statements starting with "Every time we go to the CTC . . ." when you've been there ONCE. Also, stop trying to get me to give you validation for your feelings. That is not my place, and I do not want to. I want to type my damn notes. I know you think that I am not working, but these are actually quite important. I know paperwork does not seem like an important job to you, but it is quite important to me. I know that you think you should be put to work saving lives rather than stuck in an office all day, but what I do allows people to think in ways that affect lives on a global scale. I am working. End rant.)

I was angry with Tiffany for what I perceived as her not valuing my research as work. She wanted to vent and to have me validate her feelings. I refused, instead imposing over them a view that *I* knew more about the context she was working in than she did, that *I* understood Tanzanians better, that *I* knew paperwork functioned as (neo)colonial debris,[2] and that *I* was okay with menial tasks, because *I* knew better than to be a white savior. At the same time, I supported my feelings with a similar logic to the one I read into her actions: My time is too important for this; what I do allows people to think in ways that affect lives on a global scale. My claim seems to be that I know better than to try to be a white savior in aid, but being an *ivory tower savior* is different.

The funny thing is, I really liked Tiffany. We were friends, and I enjoyed talking with her. Yet there were times when we were not kind to one another. Moreover, the negative feelings I felt toward Tiffany in this instance were anything but unique; every Western volunteer with whom I interacted had conflict with other Western volunteers at some point or another. As I casually surveyed other aid workers in the area, I found that the phenomenon was not unique to this organization, either. One local missionary informed me that this was well known in the church, and thus why missionaries were often placed separately. Rather than simply noting this as a fact of life for Western volunteers in Tanzania, I became curious: Why was there a seemingly inherent conflict between Western volunteers? And how did it relate to neocolonialism?

Nearly every volunteer I talked to at the nongovernmental organization (NGO), whether formally or informally, described the most challenging part of working in Tanzania as *other Westerners*. Most of the volunteers had some sense of how easily aid can turn into paternalism, or—at the least—how aid projects fail when they are not connected to community desires. Many also knew that being a "white savior" or a "voluntourist" was bad. Yet each Westerner seemed to feel as if they had a right to be in Tanzania when others did not.

If volunteers were to take their own critiques of other volunteers seriously, they—or, I should say, *we*—would have a very difficult time being in Tanzania. In an unfamiliar cultural and linguistic context, what does a Westerner have to offer that cannot be traced back to an assumed privilege—of country of birth, of skin color, or of both? Even with skilled volunteers, such as medical students, the lack of contextual, linguistic, or cultural knowledge should give them pause. How is it, then, that most volunteers are able to so clearly see this lack in others and go to such lengths to avoid it in ourselves?

In this chapter, I argue that the subject constitution of Western volunteers is dependent on foreclosures of our own neocolonial and racial subjective structuring. If the subjectivity of the Western volunteer is constituted through a foreclosure of the neocolonial self, accusations of neocolonialism may be leveled at others without a recognition of the same in oneself. To build this argument, I first describe the process of subject construction for US volunteers, what foreclosures it depends on, and how US volunteer subjects are racialized through fantasies of being a white savior who "makes a difference." I focus particularly on people from the United States, since nearly all of the volunteers with whom I interacted during my time present at the NGO were from there. Although the Little Community also has volunteers from Canada, Finland, Sweden, and the United Kingdom, there were not many present during my stay at the NGO. In addition, each of these countries has particular national identities that play into the process of subject constitution, and some of the aspects I trace in this chapter take a unique shape in the US. In the following pages, I demonstrate how US volunteers maneuver symbolically to avoid the dissolution and reconstitution of subjectivity that would come with traversing their fantasies. Finally, I explore potential routes of encouraging subjective dissolution, leading to haunted reflexivity.

Constructing US Volunteer Subjectivity

Foreclosures and Fantasies

My sense of foreclosure is derived from the psychoanalytic theory of Jacques Lacan, as filtered through Judith Butler and Gayatri Chakravorty Spivak. For Lacan, the subject is fundamentally constituted through a misrecognition of oneself as whole and the simultaneous foreclosure of the possibility of the subject ever actually being whole or self-knowing.[3] To be a subject requires foreclosure, a structural limitation to self-reflexivity. Butler explains that "to the extent that one is a subject, [one is] always at a distance from oneself, from one's origin, from one's history."[4] Since foreclosure is the condition that makes subjectivity possible, the subject's "veritable subsistence [would be] abolished by his knowledge."[5] In other words, it is impossible for a subject to fully know themself, recognize themself, understand themself.

At the same time, foreclosure creates the possibility for agency. A subject can act only on condition that "certain things become impossible" for them.[6] The subject develops fantasies that work to cover what is foreclosed through a narrative of possible wholeness. Fantasies "offer, simultaneously, a frame within which to exercise agency and a shield from the horror of contingency."[7] Through fantasy, a subject can narrate their past experiences in a way that produces meaning, and thereby defend themself from recognizing their own structural inability to ever be coherent as a self. These fantasies are culturally constructed, though internalized differently.[8] For US volunteers, in defining themselves as international agents of good, the primary cultural fantasy is that of the white savior.

Racing Neocolonial Fantasies

The white savior fantasy takes shape in the foreclosures inherent in conceptualizations of international aid and US national identity. As Spivak explains, "to the extent that ... the North continues ostensibly to 'aid' the South—as formerly imperialism 'civilized' the New World—the South's crucial assistance to the North in keeping up its resource-hungry lifestyle is forever foreclosed."[9] Aid from the United States to Tanzania, including volunteerism, is premised on a foreclosure of the ways economic relations with countries such as Tanzania make aid possible in the first place. In addition, prevalent cultural invocation of the myth of "American exceptionalism" indicates an underlying foreclosure constitutive of US subjectivities. American exceptionalism hails the United States as a uniquely superior nation and "allows for a unquestioningly positive construction of humanitarian aid," thus foreclosing the possibility that aid can do harm.[10]

Volunteers constituted by these foreclosures internalize the fantasy of the white savior to create a fiction of wholeness and stability that hides the terror of incompleteness. Being a white savior incorporates both the idea of national autonomy found in the conceptualization of aid and the idea of superiority found in American exceptionalist ideology. In the fantasy of the white savior, the US volunteer can "find themselves"—that is, find wholeness, be complete—in other countries by saving other people. By making a difference, I can be the self I want to be.

The fantasy of white saviorism depends on racial privilege. Teju Cole describes how "Africa serves as a backdrop for white fantasies of conquest and heroism" where "a nobody from America or Europe can go to Africa and become a godlike savior."[11] Here whiteness is tied to the nationalistic idea of American exceptionalism—where anyone, regardless of qualifications, has the ability to be a savior in Africa simply because of their national identity. The assumption of a white body is inherent in cultural narratives of the Global North as purveyor of aid, and Americans as exceptional.[12]

Yet, even as an African man living in the United States, Cole recognizes that he is not outside the dynamics of power.[13] Although foreclosures and fantasies are clearly racialized in certain ways, nonwhite volunteer subjects may still be positioned within them. Aimee Carrillo Rowe describes subject constitution as a function of differential belonging, emphasizing the contingency of social relations that form the subject and the contradictory narratives that the subject imbibes.[14] As Amina Mama argues, for Black British subjects this differential belonging produces subjects "born out of an imposed contradiction between blackness and British-ness, British-ness being equated with whiteness in the dominant symbolic order."[15] A similar conflation of the US with whiteness occurs in the context of international aid. Whiteness is an embodied phenomenon that has different manifestations in different spaces and places.[16] Since the fantasies internalized by US international volunteers assume whiteness, volunteers of color are more likely to be faced with a contradiction in their experience that may cause them to question their role abroad or construct it using different cultural fantasies than white volunteers.

Undoing and Redoing in US Volunteer Subjects

Contradictions offer a means of recognizing foreclosures that underlie subjectivity, thereby undoing both the foreclosures themselves—once they are recognized, they are no longer foreclosed—and the subject as such. The subject does not completely dissolve but becomes a new subject; they are reconstituted on the basis of a different foreclosure. As Butler explains, "while we are constituted socially in limited ways and through certain kinds of . . . foreclosures, we are not constituted for all time in that way." By addressing a foreclosure, the subject "can renew the meaning and the effect of the foreclosure."[17]

The way to address foreclosure is by traversing the fantasy that covers it. Dana Cloud, quoting Slavoj Žižek, explains that "to 'traverse the fantasy' . . . is to recognize it as a signal of unrealizable hopes, to come into traumatic awareness that there is 'nothing "behind" it, and to recognize how fantasy masks precisely this "nothing."'"[18] Yet it is not as simple as it sounds to recognize the fantasy that one has been using to make sense of one's life is "nothing." How are subjects brought to such an awareness?

Carrillo Rowe argues that "deep connections along lines of difference are a transformative source" in relation to subjectivity. When connections are forged across what she calls "power lines," it changes how subjects are formed, since subject constitution "arise[s] out of the collectivities into which we insert ourselves or are inserted."[19] As I noted in chapter 1, volunteering always includes the possibility of forming connections across difference that can force the subject to face their foreclosures and be reconstituted in ways that make them capable of acting against the very power relations formative of their subjectivity.

Yet chapter 1 also demonstrated that forming connections across difference does not automatically bring such awareness. Creating reflexive subjects requires more than simply bringing contradictions to their attention. That is, providing the critical conceptual tools to understand whiteness does not always result in subjects willing to challenge it.[20] Subjects have means of avoiding subjective undoing. US volunteers at the Little Community displayed this in two main ways: through denial of contradiction, and through an ironic rendering of themselves as outside the white savior fantasy they recognize in others. Denial is the response when a fantasy is so strongly internalized that the subject cannot (yet) question it. Irony is the response when a fantasy is recognized as such, but not as one's own fantasy.

Popular critiques of aid are currently rampant on social media.[21] Elsa Gunnarsdottir and Kathryn Mathers note that many young volunteers are therefore "fully aware of the relation between their work and parodies of it, as well as the cultural and political critique of the 'white savior complex.'" They argue that millennials' heavy use of social media has led them to "turn aid . . . into an entirely affective economy, switching emotional resonance for political and economic landscapes of inequality."[22] What is "good" in aid is individualized as positive affective resonance, leading young volunteers to find "no contradiction in being both critical of and a participant in voluntourism" and allowing them to be aware of the white savior fantasy without traversing it.[23]

The idea that one can both participate in aid and critique it at the same time functions as an experiential irony bribe. Cloud describes how "the *irony bribe* wins viewers to participation in an ideological discourse by tempting them not only with mass social and political fantasy, but also with the possibility of protection against rampant archaic desires by the reflexive *rejection* of the fantasy."[24] The irony bribe for aid tempts subjects to believe that simply being savvy about the contradictions in aid narratives will allow one to get the savior thing right oneself and simultaneously be able to reject the attempts of everyone else.

Through irony, recognition of the fantasy can counterintuitively work to shore up the foreclosures on which the fantasy depends. Irony allows a US volunteer to "avoid the traumatic encounter by imagining that s/he is somehow outside of the fantasy and its spectacular failures to deliver on its promises."[25] Precisely because US volunteers have the ability to recognize that being a white savior is a bad thing, we are able to claim that we are *not that*, and so avoid the only recognition that would allow for the reformulation of the volunteer subject as a decolonial ally: The recognition that we *are* the white saviors we love to hate.

This chapter thus traces everyday denials of haunted reflexivity and its attendant recognitions of complicity. By staging the ways in which US volunteers avoid facing the racial and neocolonial power relations of which we are a part, I hope to clarify how exactly haunted reflexivity develops in Western subjects—and how it does not. Notably, both processes, engaging or denying haunted reflexivity, rely on iterative reconstructions of the subject. Haunted reflexivity involves an iterative engagement with the ghosts created by traumas inflicted on colonized peoples. Haunted reflexivity involves recognizing and being accountable for past and present harms wrought by coloniality. It is a continual process that can never be fully realized. The volunteers in this chapter, on the other hand, display an iterative *refusal* to engage with the violences neocolonialism has wrought. Both are labored processes. There is no Western subject that does not either labor to engage with haunted reflexivity or labor to avoid it.

In the following pages, I detail ways that US volunteers avoided traversing their volunteer fantasies at the NGO and instead re-centered them. I analyzed field notes, and transcriptions of interviews and conversations with—and *about*—two particular volunteer groups. The first was a group of college students in a study abroad program run through a US public university. Although the program accepted students of all majors, the courses taught in the program were the

Swahili language, East African culture, and public health in East Africa. The students had been in Tanzania for two weeks before spending two and a half days at the NGO. The group was racially diverse, and they were accompanied by their instructors: a white woman from the United States who researched public health, a Kenyan woman professor of African culture, and a Tanzanian man who was the Swahili instructor. The second volunteer group was a group of high school students from all over the United States who had come as part of a "service and leadership" trip through a large nonprofit specializing in travel for study abroad. They stayed at the NGO for nearly a week. The two teachers accompanying them were Black women, and the students were almost all white. Rather than taking classes, these students had spent the past two weeks in Tanzania teaching English in primary and secondary schools. I also draw from interactions with long-term volunteers: Dr. Baker and Tiffany, two white medical workers who stayed for three weeks after their group left; Mary, a white high school graduate who had been working in the NGO's education department for over a year; and Sue, a young white woman just out of high school who was volunteering for a month.

Avoiding Dissolution of US Volunteer Subjectivity

Before demonstrating what happened when volunteer fantasies were challenged, I provide some examples of how these fantasies arose in context. As many of the volunteers articulated it, they perceived being at the NGO as a means of fulfilling desires to visit a place fundamentally wild and open, where they—unskilled students—could "make a difference." As I have described in earlier work, the desire to "make a difference" without reflection over whether or not one has the requisite knowledge or training to do so replicates neocolonial conditions.[26]

In response to the question of why they decided to come to Tanzania, the students answered in ways that did not directly correlate to the country at all. The fantasy of white saviorism filled in the spaces between the answers provided and the context of Tanzania itself. For instance, when asked why she had come on a trip to Tanzania, one high school student named Tracy said, "'Cause I know, like, my—like, when I die, I want to know that I made a difference. It sounds kind of cheesy, but I want to know that I impacted someone's life. And—or, more than one person." Rather than describe anything she knew about the country, Tracy answered that she wanted to make a difference before she died. Her statement implies not only that she could make a difference in Tanzania, that it provided a context where a high school student from the

United States had the ability to do something life changing, but also that this life-changing work would be enough to satisfy a deathbed criterion—that is, she saw what she was doing in Tanzania as meaningful enough that she would be able to die in peace. Her answer implies that she could not have the same impact at home in the United States. Tanzania, however, is seen as an abject space where she cannot help but impact at least one person's life in a meaningful way simply by being there.

How Tanzania is conceptualized as a space is perhaps more clear in another volunteer answer. I asked the same question of Alicia—why she had come on a trip to Tanzania:

> ALICIA: I guess I initially went on the trip, um—do you know the movie *The Wild Thornberrys*?
> SARAH: Yes. Um, well, I know *of* it.
> ALICIA: It's a cartoon about living in Africa, and I saw it when I was really little and absolutely fell in love with the idea of coming to Africa. . . . I honestly didn't come so much for service—um, that's not what really drew me in; what really drew me in was, like, the group—I mean, not that I don't want to do service, but, like—coming to Africa, and, like, giving such a chance to do something like that.
> SARAH: To meet like a new group of people or what?
> ALICIA: To go to Africa.

The Wild Thornberrys is a cartoon television show and film about a family of white Western wildlife documentarians in Africa. The cartoon focuses on a young daughter of the filmmakers who is given the magical gift of speaking to animals by a shaman. The movie particularly follows the daughter on an adventure to save a cheetah cub taken by poachers. *The Wild Thornberrys* seems to encapsulate a certain type of white savior narrative, one that focuses on the adventure to be had by white people in the yet virgin lands of Africa, which are filled with wild and majestic animals (but not usually people). Tanzania is a space where volunteers can make a difference, because as virgin land it is assumedly untouched; there is so much that can be done with a blank canvas. And the people there are ones whose lives can be impacted; "they" need "our" help.

I highlight two particular ways that US volunteers reacted to challenges to their white savior fantasies in ways that restabilized them. First, I explore how denial figures an inability to recognize the fantasy itself in volunteer explanations. Denial often functions through slippages, claims that initial statements were worded incorrectly, and attempts to decontextualize. Second, I trace how an ironic rendering of oneself as outside fantasy allows volunteers to recognize that other people have white savior fantasies but elide that recognition in themselves. In particular, I look at how whiteness grounds ironic displacements of the fantasy onto others, and assumptions that one is an exception to it.

Denial: The Inability to Recognize the Fantasy

Kristen Lavelle theorizes denial as "integral to how dominant groups are accustomed to managing both their past *and* their present." As *integral* to managing self-narrations, "denial is *normal*," an everyday activity that unconsciously and habitually reinforces normative power relations.[27] Denial allows white US volunteers to avoid facing the racial and neocolonial bases of their fantasies. There are three primary ways that US volunteers in the Little Community deny or avoid addressing the foundations of their fantasies: slippage, rewording, and decontextualization.

DENIAL THROUGH SLIPPAGE

When volunteers avoided traversing their fantasies by denial through slippage, they avoid directly answering the question that was asked by reorienting it around a minor aspect, thereby avoiding the implication that would disturb the white savior fantasy. Mary provided an example in an interview:

> MARY: Like, most NGOs are started by Westerners. So if you're looking at it from that side [that NGOs should be managed by local people]—that eventually you would be passing it off to Tanzanians. That if it was going to continue on, it would continue on as a Tanzanian-only project. And I would agree with that more and more.... That you're empowering Tanzanians to do that work that you're doing.
> JENNA: Why do you think the Westerners are needed to start it in the first place?
> MARY: Money, I would say, is probably a big thing. And then I think that it would be hard ... impossible ... to, like, give money to—like, if I wanted to start this NGO, I found Damas [a Viongozi Wa Shirika member], and I gave him all the money to start this NGO without me being a part of it at all. I don't think that that would go down very well.
> JENNA: Why?
> MARY: Um ... 'cause ... I don't think he—I can't—I don't know if there's like one person who's—who has all that knowledge. Anyway. And who'd be able to do that. Even in America. If you just gave money to one person, and they would just know exactly the best way to, like, do it.

Here, instead of facing the question of why Westerners are needed to lead an aid organization in the first place, Mary used the terms of her own answer to slip from the question of *Western* control into a question about *individual* control. When faced with the knowledge that her position was based in an idea that Tanzanians could not be trusted to handle money themselves, she denied it by slipping between Tanzanians (plural) and *a* Tanzanian. This allowed her to claim that the reason Westerners were needed to start an NGO is that one person cannot be trusted with money—a clear non sequitur. Yet, by tying this to the idea that this is true "even in America," she can make it seem as if her statement treats people from Tanzania and the United States equally, denying her implication in white savior fantasies.

Similarly, Sue, a young white volunteer just out of high school, demonstrated a slippage between the problems of Westerners paternalistically controlling Tanzanian situations and the problems of *Tanzanian* control. In an interview, Sue kept referring to the problem of "dependence" in aid—that Tanzanians will become lazy and entitled if an organization simply hands out free goods to them. As this recurred, I asked Sue questions to try to encourage reflection on how assuming dependence as a key problem in aid requires an inherent power inequity:

> SUE: I like the idea of providing resources that, like, don't create dependence, but maybe, like, resources that help people who want to make a difference in their own country. I think that could be cool. I don't know.
> JENNA: But is that really putting them in charge?
> SUE: Well...
> JENNA: Or is it just another way of screening a power relation?
> SUE: Exactly, yeah, I mean it depends on the stipulations. I think it would be cool, I mean—you know... theoretically. But that's the thing too, so much stuff, like, you know—David Giles's idea of colonialism as a way to regulate the Tanzanian government and, like, its corruption! In theory, you're, like, wow, maybe that's not so bad. But then you think about it, and you're like, you know, in practice that would just cause more corruption, that would just cause more *bibis* and *babas* [grandmothers and grandfathers] talking about the past when they were, um, not independent and could not make their own decision and had no voice. Um, and—so obviously in practice, that's not, that's not how things work. Power gets corrupted very easily.

When I tried to get Sue to think about how her formulation of providing resources still puts Western people in charge of aid work, she avoided facing the assumption of Western dominance central to her fantasy and instead reinforced it by slipping from talking about the problem of Western colonial control of aid to Tanzanian corruption in government. She even posited that, "in theory," colonialism is "not so bad," denying recognition of the inherent power inequity in colonial relations. She had recently had a conversation with David Giles (the middle-aged son of the Little Community's head, Mr. Giles), who was a vocal proponent of reinstating a British-controlled government in Tanzania. Although Sue came to the conclusion that colonialism would be bad, she got there through a route that did not disturb her assumption of Western dominance. Rather than reflect on how colonialism is *inherently bad*, Sue instead focused on how it would result in "more corruption" and complaints from older generations. Remarkably, she concentrated not on the material implications that reinstating colonial governance would have on people's lives but what they would *say* about it. Such a formulation implicitly posits the audience as Western; what matters is not how Tanzanian lives would be affected, but how it would look to other Westerners. The concern is that it might raise perceptions of corruption and complaints about loss of freedom. That is, the problem is not that Tanzanians would have liberties taken from them but that they would grumble about it.

DENIAL THROUGH REWORDING

The high school student group was particularly adept at parroting the language of the NGO leadership and their teachers to avoid both responsibility for saying something offensive or problematic and reflection on what led them to speak in that way. Sarah decided to lead reflection sessions for them each evening in an attempt to help them think through what they were doing at the Little Community and to move away from a white savior or voluntourist attitude. In part, this stemmed from recent ire demonstrated by Canadian donors who contributed a substantial amount of the NGO budget. Esther and Gail, whom I describe further in chapter 5, were so concerned about voluntourists at the NGO that Mr. Giles threatened to stop taking all volunteers in the future if Esther and Gail continued to be unhappy. Notably, Sarah did not want to host the high school group in the first place; she felt she had been tricked into it by the manager of the trip, who also conveniently was "unable" to accompany the group to the village.[28] Sarah felt both deceived and burdened with another person's responsibility in taking care of this group. The reflection sessions were a means of trying to make the best of an unfortunate situation where unskilled volunteers were foisted onto the NGO's staff, resources, and time.

Language is a structuring force, and it has the power to affect symbolic and material change. But language can also be used as a means of escape or avoidance. As Mama argues, "Adopting political rhetoric and symbolism, however earnestly, does not unproblematically lead to personal change."[29] The high school group demonstrated multiple times the power of rewording in avoiding reflexivity. Camille, one of the teachers, told Sarah and me after the first reflection session that "when they [the students] were answering your questions, they were feeding you guys back the same keywords that you were using." The students, however, seemed to see this not as avoidance but as defense. In the reflection times, the feeling of defensiveness in the room was tense and stifling. The students were so concerned that they might *say* the wrong thing that they were unable to stop and ask if they were *doing* the wrong thing by being there to "help" in the first place.

When asked to reflect, they would often instead reword their statements in order to avoid having to think about what had just been said. The implication was that they had expressed themselves wrongly, or that we had misunderstood them, rather than they had expressed a perspective that needed to be reflected on further. As an example, Neill commented in the first reflection session that he had come to Tanzania in order to "better the people":

NEILL: Well, also, because I know that I want to work with people and try to help in some way, and so that's why I came here, also, is to see how I can help to better the people, and not just how I think I should better them.

SARAH: To better the people in what way?

NEILL: In the way that they want to be bettered. In the ways that like I could be, I guess, respected amongst them because I'm listening to what they have to say and I'm getting—what they want from me, and then giving them what they need and not what I think they need.

JENNA: Can I ask a . . . question?

NEILL: Of course.

JENNA: Is there already a certain assumption—or what assumptions are being made in the idea that you can help, even if you are listening to how they need to be helped?

SARAH: So the pushback is—you said "giving them." So, the word to *give* people implies that there's a hierarchy of, also, of power, of have and have-nots. What do you think about that?

NEILL: Ohhh. Okay, well, putting it in that way, I think I would reword my—I would choose a different word. I would think more of. . . . I, I don't know. 'Cause, like, I don't want to make it seem like there's a hierarchy, because I'd rather set myself as equal. Because we're all people when it comes down to it. And I understand that, and I just want to have—to have sort of exchange, really. Because I understand that there's some issues—like, that's obvious—like, we can all recognize that there's something—like, they might need ... water, I don't know, I don't know. I don't know what they need, and that's why I'm here to figure it out. But whatever they *needed*, then that's what I want to figure out. Like, kind of just like, fill in where I'm *needed*, not to *give*, but just to ... just to be there, I guess. Just to be useful.

When Sarah and I tried to prod Neill into questioning why he assumed he could "better the people" in Tanzania, he first tried to refocus on how he would make sure to give them "what they need." When we again tried to get him to think about the assumption of US dominance in that statement, he explicitly said that in answer to us he would "reword ... choose a different word." Here Neill used attempts at rewording to avoid challenging the fantasy that he innately has something to give that can help "better the people" of Tanzania.

DENIAL THROUGH DECONTEXTUALIZATION

On the third night of reflection with the high school group, Dr. Baker and Tiffany came in to talk with them about medical matters in Tanzania and the systemic issues involved with getting people in the village access to medical treatment. As an example, they told the students about all the problems they had faced just that day in attempting to get a dying baby on antiretroviral medications for HIV/AIDS, and how it still had not yet happened. They were attempting to point out the importance of systemic inequalities to health care access, and disturb the white savior narrative of an individual being able to simply save lives alone. Dr. Baker summed up the heart of their presentation:

> When it comes down to it, it doesn't matter how smart I am, and how well-educated I am—it just doesn't, um, it doesn't matter if you don't have a system around you to support you. I need to have nurses and lab techs and machines and medicines and pharmacists and all that sort of stuff, and that's how I do my job. Here, when those things aren't available, it's tough, and you try to pull yourself up by your bootstraps—I can look up doses, I can mix medicines, I can give shots, that sort of thing—but when you have an entire *system* failure, where this mama's been to three doctors, and nobody helps her. And even now, I'm like, this baby's dying! And I don't have an emergency room to send them to. What can you do?

The medical workers did an excellent job challenging a central theme of the white savior narrative: that a decontextualized individual can, as Dr. Baker said, "pull yourself up by your bootstraps" and win the day.

Yet some of the students felt this attack on their fantasy and denied it by attempting to decontextualize the narrative away from systemic issues. For instance, at the end of the session, one of the students said to the medical workers, "And I kinda know like—I know happy endings aren't really real-world, and obviously from the stories you have told us, it doesn't happen super often. But you guys are obviously in this field for a reason, and I was wondering if you could just share a story of, just like overcoming—not a miracle, but . . ." The student trailed off, unable to find another word for what she was asking from Dr. Baker and Tiffany other than a story about a "miracle." Dr. Baker again took the opportunity to directly undermine the lone savior fantasy, answering, "When we turn the bad stories into systemic change."

The next day, I spoke to one of the teachers who thought this was a moment of breakthrough for the students. She said that after we had left, the students were silent, and Camille had told them, "You *still* don't get it." Her comment had prompted them to talk more about *why* the doctors told negative stories, with no happy endings, and how life is not like TV, and some of the them started crying and realized that "helping" is not as easy as it sounds. At the last reflection session, however, it was clear that some students still could not address the terms of their fantasy, instead internalizing that the medical workers must have "just" had a "bad day." We had asked the students to describe a metaphorical rose bloom, bud, and thorn of their weeks, or high point, new beginning, and low point. Alicia began with her thorn:

> So my thorn was actually, um, I think this last night when the doctors came and talked to us. I really liked all . . . that they were saying, and I totally understood where they were coming from, with, like, having a bad day, but, like, they kind of had a negative attitude towards helping and they kind of were saying that, like, everything was hopeless. And I'm—I'm sure that they don't normally talk like that, I'm sure that was just their bad day, but that kinda just—I think that affected everyone else in the room—just mainly, it kinda just, like, brought everyone's spirits down. Why are we here if we can't help? Why is anyone here if there's no hope? And it was kind of a rough few minutes.

Instead of reflecting on the way their hard work fits into a difficult system, Alicia dismissed the medical workers' presentation as "having a bad day," "a negative attitude," and not how they "normally talk." This, then, allowed her to have a "rough few minutes" rather than taking the time necessary to really think through the challenging aspects of their stories. Although later in the session I managed to point out that by saying the medical workers had simply had "a bad day," the students missed the lesson of the conversation, and no one picked up my comment for further discussion. Instead another student changed the subject by asking what had happened to the baby.[30]

Irony: Imagining Oneself as Outside of and Superior to the Fantasy

If denial involves being unable to face the assumptions underlying a fantasy, irony involves facing them as aspects of someone else's fantasy and not one's own. Cloud describes how irony allows subjects to recognize a fantasy but posit themselves as *"outside of"* and *"superior to"* it.[31] In this way, the very white supremacist and neocolonial attitudes that underlie the fantasy of white saviorism counterintuitively provide grounds for volunteers to avoid recognizing themselves as partakers of the fantasy and to instead posit themselves as different or exceptional volunteers. Mary provided a clear example of irony in my interview with her:

MARY: Well, I think, I mean, when you start out, I think you have like a savior complex. And so, being aware of that, and aware, of, like, how you're being perceived and what your intentions are with your work. There's been a lot of volunteers that come through that like, want their stamp of Africa. Like, I'm gonna wear African clothes every day, I'm going to eat *ugali* [the staple starch for Tanzanians] every day, and that means that I like, did something, you know?
JENNA: Do you feel like you started there, too, or that you had a different attitude?
MARY: I feel like I just came—I feel like—or at least I tried to come with an open mind and just try to push myself. To get out of my comfort zone. I'm—I think I'm pretty integrated.

Mary started by claiming that the general volunteer, when starting out, has a "savior complex," but went on to excise herself from this general claim. Although she recognized the white savior fantasy of US volunteers, she imagined herself to be outside it, different from everyone else.

Another example of an ironic recognition of fantasy is when a volunteer assumes that they are doing something worthwhile—making a difference—while others are not. Some of the college students betrayed this attitude while working on the farm one day. The students were split into three groups to work in the fields. One was using *majembe* (hoes) to dig up the ground for replanting, and the others were put to work weeding the areas where crops were already growing. I wrote about the reaction of the hoeing group to the others in my field notes:

> The students who were working with the *majembe* did not want to switch with the other students at all. I think they wanted to prove themselves capable of doing the most difficult task. They seemed to have a negative attitude . . . that placed their work above that of their counterparts. When they finished hoeing the hill and went to pick greens to cook for lunch, the students picked some leaves, stood up, and immediately said, "That only took, like, two minutes. What have they been doing this whole time?" referring to the other two groups of students. I chimed in at the same time as another student to say, "They weren't picking greens. They were weeding." However, it's interesting that the first assumption they had was that the other groups hadn't been doing real work at all, and must have just been lazily wasting time. It's such an ironic view for these students to take, here doing the work Tanzanians do *every day*, when it's a perspective that is so often turned back on Africans themselves. Just because we don't understand the kind of work they are doing, and because we have already assumed that *we* are doing the hardest work, they must not be doing anything worthwhile at all, those lazy people.

Rather than asking what the other students were doing, the first group immediately assumed that their group had been working hard, making a difference, while the other groups had been wasting time.

In the following pages, I address two primary ways volunteers demonstrated recognition of, and yet ironic investment in, white savior fantasies: through displacement onto others, and thinking oneself an exception to the fantasy rule. Displacement allows volunteers to implicitly figure themselves as *outside* the fantasy by laboring to contain others within it. Exceptionalism provides a means for volunteers to figure themselves as *superior to* the fantasy through invocation of whiteness and national privilege—the very things that should spur recognition of one's own fantasy, yet ironically do not.

IRONY THROUGH DISPLACEMENT

Through displacement, volunteers locate themselves outside the white savior fantasy by ironically recognizing it in someone else. Two key moments of ironic displacement occurred at the NGO when one of the Black teachers who accompanied the high school student group, Jalisa, attempted to engage Sarah in reflection over her position as NGO manager. Jalisa first raised a concern:

> JALISA: I just wonder ... like, how ... how do we change their mindset about being saviors when it seems like that's kinda what we see everywhere we go. Like, everywhere we've gone there's always been a group of white people that are—
> SARAH: Like church missionaries come in, and doing something, or building a building?
> JALISA: Or even like, here. It's like, all white people living in the big house. Or all the volunteers—I haven't met all the volunteers, but all the volunteers that I've met have been white. How do we—
> SARAH: Here, specifically at this NGO, or in the country?
> JALISA: Just, period. How do we change that narrative, when that's the narrative that we are seeing? You know what I'm saying? I don't know how to do that when that's what we are being presented with.
> CAMILLE: Well, I think, this kinda goes back to what Mary said yesterday, that she's training someone else to work herself out of a job. . . . And that you want to leave a group of Tanzanians that are here, able to run the NGO themselves.

When someone else entered the room, the thread of conversation was lost for the remainder of the meeting. Jalisa was attempting to get Sarah to reflect on how she presents herself to the volunteers who come to visit. As Sarah leads tours, leads the reflection sessions, is constantly walking about to monitor activities during the day, it can be easy to see her as a living embodiment of the white savior fantasy. Yet after each point Jalisa made about whiteness, Sarah interrupted her to displace her own position from the center of reflection by attending instead to "church missionaries," or to aid workers in the country writ large. Even when confronted with details about this particular organization, such as the "big house" that Sarah lived in with her family, Sarah managed to displace attention from herself onto others. Sarah recognized the white savior fantasy, but ironically figured herself as *outside* it.

In the second instance, later that evening, Jalisa again attempted to challenge this fantasy when a student seemed to refer to Sarah as having single-handedly "created" the Little Community:

> AMIRA: And I really—I really wanted to experience new things ... to see how this community—this whole community that you have created works.

JALISA: Can I ask a clarifying question? You said, "A community that *you* created." Who were you referring to?

AMIRA: You, as in every person here who's worked to create this community, and those who participate in . . . the community as an NGO. This is a different feel—this—everything that happens here, I guess.

SARAH: I, I think that—I mean, that's a tough question to answer. Is there a face of an NGO, is there, like—what does it mean? And what do communities—how do we define community as a community?

By moving the conversation into "how do we define community," Sarah missed an opportunity to challenge that fantasy of the white savior in her own subject construction. This is ironic, as it is the same fantasy that she had been consistently challenging in others throughout her encounters with volunteer groups. Additionally, this example demonstrated Amira engaging in denial through rewording. Once her use of *you* to refer to Sarah was called out, she attempted to backtrack and say that she meant *everyone* all along.

Displacement can also function more implicitly: one displaces oneself from inclusion in the fantasy by fixating on *others'* inclusion. In the following example, white volunteers labor to contain Black volunteers within the white savior fantasy in order to displace attention from themselves. For African American volunteers the white savior fantasy is disturbed by a recognition of their double presence as both *home* and *not home* on the continent from which their ancestors were taken.[32] Yet white volunteers for whom the white savior fantasy fits undisturbed have a hard time recognizing the struggles of Black volunteer subjects. Instead of letting the double experience of Black volunteers critique white saviorism itself, the unreflective white US volunteers instead level the critique at Black volunteer attitudes. By fixating on the singular dimension of *foreignness* assumed in volunteer fantasies, white volunteers are able to avoid facing questions about the *whiteness* of their subject construction.

Consider the following conversation in which Julie (the US instructor), Sarah, and I discussed the legitimacy of Black perspectives in the college group:

JULIE: There is a thing with the African American kids. Like, they're, like, "*We* can just blend in, and *we* are different." And a little bit of like self-segregation in the group.

SARAH: I noticed that.

JULIE: Yeah.

SARAH: Three of them are sharing a room together, for example.

AMANDA: I actually—they were—I don't know how they arranged themselves at the houses, but I got that—

JULIE: Like, even in Dar [es Salaam]. When Jason [her husband, the trip manager] was with them in Dar and they went to the mall, and he definitely heard a couple of them saying, "I wish we could just walk away from these white people because then we could just blend in." And Jason's like, "Wake up, honey, you're a foreigner just as much as everybody else." You know? Like, you walk different, you act different, you dress different. And as soon as you open your mouth—yeah. Anyway.

SARAH: That's interesting.

JULIE: Yeah, it's an interesting dynamic. Jason always—he says he gets that kind of chip-on-your-shoulder attitude kinda thing from the African American students all the time. Like, "What are you, white guy? What do you have to teach me about Africa? This is my homeland."

AMANDA: Is it?

JULIE: I mean, one was born in Kenya, okay. But she lived in America. One's Ghanaian, ethnically, but she grew up in America.

JENNA: Is, um, the man from Nigeria, like, *from* Nigeria?

JULIE: Yeah, but [only] until he was, like, five.

JENNA: Okay.

JULIE: They've all grown up in America.

Even when it is pointed out that three of the students are *from Africa*, they are still rationalized as within the fantasy—and thus within the white subjects' ability to judge—because they grew up in the United States. Rather than trying to engage with the students' perspectives, and address the assumptions of whiteness in our understandings of US volunteer presence in Tanzania, or the different experiences that Black US volunteers bring, we in the conversation instead re-centered the white savior fantasy by forcing others to fit within it. By focusing on Black volunteers, we displaced attention from ourselves and implicitly positioned ourselves outside the fantasy.

IRONY THROUGH EXCEPTIONALISM

Perhaps an even larger degree of irony is found in exceptionalism. When rendering themselves as an exception to the white savior fantasy, volunteers utilize the very logics of white supremacy and neocolonialism that underlie the fantasy to provide an argument for why they are *superior to* it. In exceptionalism, volunteers recognize their privilege, yet rather than using this recognition to traverse their fantasy, they instead ironically use it to bolster the fantasy's perceived necessity and naturalness.

For instance, when asked why he had come on this "service and leadership" trip to Tanzania, one high school student named Ben said, "Yeah, so, I've been blessed—I've been, like, so fortunate in my life to be able to travel all over the world, Asia and Africa, and I just feel so blessed and I just want to be able to see the different cultures, and, like—there's a stereotype that, like, Africa's so poor and impoverished—at least that's what I've heard—and um, so I've always wanted to come here and help and I feel like I've been so fortunate." Ben used his blessings and privilege as evidence for why he believed he can help "Africa." The irony here lies in the way Ben used recognition of his privilege (implicitly, as a white man from the United States with the financial means to travel regularly) to support the white savior fantasy rather than challenge it. Though he carefully noted the idea that "Africa's so poor and impoverished" is a stereotype, he still used it as grounds for why he had the ability to help—implying at least a partial belief in the accuracy of the stereotype, as well as a belief in his own ability stemming from his fortune.

On the group's initial tour of the NGO grounds, we had discussed with them the need for volunteers to have usable skills, desired by the local staff, in order to begin avoiding the neocolonial pitfalls of voluntourism. And yet, Ben ironically avoided the question of whether or not he had useful skills as a volunteer by attributing his ability to help to his blessedness. Ben used a neocolonial rendering of his fortune as far and above that of "Africa" to explain why he was there to help. He ironically used recognition of American exceptionalism to reinforce the white savior fantasy, rather than challenge it.

Ben's assumption of ability to help due to blessedness resonates with a second exceptionalist strategy whereby volunteers profess *not having the requisite skills and yet still working* as a reason they are exceptional volunteers.[33] This counterintuitive logic allows volunteers to posit themselves as exceptions to the white savior fantasy through a special ability to perform work without the requisite training, but this special ability is again dependent on the very white supremacist and neocolonial logics it purports to rise above.

Mary demonstrated how not having the requisite skills and yet still working can be used to ironically render oneself *superior to* the white savior fantasy. In her interview, Mary said, "I wasn't working in education before I came here," and described how her work had been "progressing . . . knowing that . . . I'm working myself out of a job." "Working yourself out of a job" is a common approach to empowerment discourse in aid. The phrase functions to discursively distance the speaker from the white savior attitude of assuming Western dominance. The key here is that Westerners have been trained and/or are skilled in some areas for which Tanzanians do not have access to proper education.

Claims to be working oneself out of a job can then posit Western dominance while countering its inherency. I asked Mary to elaborate:

> JENNA: You said you're working yourself out of a job. So what is it that right now you need to bring, that you can eventually train them [in]?
> MARY: Um, I think—some of the—still—like, goal setting I think is still hard. And I think I—you know, I'm still learning as well. You know? Um, and I—as I learn, I can teach. You know? So there's this always developing to it. It's not like I'll just run out of everything, and be done.

Mary belied her own statement about wanting to work herself out of a job by claiming that there will always be more that she can teach the Tanzanians at the NGO. She argued paternalistically that she will always have more knowledge than Tanzanians, and thus always have necessary skills that the NGO needs—thus reinforcing her uniqueness as a volunteer: Although she knows that good volunteers—the kind that are not white saviors—should be working themselves out of a job, *she* is the exception. She is different because she is always learning.

Mary's explanation is particularly interesting given how she represented herself earlier in the interview. When I asked why she was volunteering in Tanzania, Mary told me that she had selfish intentions, that she wanted to know more about herself, what her interests were, and what kinds of things she was capable of. She told me, "I loved the way that I felt after volunteering, just . . . as a human." It made her feel confident, and she wanted more of that feeling and to push her own potential. "I didn't try very hard in high school," she said. "I'm doing minimum wage jobs in Pittsburgh, so I'm *not*, like, going to live up to my potential at the minimum wage job!" She wanted to do something else that she could put more of herself into—"more of my heart," she explained—and, if she worked hard, to see "what kinds of results could come of that."

That is, Mary explained how she was unqualified for anything but a minimum wage job in the United States, because she "didn't try very hard in high school," but that a minimum wage job would not give her the opportunity to live up to her potential. She implied that she could, however, live up to her potential in the Little Community, even though she later described how she had no qualifications to work in education when she first arrived. Underlying many volunteer narratives is an assumption that one does not need to be qualified to work in Africa, because being a (white) person from the United States is qualification enough to help.

Amira, from the high school student group, provided another example. The group arrived at the NGO after spending two weeks teaching English in both primary and secondary schools. As Amira remarked on her experience in the first school, "At first it was like, like—oh I wasn't sure what we were doing . . . and then we got to the school and we were teaching students, and we were just completely thrown to the sharks there, and I didn't—I came late, so I hadn't met anyone either, and then all of a sudden I was standing in front of a class, [and they were] expecting me to teach them grammar, like, language grammar. And I had no idea! But I *knew* it. Like I know it, I just don't know wording." She admitted that she both did not know how to teach grammar and did not know grammar itself before backtracking on that statement to save face. Like Cole's description of white saviorism, where "a nobody from America or Europe can go to Africa and become a godlike savior,"[34] both Mary and Amira based their ability to help in an assumption that one does not need to be qualified to work in Africa because being from the United States is qualification enough. Mary, in particular, ironically used recognitions of whiteness and neocolonialism to shore up her investment in the white savior fantasy, allowing her to construct herself as an exceptional volunteer.

The Political and Practical Implications of Volunteer Foreclosures

The Racist Implications of Denial and Irony

Irony and denial are not separate, but two sides of the same coin. And once the coin is tossed, whichever way it lands, it reinforces white savior fantasies that traffic not only in neocolonialism but also in racism. By starting out suspicious of—or even not wholeheartedly supportive of—the Black teachers, the white volunteers and staff at the NGO risked repeating the dynamic that the high school students had put in place. The students did not take kindly to the teachers, instead villainizing them for seeing problems in student behavior. In short, because Camille and Jalisa were able to better recognize racial-colonial dynamics, they were often seen as the enemy when they tried to get the students to reflect.

In a meeting that Sarah and I had with the teachers to get their perspectives on the student group, Jalisa described how the students had dismissed her:

JALISA: We were on the hike at the . . . museum, and one of the girls said, "I saw a white person on the street, and I went up to him and I said, 'Hey, my brother!' Because I haven't seen"—or what did they say? "'Hey, my brother,' because I need to see some white people." Or you know, something like that.

SARAH: What?

JALISA: "'Hey, my brother'—because there aren't many of us here." Or something like that! And I—and I go and I say, "Well, how do you think we feel every day? Every day in America, all I see most of the time is white people. And so how do you think other people feel when they are out of their—you know, not around?" And then, it made me feel some sort of way when she said "my people." Because I'm standing right there—

JENNA: Yeah, and are you not "her people"?

Jalisa later explained that the students dismissed what she had to say to them, because "when these things come from me, it's like, 'Oh, there goes Jalisa analyzing race stuff again,' you know?" In this instance, it is precisely *because* Jalisa had pointed out these dynamics before, precisely because the students had already been faced with the whiteness of their fantasies, that they could dismiss it. Irony borders on denial, as the more often Jalisa pointed out race issues to the students, the more likely they were to dismiss her.

At the same time, the way that I felt the need to insert myself into this description of the racism Jalisa had faced is another form of irony—of distancing myself from the type of whiteness demonstrated by the students. I desire to be seen as innocent, not party to the racial-colonial systems that the others reinforce. But in doing so, I interrupt Jalisa and subvert my recognition of my own complicity in these same systems. In chapter 3, I examine in detail the ways that white, Western subjects—not least, myself—desperately try to hold on to a fiction of innocence in order to avoid reflexive engagement.

Camille faced a similar dismissal from the students when she attempted to instruct them in what was culturally appropriate:

CAMILLE: And we tried to address it [the group's cliquishness] the first week, and they kind of just were like, "Y'all are overthinking everything." And we became the bad guys. 'Cause, like, whatever. But I know that I have had some experiences where I have felt extremely disrespected by them. Just in the way that they talk to me. And I come from a family, and even in my classroom, it's high-power distance between myself and my students. And for them, I guess they grew up in high schools where it's low-power distance, where like kids negotiate, and like—you know—like, Ben, when he, like, picked that girl up at [the school they were working at].

JENNA AND SARAH: What?

CAMILLE: At one of the schools, he picked up a fourteen- or fifteen-year-old-looking girl. So, she was—and she was actually, what did she say, she

was a Form 4? . . . So she was a secondary student, like full breasts, full behind.
SARAH: And he picked her up?
CAMILLE: He picked her up like this [*she demonstrates, both arms lifting, one around the torso, one around the upper thighs*] to take a picture!
JENNA: That is inappropriate.
CAMILLE: I *told* him that it was inappropriate, and as I was telling him to come down the stairs and talk to Jason, he turned to me and said, "Camille, you're ruining all our fun." I'm sorry, we just had a conversation just yesterday about public displays of affection and not touching each other—you decide that you're gonna grab this girl from the small of her back and like, right, under her behind? Like, he had her like *this* [*she demonstrates again*]!
JENNA: That's *really* inappropriate behavior.

In a similar manner, Camille was seen by the students as the teacher who was out to ruin all their fun. Her repetitive act of being a disciplinarian, or of explaining cultural dynamics to them, ironically allowed them to dismiss her as a villain or enemy, thus denying her critiques of privilege in their fantasies. The disrespect and dismissal that the students showed her was tied to her unwillingness to let power dynamics stand unchallenged. When challenged, the students located themselves outside the fantasy by dismissing Camille's read of the situation as nit-picking rather than fundamental, and denying her claims.

When the high school group arrived, they were accompanied by Julie, a public health researcher who had been an instructor for the college group. Julie was not affiliated with them, but came in place of her husband, Jason, the trip's manager. We asked her what the group was like, and one of her first responses was about how the teachers were too judgmental of the students:

JULIE: Like, yesterday the kids broke out into a song. And it's a song by Black people. And [Jalisa, one of the teachers] was like, "What is this? Yesterday there were too many Black people and now they're appropriating Black culture?"
JENNA: Well, I mean—
SARAH: What were they saying?
JULIE: I don't know.
JENNA: I could see why that would be offensive.
JULIE: Yeah, I don't know. I wasn't there.

Julie had no more context, other than at some point the students had said there were "too many Black people here." Although I did not simply agree with Julie's read of the story as the teachers being too harsh, I also did not challenge it outright. Later, Mary, who must also have heard this story from Julie, brought it up in conversation with me when I asked if she had heard about the problems arising with this particular group:

> MARY: About the issues that are arising so far?
> JENNA: Yes.
> MARY: Well, like, racism? From the leaders?
> JENNA: Well, it's just like—like, "we are coming back to our homeland, you guys... can't..."
> MARY: Ohhh. That happened in that other group a little bit.
> JENNA: It did.
> MARY: Yeah.
> JENNA: Like, "You guys can't understand the way we understand." But then, at the same time, one of the examples that Julie was talking about to me also kinda sounded legitimate.
> MARY: Okay, which was—?
> JENNA: But she didn't give much detail, and I don't think she overheard exactly what had happened. But one of the leaders said something like, um, "You can't say that"—so what the leader said was—well, everybody in the van was, like, singing an artist's—a Black artist's song. And she said, "You can't say there's too many Black people here and then appropriate Black culture." And Sarah had missed the first half of this—
> MARY: You *can't say*?
> JENNA: That there are too many Black people here. And then appropriate Black culture. And Julie's using this as an example, but, like, not having heard what happened beforehand, that could absolutely be a legitimate cause of anger.

I did not simply stand up to Mary and say, "No, the teachers are in no way being racist." Instead, I used diminutives, saying that the position of the teachers "kinda sounded legitimate," and that their anger "could" also be legitimate. I had a hard time facing my fantasy head-on; I could not face that I did not understand everything with which the Black teachers were dealing because it would disturb the ivory tower savior fantasy I was holding onto. I allowed for and supported the racist gossip of the white NGO workers talking about the Black volunteers dismissively behind their backs. I chose to perform white relationality, politely agreeing rather than challenging the racist narratives presented. Foreclosing my own racist and neocolonial relations, I strengthened my fantasy of being a "good" decolonial researcher. I protected my own fantasy at the expense of Black well-being.

White Savior Nostalgia

Two weeks after the student groups left, I wrote in my field notes,

> Last night, right before going to bed, Sarah said to me, "I hope I'm not a hypocrite." I asked what she meant, and she continued, "I'm always saying that the Tanzanians are in charge, but I also hold on to some decisions myself." I told her that I don't think she's a hypocrite. We left it at that last night, but I feel like I need to explain, in these notes if not to her, why I feel that way. In my mind, it's similar to the way I think about Dr. Baker's conflict over whether providing service outside of her expertise here is ethical or unethical: should she treat these patients in a way that amounts to a lower standard of care than they deserve, since she is simply a pediatrician? Or by not treating them, is she doing greater ethical harm, when there is no access to medical care whatsoever otherwise? In my mind, what matters almost as much as her answer is the fact that she is *asking the questions in the first place*. Similarly, the fact that Sarah is concerned, and deeply concerned, about whether or not she is being hypocritical is part of what allows her to do her work here so well.

Here, even in my field notes, I again missed an opportunity to challenge white savior fantasies. I again chose to interpret the situation in terms of white innocence, rather than racist harm. In saying that Sarah is not a hypocrite, I chose to support white comfort rather than help her embrace the disorientation that comes from understanding such comfort depends on systems of racial and neocolonial violence. In writing that her and Dr. Baker "asking the questions in the first place" is what allowed them to do good work in Tanzania, I missed that inquiring whether or not one is a white savior can also be a means of eliding reckoning with the question itself—fishing for the answer we want to hear. In telling her that she was not a hypocrite I stopped Sarah from further diving into the question, further interrogating why she felt that way, further asking what she could be doing differently. In part, I did so because of my own subjective insecurities. If Sarah felt like a hypocrite, if she *was* one, then what did that make me?

It requires labor to avoid learning, to avoid facing the contradictions on which subjectivities depend. But it is a labor that white Westerners are practiced at, have become used to. It is far harder to labor to engage with our coloniality and racism, to face the fact that we are hypocrites, to face the ghosts of our past mistakes and the racial-colonial violences with which we are complicit. It's taken me more drafts than I can count of this chapter to get this far. And I'm sure I have farther to go.

Part of what makes this work so difficult is the emotionality bound up with having our fantasies challenged—or even challenging those of others. Our pulses rise, adrenaline spikes, something hardens in the pits of our stomachs. In the United States, we are conditioned to be far more afraid of being accused of racism and neocolonialism than of actually acting in racist or neocolonial ways. Because of this, it's often more socially acceptable to allow racial-colonial actions to pass by unremarked than to call out the person engaging in the act—particularly for those of us raised in white cultures of civility and politeness. I was exhausted after each of the reflection sessions with the high school students. And yet, my exhaustion was slight compared to that of Jalisa and Camille, who were far more impacted by the things the students said and did, required to spend far more time with them, and faced additional racism from the white NGO and volunteer leadership. Sarah and I were able to engage in the labor of challenging the students' frameworks because we were white, we were removed—and because we used it as a means of avoiding our own fantasies. It was emotionally difficult. But I wonder, now, if part of that emotional difficulty lay in the effort it took to continue to uphold our own fantasies even as we challenged those of others.

That is, in leading the reflection sessions, Sarah and I repeated ironic reinstantiations of our own fantasies. For me, focusing on getting the *students* to reflect removed the impetus from changing myself and placed it instead on changing others. Much of the desire for the students to get somewhere in reflection was about proving I was already there myself.[35] That is, part of what emerges from defining myself in opposition to *other* white saviors, is that I, in leading the reflection sessions, really wanted to see an "aha moment" in the students—in order to prove I had already had that moment, that I could feel like a good decolonial scholar. Indeed, even in relation to Sarah, I felt I had more knowledge. As I mentioned in this chapter's opening vignette, I often operated under the assumption that as a researcher, an ivory tower savior, I was somehow in a position to judge others caught within white saviorism. Leaving one fantasy of white saviorism behind, I had created another, one more knowledgeable, more scholarly, more removed. I foreclosed my own collusion in white saviorism through an assumption that I already understood the politics of race and coloniality in Tanzania and thus could focus my attention instead on critiquing them in others. By assuming that I had an exceptional understanding of whiteness and coloniality in aid, by assuming that somehow I could avoid the labor of reflexivity this time,[36] I enacted the same irony I was critiquing in other volunteers. I tried to hold myself outside of politics, as innocent, so that I wouldn't have to face the repercussions of my own thoughts and actions.

It would be easy to dismiss this ironic foreclosure as a simple oversight, wherein I had not paid enough attention to the data or properly reflected on my positionality. The problem with this perspective, however, is that one cannot have done with foreclosures. As a white US researcher committed to decolonial and antiracist praxis, I will continually foreclose the same questions that I study, and be faced with contradictions in my own subjective fantasies. The question, then, is not "How do I get rid of foreclosures?" but "How do I continue with them in a way that centers decolonial justice?" By facing one foreclosure, we are undone and redone as subjects on the basis of another. Only by continually attempting to face our subjective contradictions, even though we will never do so fully, can we work against racism and coloniality to make the world more just.

Yet even calling for the disruption of fantasies is fraught with problems, for the desire to disrupt fantasies *in others* can function similarly to imperialist nostalgia, where "people mourn the passing of what they themselves transformed."[37] If imperialism has done anything in its contemporary neocolonial form, it has catalyzed varied and robust resistance. When I first came to Tanzania as a volunteer, the critiques of volunteering and voluntourism had not yet reached my privileged ears, were not vocally resounding in white, Western dominant spaces. Or, if they were, I was not listening. I believed myself innocent; I was going simply to "help." Now those critiques have inundated aid spaces; no one paying attention can think themself innocent. For me, at the NGO, imperialist nostalgia functioned as a belief that I could arrive now as I did then, blessedly innocent—as Neill put it, someone who "betters the people in the way they want to be bettered." I wanted to consider myself different than these young volunteers, wiser, because I'd already made neocolonial mistakes in the past. I somehow believed myself capable of moving past coloniality. To paraphrase Renato Rosaldo, however, the conditions that allowed me to reside there had already made me complicit.[38] As Benjamin Talton and Quincy Mills note, "research travel is just as elitist as tourism."[39]

The tensions between neocolonial actions and decolonial desires that wracked the Little Community functioned not only at the level of intercultural communication and relation but in Western interactions with each other, tethered to the negotiation of subjective contradictions. In part, the

Little Community threatened to tear itself apart under the weight of (de)colonial tension because Westerners—even, or perhaps, *especially* those who attempt to engage in relations that destabilize neocolonial mores—threaten to tear themselves apart under the weight of contradiction.

And yet, at the same time, contradiction is inherent to subjectivity. One cannot be a subject without foreclosure of contradiction. If there are so many fantasy traps that we set for ourselves, what is to be done to encourage subjective dissolution, to bring about reflexivity that enables substantive change rather than ironic detachment? Rosaldo calls for "surrender to ... the recognition of our complicity," which "will enable us, not to detour around, but to move through, and hopefully beyond, imperialist nostalgia."[40] This type of recognition, however, seems structurally impossible. Although we may attempt to engage in the type of reflexivity that is "*not* an escape, a vacation, from the complexities of the world we live in, but a way of being more present in this world," we will always fail.[41] We will always find ourselves sitting at an office table, realizing that we did not see what was right in front of us at the time, that we failed to recognize our own complicity, that because of that failure we have served to reinforce the forces of coloniality rather than to undermine them.[42] We may even recognize that we will look back on this moment later, in the act of writing, and shake our heads in shame. Recognition is valuable, but there are limits to what can be recognized. As Sara Ahmed reminds us, "We don't tend to notice what is comfortable, even when we think we do."[43] Perhaps the question, then, is, How do we make ourselves uncomfortable?

How do we face what we cannot see?

Chapter Three
Haunted Reflexivity

What you believe depends on what you've seen,—not only what is visible, but what you are prepared to look in the face.—Salman Rushdie, *The Satanic Verses*

A break: it can shatter a story we tell about ourselves. If so then: we can be shattered by a story.—Sara Ahmed, *Living a Feminist Life*

An old man, a stranger, yelled at me: "*Mzungu!* Where are the diamonds? I know you're here for them! I know you know where they are!" As a Peace Corps volunteer teacher living in Tanzania, I was frightened. He approached me aggressively, and accused me of actions of which I knew nothing. I backed away cautiously, and walked quickly home.

This moment returns to me, over and over, because I cannot come up with an explanation sufficient to lay it to rest. There is something about this moment that I cannot see, cannot face. As a critical fieldworker, my research training informs me that the solution is to be reflexive, to consider what this situation reveals about power. Maybe then I can find an interpretation that provides valuable insight into intercultural relations and my own implication in restabilizing power dynamics. To "be reflexive" is more difficult than it sounds, however. What does it mean, in practice, to be reflexive?

Reflexivity is often used simply, as if activist scholars already know what it is and understand how to enact it. To those who do investigate the term, *reflexivity* usually denotes a conscious action that is done or perspective that is adopted by a particular subject in order to attempt to redress their own problematic participation in power relations with others. That is, we often treat reflexivity as something that a subject recognizes, chooses to do, and then *does*. Often this involves listing one's positionality at the beginning of an essay in terms of social categories of difference, such as race, gender, sex, sexuality, and nation, implying a recognition of one's positionality in relation to others and how it affects the way the research has been conducted and analyzed. Yet this rarely seems to substantively affect the content of the essay. Much academic discourse parallels what Michelle Colpean and Meg Tully call "weak reflexivity": scholars speak of reflexivity, but in a way that does not require thorough application or transformation.[1]

The more I attempt to "be reflexive," the less I understand how to do so. What kinds of power dynamics am I able and willing to face? How is it that some can be more reflexive than others? What allows for their greater sensitivity to power relations? What invokes the limits of reflexive practice for each subject in context? How are those limits stretched and developed?[2] Can one be unwittingly reflexive? I find that such questions underscoring what being reflexive means are rarely addressed, let alone answered. When scholars call for researchers to be reflexive, when they say they are being reflexive, when the use of the word continues to be structured by a peculiar absence of what this act entails, we find that rather than mark a presence of a concept, reflexivity marks a haunting—a structuring absence.[3]

Charles Morris III describes how rhetoric scholars have long been uncomfortable with the idea of reflexivity, as it requires a sort of "critical exhibitionism," "indecorousness," and "impiety" to demonstrate in writing how we as critics are implicated in the relations with text and context that make up our research. Morris recognizes that rhetorical scholars engage in reflexivity, but that it is not articulated in their writing. Instead, "it's as if theorizing self-reflection was for many good enough."[4] Similarly, mainstream anthropological research has long been wary of performative writing, writing that demonstrates the feeling and vulnerability of reflexive engagement. Ruth Behar writes that "the huge fear of good writing in anthropology" arises from "the assumption . . . that good writing has a scary tendency to be precious, to be too full of itself, to be self-indulgent (always a no-no in anthropology), to be a distraction from the pressing reality at hand that needs to be analyzed rigorously and unselfishly."[5] Notably, the reverse phenomenon is also prevalent: that scholars articulate reflexivity in their writing without having a clear theoretical mooring. The word *reflexivity* appears, but the assumptions undergirding its use remain ethereal. Reflexivity appears as something that everyone should understand, should already know how to do.

In both cases, reflexivity haunts our scholarship. Reflexivity marks a gap, an absence that we cannot figure. On the one hand, scholars may have a theory of reflexivity but struggle to claim it. On the other, reflexivity is claimed, but has little theory behind it. Very few scholars occupy the space between, where deep thought and gut-wrenching labor have gone into conceptualizing what reflexivity is, enacting it in practice, and putting words on paper that performatively reflect such conceptualizations and enactments.[6] Yet even these scholars realize that reflexivity is something you cannot grasp hold of, something you cannot capture, something you cannot ever know or do completely. In this chapter, I engage with reflexivity as a necessary marker of a haunting, reminding scholars of the silences, gaps, and erasures that constitute critical theory and method, calling for attention.

I develop the concept of haunted reflexivity as a repetitive and relational engagement of reckoning with one's own complicity. To the contemporary colonizer, haunted reflexivity feels traumatic. But it is not a trauma; it is the act of being faced with traumas one had a hand in creating. I argue that haunted reflexivity stages how those perpetuating coloniality and white supremacy initially feel that calls for reckoning are an attack on the self because the US subject is inherently based in ongoing (neo)colonial and racialized violence. Haunted reflexivity asks colonizers (as well as those Black, Indigenous, and People of Color (BIPOC) or colonized subjects who have invested in and internalized coloniality) to collectively face the knowledge of our own direct and indirect complicity, listen to calls for reckoning, and allow them to subjectively undo us and re-form us anew. Reckoning with ghosts is never easy, nor are we ever finished with them.

The day I first encountered ghosts began in a typical manner. I was a twenty-four-year-old Peace Corps volunteer in the Hagati Valley of Tanzania. I woke up, went to school, taught my classes. I had two other Peace Corps volunteers visiting my house, Joe and Etta. Both came because they had heard of Mbuji, rumored to be the second largest rock in East Africa, and wanted to climb it with me. It was early afternoon by the time I finished teaching, a little late to be starting out the hourlong hike that would bring us to the base of the gigantic stone, but we decided to go anyway. At the last minute, Etta changed her mind, so Joe and I set out alone. By the time we reached the rock, I was flagging. I was tired, dehydrated, and a little dizzy. I began to climb the rock with Joe, but felt off balance. I told Joe I couldn't continue, and he went on without me. I remember feeling proud of knowing my limits. I sat, waiting for him to return, taking in the beautiful green grasses edging into maize fields surrounding the rock. A long while later, I heard him calling. I turned to see him hanging nearly vertically, arms fully extended, hands gripping the side of the rock, far from me, as well as from the path back down. I froze. My body tightened, closing off. I detached. My desire for this not to be real was so strong that I felt like I was watching a scene in a movie, not something happening to my friend, directly in front of me, in real life. I couldn't face what was occurring. I knew there was no way out of the position he was in, and nothing I could do to help before his grip would give out. My ears felt stuffed with cotton. My heartbeats grew louder, echoing in my head. A few minutes later, he fell.

I am haunted by a ghost. I try to face him, but I continue to detach and hold him at arm's length, as I cannot reckon with what he tries to tell me. I try to listen to him here. Still, after innumerable drafts, a reader comments that this chapter continues to use theory to distance. Reviewers want more sensory detail. I rewrite again, trying to bring Joe, and all the ghosts, closer.

When I gained the ability to see ghosts, I had to face them everywhere. Returning to Tanzania five years after Joe's death, I had a dream one of my first nights at the Little Community, the nongovernmental organization (NGO) where I was doing research. I dreamed I was standing in a room of people surrounded by ghosts. I knew, as you can only in dreams, that my awareness had somehow shifted. I could see the ghosts all around me, all around everyone in the room. As I shrank back in fear, collapsing in on myself, it was clear that no one else was reacting. They couldn't see the ghosts. I watched others walk right through them without sensing the apparitions' presence. I felt a heavy dissonance in the air. At first I thought it was vengeance and anger, and I was afraid. But my fear dissipated as I began to realize the ghosts were not attacking, they were reaching out. Arms raised toward faces that could not see them. Hands attempting to touch, to get attention, before passing right through. All they wanted was for someone to notice them and to listen. Finally, one ghost realized I could see him. His face broke open with hope and the painful vulnerability that comes with it. He walked toward me, hand tentatively stretched forward. He touched me, skin meeting skin in an electric pulse. Our eyes met, both full of tears. And I woke up.

We are all haunted by ghosts. How difficult it is to attend to them, even those that are seemingly benign, those not crying for vengeance (as some are, and should be). We are trained to ignore them. We practice it, until the stillness is embedded. But they are still there. Our ghosts may be more or less personal, imbued or overdetermined by systems of power, but anyone reading this book has at least some connection to ghosts. This book is a part of the production and dissemination of Western knowledge systems that are dependent on the obfuscation and erasure of other epistemologies, on (neo)colonial and racial violences that were part and parcel of their collection, and on the colonial amnesia that figures their continued dominance.[7] Western knowledge depends on the making of ghosts.

Yet our relations to Western knowledge systems implicate us differentially. I speak as a white settler colonial subject in the United States, doing neocolonial fieldwork in Tanzania, struggling to divest from the ways that I reinforce whiteness and coloniality through my rhetoric and (in)action. I use the term *we* to figure complicity within coloniality and whiteness throughout this chapter. But *we* will not register the same for all readers of this work. I hope to point to the collective need to listen to the ghosts created within the structures of whiteness and coloniality of which we are all a part, while also recognizing that such structures emplace us unevenly. For those marginalized within Western academia, even written out of humanity,[8] you do not need to turn toward ghosts to see them. They are inescapable for you. It is much easier for those of us who fit with white, Western norms to turn away, to run toward a fiction of innocence and wholeness rather than face the destruction coloniality has wrought—the destruction our very selves are founded in. It took me years to gain the ability to see ghosts, because it was easier to be ignorant of their presence. The most privileged of us are able to turn away from the ghosts that others cannot unsee.

How do we gain the ability to see ghosts, to face them, to listen? Throughout this chapter, I particularly write for those for whom reflexivity is hard. Who could more easily check some boxes in the introductions of their essays—white, Western, cisgender—and continue to say what they planned on anyway. I write to challenge us to do reflexivity differently. To even let it do and undo us. I hope that this chapter offers perspectives that are beneficial to all who are caught within relations of coloniality and whiteness. But I particularly hope that those of us who could get away with listing identities and still pretending our perspectives are universal are called to pause—to stop, turn around, and face what we are avoiding, what is hidden behind easy positionality statements and paragraphs about research limitations. I hope that we can listen to our ghosts, relieve them of their burdens, and reckon with the horrors of our own complicity in their deaths.

Reflexive Reckoning

Colonial Amnesia

Reflexivity is often conceptualized as an individual act of identifying and interrogating one's identity. Yet pushing and prodding at the nature of the subject reveals that a subject's identity is not easy to describe, let alone reflect on. There is no stable essence to gaze on, understand, and represent through writing.[9] As Aimee Carrillo Rowe explains, "the work of self-representation, as with the work of self-reflexivity, arises not merely within the interior of the individual, but within the relational spaces in which the subject ... locates herself."[10] One problem with conceptualizing reflexivity as dependent on identity is that it turns our attention to the wrong thing. Identity plays a part in what one experiences in the world and how one must reckon with it, but centering identity places the emphasis on the subject rather than the damage we have wrought. As I explore further in this chapter, a focus on identity makes it seem as if some could be innocent. But reflexivity should not seek atonement for oneself, but for others.

Reflexivity, then, must draw attention to social relations rather than centering an individual subject. D. Soyini Madison describes reflexivity "as constitutive of the performative-I."[11] Instead of referring to the concept as "self-reflexivity," which invokes a unitary subject,[12] Madison conceptualizes reflexivity as a process that institutes and reinstitutes subjects. She examines how each iteration of a particular, momentary *I* is created through and with the people and circumstances that surround it. Aligning with Carrillo Rowe, such a view of reflexivity figures a "vital departure from the self-reflexive move of situating the individualized ... researcher" by instead "call[ing] attention to ... *collective practices*."[13] This, then, brings attention to the political processes by which particular subjects are brought into being in relation to others.

The task of reflexivity is not to engage with personal enactments on the level of an individual actor, separable from the rest of society and history, but with the reverberations of actions, behaviors, and feelings of one who is fundamentally entangled within coloniality, colonial histories, racial formations, and other relations of power. Although this book focuses on Western—and particularly US—subjectivity to engage with the concept of reflexivity, it does so in order to demonstrate how Western subjects are part and parcel of larger neocolonial forces. Reflexivity is complex, and larger than a single person can account for.

It is the specter of reflexivity that hovers every time a white colleague asks a Person of Color to explain their oppression. Reflexivity haunts the writing of non-Indigenous fieldworkers when they cull the uncomfortable moments that they still cannot understand from their carefully curated analyses. It floats, unnoticed, in the foreground as scholars explain their research at conferences and elucidate fundamental concepts in the classroom. Even scholars who know that they should be reflexive, perhaps even attempt to do so, often act to reinforce the racism, neocolonialism, cisgender heteronormativity, and sexism of the academy and of the West rather than deconstruct it. I have done so. I still do so.

US society is built on forgetting and erasure. Part of what makes reflexivity so difficult is that it is a process of attending to that which we are structurally unable to see, hear, apprehend, and understand—not only in our own words and actions, but in the histories of coloniality and racialization that they tap into and extend. US society relies on a colonial amnesia that explains "why when we ... encounter fragments or remnants of colonialism past and present, such as in media culture, it is difficult, if not impossible, immediately to conjure up the history of colonialism that would help us make sense of that memory object."[14] In this sense, reflexivity not only marks a haunting of our disciplines, of power relations that academics cannot quite grasp, but is itself a haunting. Reflexivity is thus a constant attempt to reckon with what we cannot ever fully know. To engage with reflexivity is to be haunted by the ghosts that the United States has worked so hard to forget. A reflexivity that attends to colonial amnesia is not the self-obsessed navel gazing that some critics assume but a haunted reflexivity, one that preserves an attachment to and for others—even, or perhaps especially, those we have forgotten: those we have figuratively and literally killed.[15]

To put it another way, the violence of (neo)colonialism affects the colonizer as well as the colonized. It is a self-inflicted poison, a desensitization, a cauterizing of care. If violence and subjectivity are "mutually implicated in the contemporary world," how does perpetually enacting violence, taking it for granted, and reaping its benefits affect the composition of US subjects, and particularly those who are relatively dominant in social relations?[16] Much work chronicles the impact of collective trauma on the victims—anthropological subjects and, more recently, on the researcher[17]—but work is also needed on the perpetrators of trauma, as violence serves to fill them with a poison that is difficult to remove and has corrosive effects on themselves as well as others.[18] The reflexivity I search for in this chapter is not one that exonerates, that allows for escape from responsibility or provides a shroud of innocence. Reflexivity should not mark the unjust melancholia of what Allan Young calls the "self-traumatized perpetrator," or shame that re-centers the feelings of the colonizer, but rather, notes Sara Ahmed, a haunting that "requires that we give up the fetish of the wound through different kinds of remembrance."[19]

Haunted reflexivity requires different kinds of remembrance because colonial amnesia has clouded our ability to understand the past. And yet, how do we face what is too terrible to behold?[20] We must allow for our selves, the selves that cannot handle knowing, to be transformed by what we face. As Ahmed elaborates, facing histories that our subjectivities are conditioned on forgetting necessitates transformation: "The 'knowledge' of this history as a form of *involvement* is not an easy or obvious knowledge. Such knowledge cannot be 'taken in'—it cannot be registered as knowledge—without feeling differently about those histories, and without inhabiting the surfaces of bodies and worlds differently. I cannot learn this history—which means unlearning the forgetting of this history—and remain the same."[21] When subjects cannot remain the same, we must be undone and redone in a different configuration, on a different basis. We must fall apart.

Haunted reflexivity stages an encounter, over and over again, with our own perpetuation of trauma and complicity in power relations that cannot yet be understood or taken in. But there are so many ways that subjects bound to whiteness and coloniality have learned to avoid facing our complicities, as we saw in chapter 2. To unlearn forgetting means we must be willing to examine, sit with, and expel each of those maneuvers we are tempted to perform—or have performed and look back on. There must be an undoing of the subject before we can re-form ourselves as coconspirators in struggles for decolonial justice. Chapter 2 also demonstrated, however, that denying our own complicity is part of what keeps US subjective coherence in place. When faced with what is too terrible to behold, instead of listening, we often run.

Moves to Innocence

The old man haunts me. I still see him, hobbling toward me, bent under the weight of years. He speaks loudly, sternly.

. . . Is it yelling? Is he bent under the weight of years, or living under (neo) colonial domination? What about this event is so threatening that it makes me feel the need to run in the other direction? In my mind's eye, now, years later, I pause. Who is it I truly fear?

Perpetrators of violence often turn our specters into monsters.[22] It makes it easier for us to explain why we're running from them rather than facing them, listening, heeding their warnings. Because we are not really running from a threat. *We* are the threat. We participate in a history of threats and violence, and we create a new threat now as we run, frantically, distancing ourselves from the specter that would instruct us in our own complicity. The new threat we write is the fiction of innocence. We run toward it, and in telling stories that describe why, we make others into monsters.

I know that I am not innocent, but still I chase it. I move toward innocence, racing—I even seek to beat other people there.[23] But innocence does not actually exist. I can say this to myself without actually admitting it. Unwittingly, I fashion a fiction of it. In the story I tell myself, the knowledge I've gained demonstrates innocence. I take this story I've made and turn it back on others, challenging them to be as reflexive as I purport myself to be. You've seen me do it; I did in chapter 2.

I know that I am not innocent, but still I defend it. Lisa Marie Cacho explains that the law makes property into a "permanent victim" and reminds us that whiteness acts as property.[24] As such, there is a "presumption of fear," a right to be afraid of anyone who threatens our property: our investments in whiteness and the veneer of innocence that glosses over their violence. So we presume fear of our ghosts, because they have come to disturb our investments in the property of whiteness and coloniality. We do not see that they are only ghosts because our investments in such property killed them in the first place.

Specters linger after acts of violence. They wait to communicate with those who had a hand in their death. But the story of hauntings are often told from the perspective of those still living, those being haunted. Those with blood on their hands.

We begin the story in the wrong place. Centering ourselves, we start not with our implication in generations of violence that created multitudes of ghosts, but with the first glimpse of one returning to haunt.[25] With our hands safely hidden behind our backs, we convince ourselves that the ghost is the monster. The specter is to be feared. And when we see our ghosts, we *do* fear. We feel it intensely, a punch in the gut, air stolen from our lungs. We think—this is what trauma feels like. But we have trained our guts to feel in ways that support coloniality, and then naturalized the feelings as instinctive.[26]

Instead of listening, we turn away. Sometimes we run.

The old man *was* yelling at me. He was aggressive. He had to be. Or else I would have to engage with the reasons his statements about diamonds shook me. I would have to stop running in order to consider how the legacies that link past and present extraction of resources and labor connect to the "need" for aid—for people like me to come, teach, "help."

When whiteness and coloniality are juxtaposed against the violence they have wrought, it may at first feel traumatic. In fact, in my initial writings about reflexivity, I conceptualized reflexivity *as* a trauma. When I read about trauma in the way that Cathy Caruth defines it, as "an overwhelming experience of sudden or catastrophic events in which the response to the event occurs in the often delayed, uncontrolled repetitive appearance of hallucinations and other intrusive phenomena,"[27] reflexivity felt like a trauma to me—a repetitive and unfathomable encounter with ghosts, often against our will. I thought that engaging with complicity could be called traumatic because it required facing the traumas we had helped create and perpetuate.

But I was pushed by many to think more deeply.[28] Just because something is perceived as a trauma, felt as traumatic, does not make it a trauma. I knew this. I had seen this. I just didn't want to recognize myself within it.

We've all seen this. We may be reminded of the woman who felt she was having a heart attack when called out for her whiteness.[29] Organizational communication scholars may have noticed the tears shed by a full professor explaining herself to me and other junior scholars after she caused a walkout when she said she didn't "have time for intersectionality." Communication scholars may remember the National Communication Association Distinguished Scholars who loudly left the organization when policies around the selection of such scholars were changed after being shown to be structurally racist.[30] We've all heard white men loudly claiming victimization, and seen white women crying.[31] Perhaps we have *been* them as well.

In chapter 2, I explored the ways that white subjects cover over their coloniality and whiteness with fantasies, and the verbal defense mechanisms employed when those fantasies were challenged. But our defensiveness does not only take the form of verbalized explanations. It is also embodied, *felt*. Our hearts beat faster, our eyes tear up, we feel the impetus toward flight or fight. It may at first feel like a trauma, this face-to-face meeting with the violent histories, structures, and actions that have brought us to this moment in time, this call to reckon with what we've been a part of constructing and continue to uphold. But it is not. It is a haunting, a call from the revenants created by traumas that we participated in causing, supporting, continuing. They call for us to reckon. In my dream, surrounded by ghosts, I was afraid. Until I began to listen. Haunted reflexivity asks those invested in whiteness and coloniality to recognize this feeling of traumatic repetition as a projection, as a means of returning to innocence, and to instead push beyond it into relations unknown.

Losing (the Fiction of) Control

Haunted reflexivity cannot be a trauma because it can be ignored. Caruth notes, "To be traumatized is precisely to be possessed by an image or an event."[32] In chapter 2, I showcased multiple ways that US volunteers can discursively reorient to pretend as if a call to reflexivity had not been issued, can paper over the horror revealed in their own subjective relations through fantasies of white saviorism. The event does not possess them, for all that it might sometimes return in the middle of the night, when defenses are low, leaving someone sleepless as they ponder what they should have said in the moment.

Ghosts do repeatedly intrude, often against our will. In doing so, they belie the fiction of an autonomous (white, Western) subject, fully in control of their choices. They re-present the liberal subject with the erasures their fiction of wholeness depends on, and ask them to reckon with them.[33] But the subject then is left with a decision, one that is often taken unconsciously: flee toward innocence, allowing a fantasy to cover over the ghosts that you have glimpsed and replace the idea that you are firmly in control; or face them, listen, and reckon with what they have to say to you, even though it destabilizes your entire sense of being. The second requires relinquishing Western subjective fantasies of control.

Elyn Saks, in her book *The Center Cannot Hold*, chronicles how she had to learn to relinquish the fantasy of control in order to deal with her schizophrenia:

> *Fight it.* You can fight it, and you can win. To be weak is to fail; to let down your guard is to surrender, and to give up is to dismiss the power of your own will. The fundamental flaw in all of this, though, is that it neglects something intrinsic to the complex real world and to complex real human beings. In fact, it is *not* necessarily true that everything can be conquered with willpower. There are forces of nature and circumstance that are beyond our control, let alone our understanding, and to insist on victory in the face of this, to accept nothing less, is just asking for a soul-pummeling. The simple truth is, not every fight can be won.[34]

We are never completely in control; rather, we deal in fantasies that allow us to think we are. Researchers with any sort of privilege, but particularly those of us who inhabit intersections imbued with whiteness, hegemonic masculinity, heteronormativity, and American exceptionalism, engage in the same type of subjective defenses analyzed in chapters 1 and 2—fantasies that allow us to maintain control even when claiming victimhood, or fantasies that cover the ways in which we practice the very same power relations that we critique. As we saw in those chapters, fighting for control is a way of reinforcing neocolonial domination. To rephrase Saks, not every fight *should* be won.

As I addressed in chapter 1, to let go of control US subjects need to approach subjectivity differently, as constituted through relational processes rather than ontological individuality. Haunted reflexivity abdicates control over the process of reflexivity—not as a way of abdicating responsibility for others but as a way of radically centering others and one's responsibility to them.[35] To think that ceding control automatically cedes responsibility is Western-centric, a perspective that assumes responsibility can only emerge from individualistic paternalism.[36] Responsibility is also a part of coconspiratorial relations. When we are haunted by reflexivity, repeatedly faced with traumas of our own making, relinquishing the fantasy of control is part of what allows us to face the horror of our own complicity. Part of that horror is, as well, our inability to ever completely understand our own complicity, a continual failure to fully know or fully reckon with what we have done. If Behar is correct that "often, in the pursuit of ethnography, you need to relinquish your will,"[37] then this requires thinking differently about how subjects relate to reflexivity.

An individualized reflexivity is not enough.[38] More than that—an individualized reflexivity is harmful to those colonized, BIPOC, queer and transgender folks, and others. Perhaps it seems as if my story of Joe's death is far too individual, too personal to have any bearing on this book. But it haunts my experience at the Little Community. It underlies the way that I engage in research. And it offers a gateway to seeing the specters that surround us—all of us who hail from the West and engage in research in the Global South.

In their powerful essay, Maya Berry, Claudia Chávez Argüelles, Shanya Cordis, Sarah Ihmoud, and Elizabeth Velásquez Estrada excoriate the individualized notion of the critically reflexive researcher, "the idealized radical subject within leftist struggles," who is "a martyr for the movement."[39] As this "self-sacrificing subject" is universalized as *the* subjectivity of the field researcher, fieldwork becomes "a masculinist rite of passage" and the violences experienced by Women of Color—violences that these authors have *all* experienced—are erased or shrugged off as par for the course. Berry and colleagues call for a fugitive flight from this individual model, for our theories to spill into as yet unthought-of liberatory spaces[40]: "How, then, can we imagine a way of doing activist research that does not reproduce violence against ourselves, as racialized, sexualized, women anthropologists speaking from places of intimate connection with those with whom we align our work? This question and others like it haunt us, yet simultaneously propel us, not toward prescriptive solutions but toward a future that is indiscernible."[41] To overflow the disciplinary containers provided for thought leaves the future radically indeterminate. Yet it is only in the indiscernible, the as yet unthinkable, that liberation can be found. By breaking apart the sovereign subject, we burst through into the unknown. Haunted reflexivity thus sets the groundwork for liquid agency, which I explore in chapter 6.

For those more privileged within their relations, jettisoning the sovereign subject may leave us feeling thrown, incoherent—in pieces rather than whole. We often fail to recognize that this shattering is not new but rather the condition of coloniality on which the Western liberal subject relies.[42] For reflexivity to work toward decolonial justice, the Western liberal subject must relinquish this dependence and fall apart.

Reflexivity's Remainders

I have also told the story like this: An old man, a stranger, yelled at me: "*Mzungu!* Where are the diamonds? I know you're here for them! I know you know where they are!" Stunned at first, thinking he must have confused me with someone else, I said, "No sir, I'm a teacher." As he continued to bellow about diamonds, I grew angry, defensively protesting, "I'm *helping*. I'm *doing good* here!" I walked away in a huff.

At the time, I saw my response as justified. I was a volunteer giving away my valuable time and energy, I thought, getting little recognition for my hard work and sacrifice. Later, while researching and writing about neocolonialism in graduate school, another version of me was ashamed at how my earlier self had failed to consider the larger context, and particularly Tanzania's history of colonization and resource extraction by peoples that I descend from and bodies that look like and carry similar historical weight as mine. Now, rewriting this chapter again, I note my wording choices, the ways the man is still posed as "yelling," even as my desperate race for innocence is impossible to ignore—the lady doth protest too much. Revising, again, I wonder what further reflexive remainders have yet to be realized. This example shows the slipperiness of context, our inability to put a vignette firmly in its place, and how even assuming that I can understand colonial histories or their present effects *in full* continues to display a colonizer's arrogance.[43] I search for what I cannot see. I try to find what I will never know. What will a future *I*, reading this chapter, find of reflexivity's remainders?

In "The Labor of Reflexivity" Madison searches "for the *fallout* of reflexivity . . . for what lingers behind after reflexivity has come and gone."[44] There will always be a remainder: a path not taken, a possibility unnoticed, a facet missed. In part, this is because we can never understand the full context of a situation. Nor can we understand the fullness of our very selves. Reflexivity becomes complicated when the identity of the *I* who experiences is neither the *I* who writes nor the *I* who will later reread this chapter. Given this chain of what Jacques Derrida would call "differential marks," the repeated *I* who is both the same and yet different,[45] which provides the reference for reflexivity?

Each time I repeat the story about my encounter with the old man, each time I reflect on it, I am performing a political act.[46] And the *I* who does so is slightly different. I re-present the story in a different context and it has different resonances, with different implications. Was the old man yelling, was he yelling at me? Did I respond gently to a confused old man, defensively in reactionary white guilt? I began, I continue to begin, by considering myself innocent, rationalizing my defensiveness, placing the blame elsewhere and otherwise. The temptation to "race to innocence" lies beneath every retelling.[47] It takes repetition to relieve me of my defenses, to force me to face that I am always complicit in coloniality, always part of the removal of diamonds, even if I have never touched one myself. A singular reflexive moment can never fully capture all power relations and implications of a situation, because the context can never be fully known, let alone represented or put into words. Reflexivity as a political act aimed toward justice will always fail. I will always fail. I can never know. Yet, as Kamala Visweswaran reminds us, failure is not an end, but a beginning: "For our failures are as much a part of the process of knowledge constitution as are our oft-heralded 'successes.' Failure is not just a sign of epistemological crisis (for it is indeed also that), but also, I would argue, an epistemological construct. Failure signals a project that may no longer be attempted, or at least, not on the same terms."[48] Failure can signal a new beginning, a shift in perspective that makes a political difference. Notably, engaging productively with failure means not only reconceptualizing our academic projects, but also "remaking self, home, and field."[49] And yet, I am troubled by the way that the promise of remaking anew also holds glimmers of innocence that I wish to grasp. I feel my hand reaching out before I catch it, tuck it back at my side, attempt to turn once again toward failure as the undoing of innocence, toward knowing that I will never know—toward openings for decolonial justice.

Each time we engage with reflexivity, and each time we fail, reflexivity's remainders produce a space where our very selves might be remade—but will never be remade perfectly. There is something important to be found in the way that haunted reflexivity is not only, or primarily, subject led. It is not about control, but it does include a decision. Haunted reflexivity requires choosing not to turn away, choosing subjective dismemberment over a reprisal of a fantasy, choosing to give up the fiction of control. It is precisely at the limits of our understanding—of context, situations, and selves—that we are able to confront the ghost of reflexivity face-to-face and succumb to what it brings. How might reflexivity itself, in both its successes and failures, institute something—*someone*—new?

The remainder of this chapter stages an encounter with ghosts to see who might emerge from the other side. I turn toward the revenant of reflexivity that haunts academia through writing about the ghosts that haunt me and my work in the academy. The following pages engage with three facets of haunted reflexivity, facets that are mutually implicated, nebulous, entangled: turning toward ghosts, witnessing (to) the encounter, and pushing beyond reinstantiations of innocence. Turning toward ghosts, my field notes perform my own falling apart as a subject in the process of facing neocolonial complicity. In witnessing (to) the encounter, I examine how reflexivity is not truly *mine* but is situated in relation to colonial amnesia. Finally, rather than concluding, I end on the opening that I can glimpse once I push through the urge to flee toward innocence, and instead stay and wait to listen further. But I will never be able to fully know all the things that I have missed. The ghosts will always return; haunted reflexivity only continues, never concludes. For we cannot have done with ghosts.

Turning toward Ghosts

The first facet of reckoning with ghosts is to turn toward them, changing our orientation that we might see, face, listen. In my first week at the NGO, having returned to Tanzania for the first time after Joe's death, I went with a group of Western and Tanzanian NGO workers to a rugby tournament in town. As I wrote at the time,

> We sat on *mikeka*, large woven reed rugs, for the rugby tournament and did very little actual watching of the sport itself. Instead I had a lot of conversations with the three US volunteers who came for a month to live with Sarah and Tim—Amanda, Nancy, and Sue—and the US volunteer who has been here for nearly a year and a half, Mary. We met a few other people of interest at the tournament as well. One was a man named Lex, from Austria. He just came and sat down on the mat with us, and introduced himself. He's been WWOOFing around Africa, and came to work on a farm in a nearby town.[50] When I told him I used to be a Peace Corps volunteer, he asked if I had heard about the bus accident on Sunday. I said, no, I hadn't, but Tim chimed in that he had.

A bus carrying four Peace Corps volunteers crashed. It apparently, from rumors that I've heard, flipped over. One volunteer died, and the other three are in the hospital with broken ribs. There was a memorial service in Dar [es Salaam] on Friday.

Tim immediately offered up the information that this had happened before in the Peace Corps, a volunteer death, and looked to me to see if I remembered.

Of course I remember. I can't forget.

... The sun shining down, people around us drinking beer and laughing, I stiltedly explained that Joe had died when climbing with me. Tim interjected to offer the name of the rock—Mbuji? Yes, Mbuji. My explanation was a jumbled mess. I said something like, "We were climbing. He fell." A girl, maybe Sue, said, "And died?" I simply said, "Yes." After a moment I related how I then went and sat in a villager's kitchen for hours, alone, staring at the dying embers of a fire, waiting for the police to arrive. And how Etta had been at my site, planning to come with us on the hike, but she backed out because she didn't feel spiritually comfortable coming with us to climb that day. And how she and Marysunny came to wait with me, there on the rock. I don't know how it must have sounded to those who don't have the capacity to fill in all the other details: who these people are, how far it is between these places, how the Peace Corps office didn't believe me at first, thinking I was hysterical.

... It would be too simple, to make this reoccurrence of Peace Corps volunteer death about me, my research, my emotional and intellectual project of understanding what is impossible to understand. But at the same time, I don't discount the synchronicity of the universe, nor the repetition of the inevitable under neocolonial structures. The continuing refrain of "To die so young, so far away, trying to do good, to serve, in Africa" echoes through media, through a stranger's explanations (this one is basically taken from Lex), through expectations of what should be said. This refrain is in constant tension with the nagging understanding that many Tanzanians probably died too, Tanzanians die all the time in bus accidents, and that Westerners have simply come into contact with a constant of travel here. No one mentions the obvious, that it could just as likely have been a car accident in the US that took this young volunteer's life. Somehow, it's supposed to be more sad here, where he was "serving," as opposed to simply living.

... I wonder if the three others, currently in the hospital, are in counseling right now. I wonder if they brought over the same emergency counselor from the US that they did for me. I wonder if, perhaps even right now, he is leaning over a hospital bed, explaining to a crying man with broken ribs that it wasn't his fault for suggesting this bus company over another, or this time over a different one, or this excursion in general. The same way that he explained to me, until I would parrot the words, that it wasn't my fault, that it was Joe's decision, that he was an adventurer, and I couldn't have stopped him.

Falling. Joe falls. I see him, but I can do nothing. I have already done something. I didn't go with him.

I turn toward him as he falls, and my self falls as well, reflexively trying to refigure the event into something that is understandable this time. Failure. "Seizing hold of repetitions,"[51] I turn around, narrate again, hoping this time the story can be told with a difference that makes a difference. I foolishly attempt to push past the limits of language, make sense, final sense, of an event beyond sense making; witness to an event I did not see, could not fathom when it was happening. Can I not lay the dead to rest? Is it obscene to want to do so, to think I can here? To think I can now?

I see his hands slip from the rocks. I return to him falling, this moment, because "to repeat something is always to open up the (structural) possibility that one will repeat something with a difference."[52] I try to understand, although I know that understanding will never fully arrive. Yet I continue to attempt to figure stories that make understanding possible, to witness (to) the event in a manner that withstands betrayal, capturing an essence that does not exist. I fail, and try again. He was an adventurer, he knew what he was doing, and the risks he took were his decisions alone. Failure. Turn toward him again. It was all my fault; I knew better and I should have stopped him from going farther by himself. Failure. Turn back, try again. It was a tragedy, a uniquely horrible death. Failure. Turn. It was a death, like any other, like any Tanzanian's death. Failure. Turn.

Falling. Joe falls. I don't see it. I look away, but I know he falls. Like the father dreaming of the burning child, I wake up and it's already too late. Caruth reminds me that each failure "is not, however, a simple repetition of the *same* failure and loss . . . but a new act that repeats precisely a departure and a difference." From each new failure emerges a different self, one who might see better, hear more, apprehend again. By witnessing (to) the limits of understanding as others listen, my witnessing "hand[s] over the seeing it does not and cannot contain to another (and another future)."[53] My failure to see, my lack of understanding—when placed in relation to other contexts, events, lives—provides a crack in a facade through which racial-colonial structures and histories can be glimpsed. This death is not simply about Joe, and I am not the only one who is haunted (although it is, and I am). Joe, me, and what I missed when it happened provide an uncanny resemblance: particular and situated, but hauntingly resonant with other times, places, and people.[54] Taken together "in their inconsistent plenitude ... memories eventually unravel the ideologies they so vividly animate."[55] Haunted reflexivity subjects us to repeated failure in order to draw our attention to what structures the repetition, to the means we employ to attempt to avoid facing our complicity, to the ghostly shadows in the background that we cannot quite grasp.

For Avery Gordon, speaking and listening to ghosts is what makes all the difference between repressing them and reckoning with them. Facing ghosts is an encounter with the uncanny, when something becomes alien precisely because of its familiarity. The uncanny frightens because it presents a resemblance we are not ready to admit, whether in relation to our theories, cultures, or selves. We must speak with specters, rather than run, as facing this troubling resemblance is the only way to transform; in speaking with specters we face what we are not equipped to understand, and the potential emerges for reconfiguring ourselves with a better apprehension of justice in relation.[56] Similarly, Derrida claims that speaking to the specter is "necessary," as without this experience, both ethics and justice are impossible.[57] For Derrida, speaking to the specter represents an encounter with the undecidable, as the ghostly apparition floats in the undecidable realm between *being there* and *not being there*, and between representing things future or a return of the past.[58] Facing the specter requires us to face our failure to ever be fully ethical or fully understand power, and yet also, as Gordon demonstrates, is the only way to move toward more ethical and just relations.

I still hold him at a distance. Too far to hear what he's saying. Too far to understand why this is important in a book ostensibly about an NGO. I turn, and am caught in the memory of what happened after he fell.

An old man, a stranger, yells at me. "*Mzungu!* Are you taking more of your friends to jump off that rock?" I freeze, walking back from the market just a few weeks after Joe's death. He laughs with his friends, sitting and drinking outside a *duka* [shop] in the village. I shake with anger. Tears stream down my face as I pull myself loose and hurry home.

Different men, different paths, different times, but similarity strikes me like a blow. I cannot understand. I am defensive out of fear—at first I tell myself I am afraid of the men, of their vehemence that seemed to hit me out of nowhere, but it is a story held as a shield. I am afraid of myself, of what little I do understand, of what precipitated this painful taunt. If I look hard enough, far enough, I can see that I am a part of a history that dealt many first blows, blows to which this one responds.

Yet I continue to run toward innocence, eliding the necessary reckoning. I lash out at others instead. I tell myself I'm not a joke; I'm a victim of a tragedy. I'm not a mine mogul; I'm an innocent schoolteacher. Uncomfortable resonances between the two old men, yelling as I pass by, present an uncanny resemblance I can't quite face. I don't see it.

I fail to see in time.

Witnessing (to) (Neo)colonial Haunting

The second facet of haunted reflexivity is witnessing (to) hauntings. Witnessing (to) incorporates the double sense of witnessing that Kelly Oliver describes: "*eyewitness* testimony based on first-hand knowledge, on the one hand, and *bearing witness* to something beyond recognition that can't be seen, on the other."[59] The undecidability of the specter requires a witnessing (to) that describes both the experience with the ghost and the uncanny resemblance it brings to light that cannot quite be pinned down, that will never be pinned down. For reflexivity, this means explaining the circumstances and relations in which we have taken part in a way that brings to light power dynamics otherwise unfathomable—and yet recognizing that what is written will always fail to capture circumstances fully. Witnessing (to) such excessive experiences is transformative because reckoning requires transition: "the precarious but motivated transition from being troubled, often inexplicably or by repetitively stuck explanations, to doing something else."[60]

If it is true that "to be haunted is to be tied to historical and social effects,"[61] then one's haunting is never simply one's own, but located within and structured by histories, contexts, and cultural dynamics of power. I tried to reckon with this in my pre-fieldwork notes, preparing to return to Tanzania for the first time since Joe's death:

> As we made our path through the mountains, to find the rock, Mbuji, Joe said that he felt like he was in *The Lord of the Rings*, traveling the long road from the Shire to Mordor. I had forgotten that, until just now. Sitting here to write.
>
> He was not so very wrong. Something was destroyed, in the end, but not a Ring. One life, and one perspective on the world.

And so we came to Mbuji. But why? Why, really, did we decide it would be fun to go climb a deathly rock, with no guide, no rope, and little time left before sunset? Why, when I tired, did I let him go up alone? How could neither of us have seen that it was a stupid, stupid idea?

And an answer that came to me, after years of endless asking, is that the attitudes and ideas of that day were not simply those of Jenna and Joe, the individuals, who made stupid mistakes. They are, surely. But they are also more. In thinking back on that afternoon, I often think that I would not have done it here, in the United States. Hard on the heels of that thought usually comes, "Stupid, stupid Jenna—you should have known better!" But the vehemence of the following thought hides an insight that I don't let land: I would not have done that in the United States. I do act differently here than there, and vice versa. And so, most likely, did Joe.

As Carrillo Rowe argues, we need to think about politics, desire, and subjectivity relationally.[62] What Joe and I did when we went "adventuring" was not the simple outgrowth of two sovereign subjects' choices, but rather the culmination—for us, for the people we were in relation to each other and other others—of resonances of coloniality. Chela Sandoval argues that the fractured Western postmodern subject that must deal with its own death is only finally facing a similar pain, insecurity, precarity, and sense that it can never and will never be whole that those subject to coloniality have had to face for centuries.[63] And yet, the experience of fracturing in Western subjects is nothing compared to the visceral, embodied, horrible violence that such subjectivities enforced on others in their quest to be whole.

And yet, Joe and I did not occupy the same subjective space as Westerners. As an Asian American man growing up on the US East Coast, planning to be a doctor someday, he was not implicated the same way in coloniality as I was as a white woman trained in those insidiously violent midwestern politics of nice, doing my best to help (read: save) others.[64] Even in Tanzania, our experiences as people from the United States were different. He was often called *mchina*, person from China, or lumped in with Japanese volunteers. He had to explain his Americanness; mine was always assumed. What can I know about how the United States trained us both to think about Africa, volunteering, and why we were in Tanzania? I didn't get to have these conversations explicitly with Joe; I cannot ask him to reflect with me over his death. Or, I can *ask*, but his answers are now difficult to ascertain. I will certainly fail to hear them.

I worry that the attempt to reflect, to write, to understand is a betrayal. I know that it must be a betrayal. Any witnessing (to) will betray Joe, his memory, his positivity and excitement, his goofy love of *A Boy and His Dog*. I write anyway, because it is necessary. As Visweswaran reflects, betrayal carries us toward critique, toward "showing how baldly what we come to know is engendered by relations of power."[65] Perhaps then, if failure is potentially productive, it would be a larger betrayal not to see what can be brought forth from it, from the turn toward critique in the aftermath.[66] And so I write about how we were, or might have been, extensions of US neocolonialism when we climbed the rock that day, how the violences of neocolonialism resonate differentially, but in all involved. What did we carry with us? One chilly morning in the Little Community, sitting alone with my coffee, I wrote:

> Perhaps Joe's death was the culmination of the effects of colonialism and imperialism in our bodies and our minds. Joe and I went on an adventure that day—as we both had, separately, many times before, partly because of who we thought ourselves to be in relation to the place of Africa. There are two aspects of this relationship at the forefront of my mind: who we thought we were there, and what we thought Africa to be.
>
> We were adventurers, saviors, heroes. We came to save students from scholastic failure, to teach knowledge that only we had to give, to give of ourselves selflessly—or so we thought. How ironic! And we came for adventure. Africa is the land of the Serengeti, of majestic animals, wide plains, and fierce jungles. The land where danger is always present, but always overcome in the end. How could it not be? We were the heroes. In this story, the people of the land figure as side notes, scenery—necessary only to the extent that we have something to save, to change for the better. We were here for two years and three months, and then we would go home. It was a time-out from "real life" that would give us valuable career experience so that we could write things about how we had experience "working with limited resources" on our résumés. But we would come back. Because nothing that happens in a dream counts. And we had not been trained to view Africa as a real world.
>
> I'm painting too grandiose a picture, too pure an idea. Of course, we did have friends. And it was life. And we did love our students, and build relationships with them, too. But the fantasy, the fairy tale, the story of the hero was there in the background. A legacy of colonialism—the telling and retelling of heroic conquest, or who wins in the end, with the same type of people as heroes. No US subject can escape the resonances

of colonialism and imperialism in the way we are taught to think of ourselves in relation to the rest of the world, and especially of ourselves in relation to Africa. Unrecognized, the story structures our thought, at least partially.

Enough for Jenna and Joe to think that Mbuji was for their pleasure. Not to consider what could happen, because heroes don't die this way. Not meaninglessly. This could not be the ending. And so it was not even considered, not even thought. Africa was not the real world. We were going home in a month.

I wrote this note years ago. I would certainly temper it now. But the point stands that this experience is more than mine. The excess, going beyond individual ownership, points to a cultural haunting. Both Joe's death and the encounters with the two old men place me face-to-face with the ghosts left in the wake of (neo)colonial traumas. I try to face it, but I often find myself running back toward the comforts of the story I tell, the one where I'm innocent. There are uncanny resemblances that I cannot face.

Analyzing Sigmund Freud's understanding of survival, Caruth argues that his notion can only be grasped "when we come to understand how it is through the peculiar and paradoxical complexity of survival that the theory of individual trauma contains within it the core of the trauma of a larger history."[67] To survive and continue on in a manner that does justice to the traumas we turn toward, witness (to), we need to engage the trauma of this larger history. (Neo)colonialism haunts all Western relations with Africa, albeit in differential ways. When we listen to Joe's ghost we can hear whispers of historical attitudes and relations toward Africa, of the way volunteering can figure as adventure, and the way African countries are decontextualized from global relations to maintain a fantasy of a playground for Western dreamers.[68]

Of course, to figure this experience as simply another resonance of colonial histories would be just as reductive as claiming it involves no more than two individuals. Placing all blame on colonial history can be another means of securing innocence by displacing attention from the ways that I reinforce coloniality and its legacies in my (in)actions and discursive articulations. By witnessing (to) Joe's death in this manner—drawing connections between my encounters with two old men, placing my own experiences within shifting understandings of context, demonstrating how I retell the story over and over in ways with different political resonances and goals—I attempt to produce a reflexivity that is not individual but collective. One that emerges from situated contexts and relations, and requires repetition in relation to others, in response to others' promptings, to even partially understand. I witness (to) what I missed at the time, what I continue to miss. As I have realized from sharing and re-sharing this chapter with friends, colleagues, and reviewers, the "performance of testimony says more than the witness knows."[69] Others notice more within what I write than I am able to. I continue to fail to understand my own stories, I continue to fail to represent them fully in words, I continue to fail to see in time. I continue to hold myself just far enough away that I maintain a semblance of innocence. But each failure brings a difference, and each listener brings the possibility of a more just future.[70] As Gordon reminds us, "endings that are not over is what haunting is about."[71]

"*Mzungu!* Where are the diamonds?" "*Mzungu!* Are you taking more of your friends to jump off that rock?" The two men were yelling different things, but they leveled the same accusation: "You *wazungu* [white people] come and you take what you want from us, whether it be diamonds or adventure." I was devastated when the old man laughed at me, laughed after Joe had died, laughed when I was still there, broken. Though it was unintelligible to me at the time, I have come to understand, perhaps, through the uncanny resonance between the two old men: laughter makes sense as a response when the (neo)colonial taking and taking and taking has in one way finally failed.

I still fail to see. I do not understand. I still cannot witness (to) what happened. I still read the men, old men, as yelling at me, accusing. I center myself and my feelings of defensiveness inculcated by coloniality.

I fail to notice that they took it on themselves to reach out, that the fact of even speaking to me—a stranger—is a type of gift. It was energy and attention that they did not need to exert. Yelling, they pushed their voices to be heard. Why gift me with such exertions? What is it I have missed?

Beyond Innocence, beyond Conclusion

Perhaps I may tell the story like this: An old man strains his voice to reach out to me—a stranger—to share knowledge—of extractive histories, of the lies coloniality tells us. An old man takes it on himself to instruct me—a stranger, one he knows may not listen. But still he implores me to understand. "*Mzungu!* Where are the diamonds?" "*Mzungu!* Are you taking more friends to jump off that rock?"

Mzungu! Where are your priorities? Why, oh why, have you set them in such violent systems and logics?

Mzungu, face what you—all of you—have done.

I fail to see in time.

I write about Joe, about the ghost that enabled me to sense all the others, because I need to in order to face the sum of what I have done—of what I continue to do, and how it impacts my work. We all are haunted by ghosts in our research. For some of us, they may not appear as literal, personal deaths. But not sensing them doesn't mean they're not there.

As I was revising this chapter, again—returning, repeating—I searched for Mbuji on the internet, hoping to gain more context, another foothold on the rock. Rumored by my students to be the second-largest rock in East Africa, Mbuji would surely show up in one form or another. I had performed an academic search and found next to nothing—only a creative nonfiction story called "The Search for Magical Mbuji." It mentioned Joe; or at least, I assume it did when it spoke of an "American explorer" who had died there.[72] I searched again, more generally.

The breath was stricken from my body.

We had climbed the rock without permission from the elders. According to local lore, those that do so risk punishment, even death.[73] One blog says, "already there is a European who came in favor of tourism, climbed the rock without permission and he was found dead."[74] I can only assume it is referring to Joe.

"*Mzungu!* Are you taking more of your friends to jump off that rock?"

It was not the first time I had climbed Mbuji unsanctioned, with friends, *wazungu*. A group of us had climbed the stone a few months earlier—without stopping to greet the elders, without securing a local guide. I had gone with a local guide the first two times; I didn't think we needed one again.

What arrogance.

What (neo)colonial arrogance, to think that I should simply have use of the land.

I write about Joe because listening to him helps me to understand the ways that I continue to display (neo)colonial arrogance in my research, continue to run toward innocence even as I critique the ways that others do the same thing—as white people, as Westerners in Tanzania. If my research is truly to be decolonial, I have to face this attitude, reckon with it, and allow the researcher subjectivity that I have constructed on top of it to be torn apart by the contradictions it reveals to me.

In part, my attitude reflects the results of epistemic injustice. Coloniality has erased African ways of knowing as knowledge, making it legible only as tradition, "instincts," or "data" to the West.[75] For this reason, Ndlovu-Gatsheni argues that thinking itself must be rethought: "Rethinking thinking is fundamentally a decolonial move that requires the cultivation of a decolonial attitude in knowledge production. It is informed by a strong conviction that all human beings are not only born into a knowledge system but are legitimate knowers and producers of legitimate knowledge."[76] When I went to climb Mbuji that day with Joe, I did not even consider local ways of knowing, engaging with land, and what they might mean for our excursion—not even when Etta, attuned to some other wavelength, decided she was not coming with us. I did not see until it was too late.

In the following chapters, I examine the way that epistemic injustice in the context of the Little Community impedes the ability for Westerners to understand Tanzanian ways of organizing and how Tanzanians relate to land. In their lack of understanding, Westerners cause problem after problem for the NGO. Part I of the book, culminating here, has set the groundwork for understanding how this occurs. Western subjectivities are conditioned by coloniality and whiteness such that Tanzanian ways of knowing are erased, or made to seem unreasonable or unintelligible. And when challenged, Western subjects often chase after innocence rather than accountability.

Epistemic injustice causes tragedies every day.

I can repeat that I should have known better, that this is my fault, over and over until my voice fails. I did, the night that Joe died. I am not wrong. But I would be stuck, immobilized by a statement that seemed final, a concluding answer: all my fault. To become stuck in the repetition of my personal responsibility fetishizes the wound and re-centers myself, a self that can seemingly be divided from the world around me and the political relations of which I am a part. Such a repetition allows me to produce a fiction of innocence through perpetual self-flogging—that I can reach innocence if I repeat my guilt enough times, provide enough penance for my sins. But as I do so I become stuck there, circling in a rut, unable to be moved or transformed. Rather than holding tight to this fiction of subjective unity, I choose to witness (to) the excesses I still cannot grasp. To what I will never be able to grasp. I give in to haunted reflexivity, and fall apart. The *I* that I know is undone.

It is undone in the face of relations. Undone because I cannot face them, cannot face how I reinforce whiteness and coloniality, from my current subjective orientation. Undone because facing them undoes the "me" I have been. I could run for the cover of innocence, but I choose to let go of the self I know, the self I recognize, instead. Or, at least, I try.

We must let go of the fiction of coherence and individuality to see the networks of relations out of which we emerge as subjects and through which we act. To witness (to) Joe's death means so much more than simply claiming fault; it means sifting through the layers of what coloniality, whiteness, and American exceptionalism have wrought in my life and that of others. It means letting the subject that I thought I was fall apart to make way for someone new. Someone who can witness in new ways, to new things. Someone who glimpses a little of what they missed at the time. But someone who is still complicit, still attuned to their own lack of innocence. Someone who attempts to meet with their ghost over and over again to listen to difficult truths, hear new facets, and continue to be torn apart and re-formed. I will never be finished doing so.

The final facet of haunted reflexivity is to push beyond innocence, to the space where we are remade as a subject—the same, but slightly different. And yet, there is always more to witness (to), more that we have failed to see, more to hear from our ghosts. Reckoning is never finished. Derrida refers to specters as *revenant*, meaning "that which comes back." We can never meet all aspects of our responsibility to a ghost, all its needs and desires. There is always a remainder: "A ghost never dies, it remains always to come and to come-back."[77]

To be haunted by reflexivity does not require experiencing death firsthand. But it requires recognizing that we are all implicated, in some way, in death. The United States functions as a nation because of death. Death secures the resources, global authority, and capital that the United States requires to function.[78] We live the way we do, in all the differential implications of that phrase, because of death. Some of us profit from death. Some of us experience a higher burden in relation to it. But we all witness it. By our connections to these everyday tragedies, we are all witnesses to injustice. We carry a responsibility to witness (to) what we experience, to attempt to relate how racism, coloniality, and other forces of power are woven in and through what we saw and what we missed at the time. Haunted reflexivity requires facing moments that we cannot handle, cannot understand, over and over, recognizing that each time we will be tempted to run toward innocence rather than listen to what the ghosts wish to tell us. And there is always something we will not be able to grasp in their communication, an excess that spills forth and will return. Each time we meet the revenant, witness (to) the encounter, and push beyond innocence to perform a haunted reflexivity, we hope to speak more truth than we know. And however we fail, we know that there is always another chance.

Let us turn to face the specters lying in wait. In this chapter, I have argued that we need to engage in a reflexivity that is haunted, that continues to haunt, because this repetitive engagement with our implication in collective relations is the only way we will ever choose to turn away from the seductive pull of innocence. Through haunted reflexivity, we can face the horrors of our own subjective constitution, and choose to fall apart and be redone as subjects on different grounds, however slightly, however imperfectly.

We choose to face the specter. To listen as it undoes us. Again and again. For we cannot have done with our ghosts.

Part II

Chapter
Four
Water in
the Cracks

Indigenous conceptions of space deny dominant models of imperial subjectivity, dismantling colonial attachments to particular geographies and revealing elements of spatial colonization. These epistemologies also oppose colonial imaginaries through rhetorical practices that challenge imperial narratives and naturalizations of place, power, and linear time.—Tiara R. Na'puti, "Archipelagic Rhetoric"

The community hall lay separate from the rest of the Little Community, about a mile or so away, through the rolling hills and past the eucalyptus forest. It was the perfect location for a meeting space, nestled between the village proper and the elementary school standing on the hill above. I don't know what I expected to find there the first time I visited, but I know that I did not expect such loneliness.

The mood of my visit to the community hall is deeply ingrained in my memory: a hollow emptiness heralded by darkness, echoes, and layers of dust. The broad hall lay still and quiet. I walked through the large, open space that composed most of the building before being let into a locked room at the back, behind the stage. It was a computer lab—when it was functioning. I swiped a finger across the dust atop one of the machines. Damas would later relay to me that gathering dust was the computers' only function these days. Some enterprising donor had bought them for the nongovernmental organization (NGO), the Little Community. Never mind that neither the village nor the NGO had access to an electrical grid. Never mind the money it cost to procure a generator and keep it running. Never mind that few in the village had the skills necessary to teach computer usage to others—or of course, that they would need a salary to do so. I wondered what the donor who had provided the computers thought about their current state—or if they knew, or if they even thought to ask.

I could understand the emptiness of the computer lab. But I wondered why the community hall itself stood unused. When were the meetings? What did the people do there? I would have these questions answered later in my interview with the two caretakers, Mama Isaak and Peter. In short, the NGO had fallen short of funds, and in order to keep the community hall open—and its caretakers salaried—the organization started charging fees for using the space. Yet many times the community members could not afford to pay them. Expressly forbidden from taking anything lower than the rate set by the NGO leadership, Mama Isaak and Peter felt caught in an uncomfortable bind, particularly as they were afraid of the consequences for the community members when they were denied a space to gather together:

> MAMA ISAAK: We had lots of older women who had gotten used to gathering here every month. And now every day we see them they demand to know when they can meet again. It's like they became used to meeting to greet each other and talk about how they're doing . . .
> PETER: It was their goal to exchange ideas and trade stories about their lives. For example, maybe there is someone who lost all their relatives. . . . If they're alone, they cry every day, "They're all dead. What kind of life is this?" But if they meet with others, maybe someone else says, "*Bwana, this is the way it is.*" *Basi*,[1] they get the strength to keep living. . . . And it really happened that some of the older people have died because those thoughts come to them, and they pass away. How many is it that have died?
> MAMA ISAAK: Two people.

In a report, it's easy to track how much money is brought in per month by renting out a community hall. It's simple to count how many meetings are held, or even how many people went to those meetings. But it's much harder to track what those meetings did for people in the community, how it made them feel, how it functioned as a space where despair could be fought off for a while.

When the NGO leadership decided to start renting out the hall, Mama Isaak and Peter had to shoulder blame and guilt that should not have been theirs to bear. But who was to blame? Was it the fault of the NGO, for taking on a project that it was unable to financially keep up with? Was it the fault of the donor that wanted to build such a place in the first place? Or, perhaps, blame for the misuse of the community hall does not fall squarely on anyone's shoulders, but rather gathers like rain on a sidewalk, filling the cracks—the places where incompatible structures meet.

Part II of *The Center Cannot Hold* examines what happens to the organization itself when the Western subjectivities analyzed in Part I collide with Tanzanian structures of meaning. If Western subjects are necessarily based in foreclosures of their own neocolonialism, and it takes unending reflexive labor in order to even begin to re-form subjectivities in alternative ways, what kinds of epistemologies do such subjectivities hold? How do they recognize or fail to recognize knowledges? Sabelo Ndlovu-Gatsheni argues that the ontological erasure of African being, through systems of coloniality and anti-Blackness, concomitantly holds an erasure of African epistemologies. Under logics of coloniality, African knowledge cannot be recognized, because Africans are not seen as being able to produce knowledge themselves but only to consume it.[2] At the Little Community, Tanzanian epistemologies often failed to register with Mr. Giles (the head of the board of directors of the Little Community) and Western donors, leading to an imposition of Western knowledge systems on contexts where they do not necessarily work. Over the next three chapters, I look to the ways that clashing epistemologies of organizing, and relation to land, eventually led to the Little Community falling apart.

While donors build halls and purchase computers, the needs of the village are much more fluid and dynamic. Liquid organizing functions in specific African contexts as a way to react to the challenges that arise in contexts of economic marginalization, allowing people and organizations to shape-shift for survival. But these liquid organizational logics are opaque to Western donors, who instead suggest solid solutions. The problem with this, I argue, is that it ends up adding to the very burdens that liquid organizing tactics are trying to eliminate. And yet, there are always trickles of water, acts of Tanzanian agency flowing through the unseen cracks in the solid structures Westerners attempt to erect.

Clashing Approaches to Organizational Logics

Organizing often takes liquid form in many African contexts, and particularly those economically marginalized in relation to global systems of finance, business, and trade. African organizing is "so intertwined with political, economic, and cultural contexts ... that it shape-shifts and moves like a liquid."³ Such liquid organizing both emerges from African epistemic systems that prioritize communality and situated action and responds to global contexts that place many African subjects in positions of economic insecurity. Western understandings of organizations and organizing obscure the value of liquid logics, however—even to the point of disavowing liquid organizational strategies as rational logics at all. Thus, when liquid worker strategies run into solid donor desires, problems ensue for the Little Community.

On the one hand, liquid organizing in African contexts emerges from epistemologies that center context and community. Organizational scholars in the Global South demonstrate that "the values espoused within the peripheral environment [on a global scale] are arguably fundamentally different from those promoted in the mainstream economic discourse," referencing how African and South American actors often prioritize solidarity rather than competition, community survival as prefiguring individual survival, and creative emergent strategizing.[4] African organizing strategies are "trust-based," as opposed to Western "resource-based" structures, grounding individual action in communal relational frameworks.[5]

Yet, liquid organizing is not freely chosen by those who use it. Quick decision-making and changes to plans are often necessary for African survival in global contexts of injustice and marginalization. Joëlle Cruz and Chigozirim Utah Sodeke powerfully render the ways that African actors "resort to fluidity involuntarily to escape hostile conditions and make a livelihood," highlighting how "oppressive conditions fuel liquid organizing for poor actors, who have to be both reactive and proactive to threats."[6] Liquid organizational strategies work because they emerge from localized cultural knowledges, but the need for such strategies reflects inequitable global economic systems that force African subjects into precarious positions requiring rapid and continual reappraisal of planned action. Elsewhere, Brenda Berkelaar and I discuss how career discourses take on different forms in Tanzanian contexts, where the resources, goals, and trajectories of work and survival are very different from what Western rhetoric describes. Entrepreneurship takes on local and improvisational characteristics in impoverished Tanzanian contexts.[7]

Liquid organizing is important to survival in African contexts, but Western epistemologies obscure and deny its rationality. Cruz and Sodeke ran head-on into this as African scholars, trained in the West, attempting to study organizing in Nigeria and Liberia. They came to realize how little their Western doctoral training had prepared them to understand the way that different African actors engaged in fluid and relational strategies that refused to be bound to a place, shifted and changed, and even dissolved into the surrounding landscape in ways that were difficult to fix and examine. Cruz and Sodeke mention that "we were not prepared for the realities of researching organizing in motion due to our training that predisposed us to immobility," to rendering "organizing as 'immutable' or fixed," and to "framing life and organizing as discrete categories."[8] Notably, these Western epistemologies do not only affect how researchers engage with organizations but also how employees, volunteers, and donors construct and act within them.

There are many ways that Western epistemologies emphasize solidity to the point of liquid erasure within NGOs. For one, Western legal and organizational structures encourage attention to solid, "measurable" outcomes, with little regard for whether or not these countable measures actually serve the communities they are meant to assist. Referring to this as "technical rationality," Dennis Mumby and Cynthia Stohl explain that this orientation to knowledge "privileges a concern with prediction, control, and teleological forms of behavior."[9] Prediction and control are difficult to hold onto in contexts where resources may not necessarily be available when needed, unexpected budgetary expenditures often occur, and the community has emergent—and *emergency*—needs that often must be quickly met. In addition, as Kirsten Broadfoot and Debashish Munshi point out, discussions couched in terms of rationality leave little room for emotional logics,[10] which are essential to the human care work performed in NGOs. As Peter Jensen examines in his research on anarchist homeless shelters, those NGOs that wish to engage with alternative epistemologies of accountability and emergent human care may be forced to divest entirely from Western legal structures to do so, as reporting to such structures requires prioritizing metrics over communal value.[11] The perceived solidity and unarguability of countable achievements is valued in Western systems to the detriment of fluidly responsive aid.

The domination of technical rationality in NGO structures reinforces neocolonial relations of power. In particular, NGO structures often shape themselves to fit donor control over community desires.[12] Rather than delving into the nebulous arena of urgent issues that arise within the moment and unforeseen problems that require creative solutions, Western organizational logics instead value alignment with previous plans laid out by donors for how their money will be spent. Under these logics, Western NGO leaders often attempt to stymie what they perceive as "mission drift," positing that the answer to this "problem" lies in more heavy-handed control. One such author writes, "The multiple sources of mission drift cry out for a control mechanism, some way of keeping nonprofits targeted on their announced objectives."[13] Donor control becomes a form of solidity as it values the maintenance of donor planning over fluid reaction to contextual demands, making Tanzanian NGO worker organizing more difficult.

The Western inability or unwillingness to apprehend liquid organizational logics is a matter of epistemic justice that has material effects. As Sabelo Ndlovu-Gatsheni defines it, "Epistemic justice is about [the] liberation of reason itself from coloniality."[14] Western organizational logics, which stem from coloniality, are unable to recognize some African forms of organizing *as* organizing. Instead it is seen as a form of disorganization, or even a complete lack of organizational logic.[15] In order for NGOs to delink from neocolonial frameworks that erase organizing couched in social, historical, and material African contexts, liquid organizing must be named and valued. Jensen argues that "deliberate disengagement from dominant epistemic frameworks may lead to more creative and more just organizational praxis."[16] I would add that such deliberate disengagement is also necessary in order to decolonize organizational structures and the ways they operate in relation to African lives.

The problem that epistemic injustice inflicts on the Little Community is not simply solidity per se. To some extent, solidity is necessary to any organization. There must be some consistent sense of processes and procedures for the organizational staff to be able to work together. Problems arise when Westerners are unable to recognize the value of fluid organizing, and ways it may complement, replace, extend, or ameliorate solid solutions. If decolonial thought works toward "a world in which many worlds could coexist,"[17] part of decolonizing organizing processes would be conceptualizing liquid and solid organizing practices as intertwined and constantly negotiated in relation to one another. Sometimes we need structures, and sometimes water must sweep them away.

What happens when liquid organizing in the Little Community meets the solid expectations and desires of Western donors? What happens when liquid organizing runs into walls, both literal and figurative? In the remainder of this chapter, I draw from interviews with the leaders of the departments within the Little Community, who together form its steering committee, the Viongozi Wa Shirika, to describe the ways that the NGO both engages in liquid organizing strategies and runs into solid walls and expectations. I argue that liquid organizing functions in a context of intimate relationalities to meet complex and ever-changing needs imposed by resource scarcity, and yet is met with a Western desire for solidifying organizational processes that simultaneously undermines liquid processes and makes them even more urgent and necessary. I first examine the contextual circumstances that underlie liquid organizing.

I then provide examples of how the organization has engaged in liquid organizing processes before finally turning to the ways donors attempt to impose solidity on the NGO. I conclude by examining how this analysis relates to epistemic justice.

Contexts of Liquid Organizing

Liquid organizing arises from two main contexts. First, precarious circumstances create the need for fluid responses to unpredictable contexts that create conditions of vulnerability. Second, relational networks allow for the trust necessary to engage in dynamic processes of organizing.

Precarious Circumstances

Precarious circumstances create a need for liquid organizing. This is reflected not only in the ways the organization reaches out and engages with the community but also in how it engages with its own staff members. Even within the organization, emergent needs may require shifts in budgetary allotments, placement of staff, or time spent on certain tasks. For instance, Nuru had never heard of the Little Community before she was called there from a village an hour away by car to help care for her brother's child. At first, she felt out of place:

> I didn't know this place at all; NGO orphanage, I didn't know it. When they brought me here, I thought this seemed like a harsh environment because I didn't know how to care for the child, I wasn't comfortable at all, and I felt very bad. I even tried to get my relatives to find someone else ... But I am thankful the guardians helped me, gave me advice, comforted me. ... After a while, I got more comfortable, I felt really good. After continuing to stay here, I was really excited to continue working here because the people here helped me learn. And I found I really liked the work of caring for children.

Nuru only came to the Little Community because of the precarious circumstances of both herself and her brother's child. She had no better job opportunities at the time, and was thrilled to learn a new skill. Notably, she was happy to learn it *after* becoming accustomed to the people at the NGO, how they worked, what life there was like—after becoming more intimately connected to the networks of relations around the NGO. Fluid organizing both responds to vulnerable conditions and depends on networks of relations to work.

The NGO also works in liquid ways to respond to vulnerability in the surrounding community. Upendo passionately articulated how she had seen children who would have died if not for the Little Community:

> UPENDO: I have totally seen, with my own eyes, that there are children who have come here who were in a very bad state, to the point where if they had stayed in the village there they would have lost their lives. I have seen it with my own eyes. I've been amazed.
> JENNA: Why have you been amazed?
> UPENDO: I was amazed because of the good guardianship here. They really help. A station like this really helps the children so much. That, *kumbe*, there is a possibility that they won't lose their lives.[18] That there they were in danger, but now they have reached a place here where they've turned around completely. Since then they've continued to have great health, to heal. And their parents are able to come again to take them back home. So it's something that this station totally helps with.

Not only does the NGO help with children in vulnerable conditions—where parents are unable to care for them because of work, health problems, and so on—but it also does so in a way that is liquid, responding to changing circumstances. After receiving the care that their parents or guardians are unable to provide, the children return to the village when they no longer require such care. In this manner, the work of the NGO is significantly different from how Westerners might typically imagine orphanages to be—the children are never permanently separated from their families or guardians but rather cared for until such time as they are either out of danger, able to care for themselves, or others are now able to take on the responsibility of their care.

Networks of Relation

Nuru was not the only one brought in to work at the Little Community due to relational connections of some kind. Peter and Deo were asked if they wanted jobs because they were regular students in the adult English classes that Sarah taught in the village. Mustafa was recruited by a Western volunteer doctor who resided for half of each year in the Little Community. Upendo and Mama Isaak first worked for the Giles family before asking to be transferred to the NGO. Sarah met Fadhili in town when he helped her find a shop she was looking for in the market. Making decisions that respond to ever-changing and emergent circumstances has to be based in close relational ties; as I noted above, some African organizing has been described as "trust-based."[19]

Here this rings true—so much so that sometimes the solution to organizational problems at the NGO is not material but rather lies in reaffirming relations. Relational connections enable the success of liquid organizing. On an intraorganizational level, this means that connections must be built between the staff members themselves in order for them to understand each other well enough to entrust others to take care of emergent needs, whether among the staff or in their community work. Although this is the case in all organizations, it is particularly necessary where budgets are variable and resources scarce. For example, Nuru explains how she and Regina, the head of the Guardian Department that oversees housemothers and -fathers, initially butted heads when she first became the head teacher:

> NURU: You know that with needs like soap and other supplies it's the guardians who buy them. So sometimes if I went there to ask for maybe a box of soap and a pack of foam for this month, I thought I needed to ask Regina if she bought them for us or not. So, it was my understanding that they would buy what we needed for the classroom for us. So sometimes I would go ask, and she would answer, "I didn't buy them." Getting an answer like the one that she gave, it had a negative effect. . . . So when the soap ran out, I didn't know what funds were for education and what funds were for guardianship! It was like everything was mixed up together. *Basi*, because the teachers needed to use the soap right away I asked if maybe the guardians could loan us some and we would pay them back in the next month's budget. But she told me, "No, I can't loan you soap. It's only for our use." So our communication was not so great. And our relationship was also not good. So when we took the issue to Damas he helped us so that now we get along great, after sitting together to give each other advice about the relationship between our two departments . . . we've seen great changes.
>
> JENNA: So what allowed you to make those changes? What needed to be changed?
>
> NURU: Mostly the way we answered each other. If I came to you with a problem and then you answered me with, "I don't know anything about that," or if I came and maybe greeted you, "How's your morning?" and you said, "Good." There's an expectation that if someone comes to greet you in the morning with "How's your morning?" you look them in the face and say, "Good." "I have a problem." "Okay, what is it?" But if you say "How's your morning?" "Good," and you continue working without even listening to me, that's scornful. So when we tried to explain that to

her, she owned up to it, and took responsibility for the guardians on the whole. The leader then truthfully said she won't do it again. So that led to some great changes. Now we greet each other nicely, and I respond well. If we need something from each other, we answer each other well.

This is not the only instance I heard from employees of confusion with the budget because multiple departments needed the same supplies, but each supply run was done for the NGO as a whole. After the run, sometimes it would be difficult to remember how much of one thing each particular department had requested. The solution to solving this confusion is not perhaps the one most Westerners might expect. Nuru didn't describe better methods of keeping track of orders or counting the number each department requested. Instead, the problem was solved through developing a better relationship. Once she and Regina were able to sit down and talk, to understand each other better, and to greet each other better each day, they were better able to work together to figure out issues like running out of soap.

In the same vein, NGO workers continually reiterated the necessity of knowing and understanding the community in order to work within it well. Arnold put it succinctly: "If you don't know what the community needs, you can't work to help them. Yeah, and you can't see the important things that need to be done. Yeah. But if you recognize the needs of the community you'll see what needs to be done." It may seem obvious that someone needs to understand what the community needs in order to help it, but it was often this understanding that was described as differentiating NGO workers from the donors that supported them.

Damas tied this to the importance of being "on-site" for financial decision-making in the organization:

> I would advocate that the people who use the money should be the ones who decide how it's used. That is, I mean that the people on-site all the time are the ones who represent the projects. They are the ones who should have the ability to decide how the money is spent. Because the Viongozi Wa Shirika sits and discusses the problems here—without the board. We discuss problems and we see a lot of things that are accomplished here in the community. And we can say, "Maybe we can help in this way." But we can see this, and when we bring it up, we're told there's no budget. But we are the ones who've seen how important it would be if we helped there.

Damas suggested that the members of the Viongozi Wa Shirika were better positioned to decide how money was used in the community because they were the ones who could see important problems as they arose—problems that those separated by distance could not notice or predict. The positioning of the Viongozi Wa Shirika on-site allowed for it to respond to changes in context or condition as they were occurring, in a liquid manner that enabled support in a treacherous environment.

Deo expanded on Damas's point, describing how the detachment of donors could lead to problems in the solutions they suggested, but also emphasizing again the importance of understanding and being in close relation with the people one works with:

> DEO: If you've planned to help me, and then you ask, so, your problems are what and what? I'll explain to you every one of my problems. Isn't that right? Then you say that you think you can help me with this certain problem. Okay, you'll have helped me, but you haven't reached the primary issue. Because if I explain to you all of my problems, the next question needs to be, Which do you think we should start with? Then, you've really helped me, because I can be completely open about which one I think needs to be addressed first—because it's the one that affects me the most and it's one that I see that really needs to be implemented soon.
> JENNA: And do you feel free to say this to a guest who arrives here at the NGO?
> DEO: Yes, I feel completely free. That is, I feel completely free because I know the people that I live among.

For Deo, it was knowing and being comfortable with the people around him that would allow him to disclose what projects are more of a priority than others. That is, if someone only asked "What are your problems?" without also following up with "And which is most important?," they might provide help with something that actually wasn't such a big deal or help that was not the most useful at that time. Deo further reinforced the importance of cultivating close relationships with the people the organization works with—both within the NGO itself and in relation to the community.

Engaging in Liquid Organizing

Within the Little Community, Tanzanian workers engaged in liquid organizing in two primary ways: willingness to shift goals and change direction dependent on emergent needs; and engaging in action as a collective network rather than to specifically meet individual goals.

Meeting Emergent Needs

One of the questions I asked in each interview was what the employee saw as the primary goal of the NGO. For an organization with multiple branches that seemed to keep adding projects depending on what the community needed, I had a difficult time pinning down what, if anything, was the primary motivation for each person's work. Most people I interviewed simply responded, "To help the community." With this broad definition they both encapsulated the Little Community's work and also hinted at why it continually seemed to be shifting and changing. If the work of the organization is to help the community, what that help looks like is going to depend on context, timing, and available resources.

Deo helped to clarify the way that the organization's goals continually changed. When I asked what he saw as the primary goal, he began by explaining the initial urgency of the HIV/AIDS crisis in the village, which left many children orphaned, others unable to be cared for because their parents were so ill, and an urgent need for not only HIV medication but health care in general to combat secondary complications. Deo continued, "Already you can see that the first goal [of the NGO], the one that's the primary objective, you know that it isn't finished, but there are other things that have come up. So, for me, I think that these services on behalf of the community should be given the power to continue. They should definitely be continued. That is, they shouldn't be left behind." Deo explained that even though the NGO certainly had not met its goal of eradicating HIV/AIDS from the area, there were other needs that had arisen in the meantime that also required attention. From his perspective, it was important to keep working toward the original goal and to also make sure that the emergent needs of the community were met. None of these things, he emphasized, should be left behind.

In addition to describing the fluidity necessary to meet the needs of the community as they arose, Deo also noted that there must be a fluidity within the organization itself in order to do so: "It's the kind of thing where I'm here today, but there will be a tomorrow or the day after when another person may come. But because we're doing things that help the community, we need to look hard at how we can make sure the NGO continues to do its work for the community. Like I said, there are many things we haven't yet accomplished—that is, every time you try to finish one thing, you find that others come up." He asserted that the NGO needed to be fluid in its operations, to ensure that even if the organization fell prey to financial or physical vulnerability in the future, it would continue to be able to do its work. In that way, even the shifting context of the Little Community itself and those who worked there must be taken into account when examining and reacting to dynamic and changing needs. Even though Deo was there today, he might not be there tomorrow; but the organization would still be needed. It is important to note that he was not advocating for emplacing a more strict or tight structure in order to plan for the future possibilities that might arise, as might be expected within Western epistemological frameworks. Instead, he advocated for a more situated and recurring "hard look" at the ways the NGO could continue to work in the community.

For Arnold, the Viongozi Wa Shirika is what allowed them to solve problems as they arose. He described the importance of the NGO leadership working together in response to issues: "When there is something going wrong with administration, maybe with a certain department—from the Home-Based Care, or whatever—when it reaches the point of a final decision, when it hasn't been successfully resolved yet, we bring it to the Viongozi Wa Shirika. The delegates there help to—*what*?[20] To make a decision that will provide a little something for everyone. When they make a decision now, indeed we have a path to move forward with that issue, to push forward." The Viongozi Wa Shirika acted as a place where every department could *participate* in making the decision together. I want to note the use of *participation*, here. The word in Swahili has a deeper significance than it does in English: securing everyone's participation, making sure everyone is working together and on the same page, that they are there supporting one another—these things mean much more than simply being present in a certain activity. There's a weight to the connotation that hearkens back to the importance of relational connections in liquid organizing. In Swahili, *participation* implies a shared goal and orientation, as well as a willingness to pitch in similar amounts of labor and money as the others involved in participation.

Here then, Arnold was describing how the Viongozi Wa Shirika acted as a means of securing participation in decision-making from each department of the NGO, and how it became necessary as problems arose that touched on more than one area, or where one department was confounded. The decisions of the Viongozi Wa Shirika, he implied, took everyone into account. This is also important to note, as it disturbs possible Western assumptions that liquid organizing is haphazard or that decisions are made on a whim; on the contrary, long histories of trust and participation created the ability for Tanzanian staff at the NGO to make necessary decisions at the moment when they were needed. Collectivity is also important to creating the context for liquid organizing, as I examine in the following pages.

Engaging in Networked Responses

The NGO often used fluid networks to meet community needs, drawing together the importance of relational grounding with recognizing and attending to emergent issues. On a day-to-day basis, this meant spending a lot of time in meetings, or simply being with one another. Over and over in the interviews, NGO employees emphasized the importance of sitting with each other, meeting to talk through plans, meeting to talk about problems—sitting and talking was perhaps the most repeated part of how problems at the NGO should be solved and why work at the NGO proceeded well. In chapter 6, this is discussed further as one reason the Western managers of the NGO, Sarah and Tim, understood and valued the Tanzanian staff and their perspectives. Sofia put it simply: "Communication [in the NGO] is great. Because whenever something happens, we always come together to address it."

For the NGO workers, the most important part of addressing emergent problems was to talk with each other about it. Transportation came up multiple times as an issue. (It will be dealt with further in chapter 5.) Since the Little Community worked with villages across three wards, employees often needed to travel to meet up with community leaders and those in need. But they couldn't simply plan to up and leave without working together with others in the organization:

> ARNOLD: To solve a challenge like transportation, how could every department leader plan their own schedule by themselves without participating with—*what?*
> JENNA: Others.
> ARNOLD: Participating with others. The work of the Viongozi Wa Shirika is to make sure that everyone's schedules are known to everyone else, and to prevent the loss of monetary assets.

Sometimes this was more difficult than it sounds, however. For someone like Mustafa, the head of the Health and Medicine Department, transportation needs were often unexpected: "People come find me at my house all the time, saying there's this thing, this thing, this thing [that needs to be addressed]. There's a certain sick person in this particular village, and I have to make a decision right then and there to go and help them. Say, to go get that person and take them to the hospital right away." Although Mustafa's needs were more obviously urgent than others, he was not the only one who had to make snap decisions about transportation and travel with little prior warning. Thus, the NGO workers had to rely on the relational networks that they'd already put in place by sitting, talking, and planning together, in order to entrust each other with the sorts of decisions that have to be made in the spur of the moment.

This trust then allowed for a flexibility in operations. As Fadhili described it, it was the amount of time that they had sat together and discussed within the Viongozi Wa Shirika meetings that allowed for enough trust to delegate decision-making throughout the organization:

> FADHILI: The way we started Viongozi Wa Shirika was very good, because we discussed lots of issues; what should we do, what should we do, what should we do?
>
> JENNA: Do you think the Viongozi Wa Shirika has helped with communication in the NGO?
>
> FADHILI: Yes, it has helped a lot. Particularly because the departments have been arranged well, with someone in charge of each. It's definitely helped Sarah and Tim. People don't come to them anymore, "I've come to ask for work" [*laughter*]. *Kumbe*, now the departments are well-arranged! If you want work, you just go to ask that person there. *Eeh*,[21] if you want a certain thing, go ask that person there. If you want to bring a child to study sewing, go talk to Fadhili. If you want to bring a child to the kindergarten, see Nuru. If you want to bring a child here who needs care, see Regina. Health-wise, if you have a problem, ask Mustafa.

Not only the managers but each department head trusted the others to do their work, because they had spent so much time building the relational networks required to earn that trust.

The importance of building networks in order to respond to emergent issues does not end with work for those at the NGO; it is also a life strategy. As Cruz and Sodeke remind us, there is often little differentiation between work and life in fluid organizing contexts.[22] Arnold explained to me, "So, the way I see it, all people are connected through life's connections, relations between one person and another. So I think that it's best to continue to help others because you can't know how you will meet them next. Who this person will be to me next, how they might help me, how they will help. Yeah. At another time they might not meet me, but my child, or my relative, or maybe my younger sibling. Yeah. So, if you do good, helping children, I see that it will pay for itself well later." Good relations with others are not only important to doing good work, but also to having a good life. And liquid organizing is something that Arnold saw occurring not only in the way the organization related to the village but also in the way he related to everyone; all of our connections with each other are constantly shifting and changing in ways that require response.

Running into Solid Walls

Western donors often lack the tools to recognize or understand these fluid relations, however. For Cruz and Sodeke, as well as other organizational theorists like Jensen, the problem is primarily one of epistemology. Normative Western frameworks for understanding organizing are based in solidity, immobility, differentiability, and other assumptions that make it difficult to attend to dynamic demands. In the Little Community, this is especially evident in the ways donors relate to and attempt to control projects. Here I demonstrate how solid expectations emerge from a lack of contextual understanding, which results in donors imposing solidity physically through a preoccupation with building and figuratively through a desire for control.

Lacking Contextual Understanding

Donors are unable to understand the need for liquid organizing because they do not have a close enough relationship to or involvement with the ever-shifting local context. For example, Damas originally started working at the NGO because he saw posts about it on Facebook and left a message with the person who runs the British donor account for the Little Community. The person in Britain connected Damas with Tim, who asked him to come visit the NGO. When Damas arrived, he found some things to be different from what he expected:

> When I arrived here, everything I read on the internet—when I arrived here I noticed that things were a little different. Because the person who wrote it was not someone here. I came to realize that there are lots of things, yes, they're here, but the reporting about them is off.... Even if you go to the village for outreach, you will see that these things were explained, I've read about this thing here, but if you get the deep story of it and return here you'll realize it was reported differently than it really is. So I'm happy to work here first because we work directly with the community. And I encounter many things, lots of challenging cases. So, from my perspective, I get lots of great life experience.

It came as a surprise to Damas to find out that the things he read about the NGO on the internet were technically true, but not in the way they were reported. He interpreted this generously as a problem of proximity—that the person writing the posts for the NGO in Britain didn't have all the information regarding what was happening on the ground. Damas then used this as a point of differentiation for the work that he did, which was done "directly with the community." That, he emphasized, is what made his work important—that he worked directly with the community and the challenging cases that arose within it.

Regina also recognized how donor distance could be problematic: "The donors can decide that they want their money to be used maybe for uniforms, but those of us who care for the kids, the Viongozi Wa Shirika, Sarah, Tim, they need to examine if this is okay—using this money for a certain thing. But you see there's a need that's more important than that one. So the donors can give their ideas, but they need to listen to the perspectives of the Viongozi Wa Shirika as well." She also reiterated that the proximity to and involvement in the day-to-day NGO operations mattered for understanding what people needed. It was those on-site that had a better idea what was most important for life at the NGO at that moment versus something that could wait.

Donor lack of contextual understanding could also take more intimate forms. Even for those donors who stayed at the NGO for a period of time, there could still be cultural misapprehensions that caused problems. Or, in the case of the next example, not even a cultural misapprehension but a lack of awareness of the ways that culture can structure experience and expectations differently:

ARNOLD: We've already had some small challenges with the children here because guests—a guest can, for example, choose one child here to build a relationship with. If they build a relationship with a child, they have a certain style of how life goes between them, and it's different than the other children. For example, we had one volunteer here who was called Grandma Lina. Grandma Lina built a relationship with a child named Musa, who's still here. She stayed in the guesthouse when I lived in House A [with Musa]. She would call Musa over to the guesthouse and give him lots of things like candy and presents. Yeah. So, it was like she exposed Musa to the environment of the guesthouse. So Musa now knows candy is there, other things are there. You see? Different things that you won't find in House A.

JENNA: Mm-hmm. He got used to getting things like this?

ARNOLD: Yeah, and when she gave things to him she only had good intentions. But she would give him things and tell him to hide them, and not give them to the other children. She told him to hide. You see?

JENNA: She built bad behavior.

ARNOLD: Yeah. So . . . this brought many harms. He stole things from guests. And he started [stealing] from Grandma Lina herself. He even stole medicines from her, thinking they would be sweet. He stole her medicines and ate them himself. So this could bring harm to the child too.

Arnold made it clear that Grandma Lina only had good intentions in her relationship with Musa. She just wanted to pamper him, perhaps make him feel special. But she didn't realize the effects that her singling him out would have on his life and behavior—particularly after she left, and he was no longer receiving the special treatment he had gotten used to. Having acquired a desire for special things, Musa started stealing, and even stole and consumed Grandma Lina's medicines. Her treatment of him not only taught him to value his own desires over that of the community but also led him to endanger himself while looking for his next treat.

Imposing Solidity through Building

Given this lack of contextual understanding, donors often aren't aware of or interested in the dynamic organizing processes that shift and change depending on context. And, because Western epistemologies emphasize permanence as the foundation for meaningful change, donors often attempt to impose solidity on NGO processes. One way in which they do so is to prioritize building structures.

Damas gave an in-depth and valuable explanation of both how donors seem to love building things more than participating in other NGO facets and also how this causes many problems for the organization:

> JENNA: Are there other problems keeping the NGO from reaching its goals?
>
> DAMAS: Another problem is money, perhaps. It's not enough to maintain all the projects that we need to reach our goals. For example, one big challenge is that if you go to Home-Based Care they will tell you they don't have enough medicines or supplies. But the donor over there doesn't see it. They tell you they want a certain classroom to be built, but in reality we need to buy antibiotics. What should we do when we don't have any other money to buy antibiotics? So you might hear that they have added more complaints, every report every month you read they don't have antibiotics, they don't have supplies, they don't have gloves, they don't have this other thing. So it's losing money to maintain projects that we've already started. It takes us backwards . . . I don't understand why they only think of building. . . . I see so many of them bringing this sort of help. To build. Let's build this thing, build this thing. But I still don't know why they love to put down buildings.
>
> Because if you say, "Let's build a school, first," for example. . . . Okay, we'll build a school but we'll need teachers. And they will need to be paid.

Also maybe we'll need to register it and that also requires more fees that they haven't planned for. They only gave the money to build the building. And if they come and see a building standing, finalized, they will say, "*Basi*, I'm finished." But we still don't have furniture. So this is a challenge. We can say maybe, okay, we'll build a another classroom there in Mikoda. We build them a classroom but their feedback to us is negative. We didn't have the participation that we depended on from them. And many times, the places where they provide help end up having major problems, because they expect that now we'll do everything ourselves. They built a library, so we said *basi*, one teacher should be placed at the library. They [at the school] say, "There's no one to teach here, employ one yourselves and pay their salary." And that is another expense again. So, I don't know why they love to build things.

First, Damas recognized that the NGO was responding to contexts of austerity and did not have enough money to do everything it would like to do in order to help the community. As such, it needed to make decisions about where money goes. But when a donor forced them to use it for building projects, it not only used money that could have had better effects elsewhere but also required many extra fees that the donor themself didn't plan for. And the NGO workers still had to listen, unable to help, as they heard how the Home-Based Care workers didn't have enough medicines or supplies to help keep people in the village alive.

It might seem like the NGO workers could simply tell the donors that there were more pressing issues at hand. But Deo pointed out that even when told, sometimes the donors still responded with the desire to put the money into a building. He suggested that there needed to be more discussion, sitting with the donors so that they had a better understanding:

> What we want, even if a guest wants to help the NGO, they shouldn't say "I want to build a well," or "I want to build a hospital," or "I want to build" . . . I don't know, a school. No, what we want is for them to arrive, to sit with them, have them say their idea and then we talk, and they ask, "What problems are you having here?" We can explain—because we are the ones who know our community, better than a guest who comes here. They come with money and a plan of how to help, but it's best if they wait for an announcement of how their money will be used.
>
> I don't think that if your leg is hurt, your head should be treated. It won't go anywhere. It's the person themself who knows more. If they're hurt in the leg, they need to be treated in the leg. . . . But if you meet a

sick person and then tell them, "*Bwana*, I've come to buy you a notebook so you can go to school," you're already going in the wrong direction. Yeah. And we love ... for lots of different people to help in the NGO. But we also love to build close relationships. That is, to do things in a participatory way.

We don't deny that guests can see the problems we have. They can see the problems we have, but we should sit together and discuss them.

Sometimes the donors were stuck on the fact that they did, in fact, see something that was a problem with the NGO, and thus failed to listen when the Tanzanian workers explained that yes, it was a problem, but it was not the most pressing issue at the moment. Instead, the Tanzanian NGO workers continued to encounter people who, when hearing that someone's leg was hurt, insisted on healing their head.

Imposing Solidity through Control

Deo hit on a facet of donor solidity that transcends the desire to build things: donors also seem to desire to maintain control. To acquiesce to Tanzanian staff suggestions for how the money should be used would be to give up power, to admit to a lack of knowledge. For Western donors, this is difficult, and many refuse. Damas described how when a nearby school needed a hostel so that girls studying there from villages farther away would not need to walk home late along dangerous paths, the donors instead insisted on building a library. He claimed it was because they did not want to listen to the Tanzanians at the NGO:

> They don't like to listen to what we say. What we want to do. But we know that if we get this money we would like to use it in a certain place. But they say they want to use it to buy books. Maybe the school doesn't have any need for books. Or they came and said, "Let's buy computers to bring to a certain place." And the computers sit there without being used until they break down and fill with dust. We take them and get them repaired for a fee and return them. They're still not used. There's no need for it.
>
> For a good example, take the school at Lulongu. They needed a hostel, but the donors came and built a library ... libraries are important, but it wasn't what they needed at the time. Now the library isn't used, or it's used poorly. Maybe, for example, they might take a student and lock them inside. One day when we went to check on it we found lots of sticks [for hitting students], like it was a room for punishment. But the books that

they arranged looked like they hadn't been opened and there was no supervision.

This is a still a challenge, but we've started to try to provide our own ideas. Hopefully, they will receive ours and we will receive theirs. But we're looking especially at—what are our needs? We've done this a lot of times—that they come, they give us money, and say "Build a certain thing." Sometimes we use the money instead for something that we need to do now. If another person gives us money, then we put it back there. But the problem is that the person who gave the money in the first place comes to visit their project—before another person has given us money to replace there.... Yeah. So my perspective is that the NGO should be given the power to make its own decisions on how to use funds.

Through maintaining strict control over how money is used, the donors procured power over the Tanzanian employees. Although Damas seemed not to understand why they wouldn't want to listen to workers' ideas, I suggest that this is an outgrowth of the neocolonial mindsets we've seen volunteers exhibit in previous chapters. Donors maintained control over funds as a means of bolstering neocolonial power structures of epistemic injustice that rejected the Viongozi Wa Shirika's input. A particular outgrowth of this is the inability to recognize liquid organizing processes as legitimate under logics of coloniality.

Donor control left the members of the Viongozi Wa Shirika in the place of having to ask or beg for their thoughts to be heard. Peter explained,

I don't really understand the work of the board. But their work is to plan for all the money that comes in from the donors, saying that they think it can help here. They're the ones that start thinking about what things should get first priority. If they're given a priority, *basi*, those of us on the Viongozi Wa Shirika come together to explain that "*Jamani*, we think after the donor decides if they're giving money, we think we should do this or that."[23] Here, we approve it, we either say yes or no. [We say,] "We think it would be great if it was like this."

So we either agree with those that brought ideas to us or we say, "*Jamani*, we beg for you to adjust this."... For us here, we're just able to accept what comes from them. And we don't have the power to say, "*Jamani*, we'd like to ask for—." No.

Peter didn't see the Viongozi Wa Shirika as having any power to challenge the decisions made by the donors and communicated through the NGO board, which comprises Mr. Giles's family and close personal acquaintances, including only two Tanzanians. Damas echoed this sentiment in his interview, saying, "The Viongozi Wa Shirika is already caught, unable to decide differently."

Arnold also articulated this feeling of being stuck with what donors wanted, and the problems that caused:

> It would be best if we had our own projects. We should have our own projects because we can decide the style of how we'd like to help. Yeah. Because sometimes help comes with conditions. *Eeh*. It can come with such conditions that many times it's not very successful with the community it's involved with. But when it's you, yourself, you have it yourself, you use it yourself, it's easier to know how we should use it—to make decisions about its use.... It can happen like that, that they want it to go this way, but, *kumbe*, that isn't what people need. *Eeh*. So it can bring problems.

Arnold described how donor help came with conditions, and how those conditions could sometimes make it impossible for the projects to succeed. He suggested that if the Viongozi Wa Shirika had more control over the ways money was spent, then it would be able to have much more successful projects, ones more attuned to community desires.

The final impact of donor control was that it didn't allow for the Tanzanian employees to practice creating and expressing their own ideas, which led to atrophy of communication between the organization and the donors, as well as a lack of creative solutions. Damas suggested that there would be more and better ideas put forth if they were only allowed to be heard:

> And even ideas can broaden more, because when someone gives their thoughts they don't know if their idea will be listened to or not. But if someone sees that their idea was received, they can build an argument on behalf of another [idea]. They will come to think more broadly because now they recognize, "I have worked, maybe I've been put in charge of a project, what should be done there is indeed this thing."... But they don't have any reason to think about, "What if we create a certain project?" To suggest we do it. They know, even if they create something, who will receive it? You see? So the person can sit there and their ideas end on the paper in their notes.... So if they're given the power to share their ideas and put them to work in reality, it can give people heart and they will have even broader ideas.

Damas was certain that if the Tanzanian leadership of the organization were only given the opportunity to speak and be heard, the staff would not only be more committed to their work but there would also be more interesting and creative work happening. If liquid organizing were allowed to flow, the results would be astounding.

Donor Control as Epistemic Injustice

But clearly something was standing in the way. "So, for you, where does the problem lie?," I asked Damas. "Is the problem with the board, or—?" He answered, "For me, the problem is right there in the structure of the organization."

The desire for control that was reflected in the donors was an outgrowth of the structures of coloniality. Donor control and desire for solid outputs functioned through an epistemic injustice that dismissed African epistemologies of organizing. Ironically, in doing so, donor control ended up materially reinforcing the very problems that liquid forms of organizing set out to ameliorate: precarity, vulnerability, and austerity.

The community hall was certainly important, though its importance lay not in the fact that the building was there but that it offered a space where people could gather together, participate with one another, exchange ideas—be together in the moment. It was the relational function of the community hall that benefited the community, and precisely this function that was taken away when the money necessary simply to keep the hall open was instead redirected to other, more permanent-sounding, projects.

Donors were missing the key part that relational understanding, situated in the moment as things are happening, played into the work of the NGO. Western logics of countable measures of success, lists with checkboxes ticked off, could never register the importance of simply being together with one's community. And without that understanding donors would continually be unable to apprehend how their ideas for projects and control of funds lead to atrophied community relations and solutions to the wrong questions: medicine for one's head instead of one's foot.

While the donors misdiagnosed problems and offered problematic solutions, people suffered—people who could have been helped simply by connecting to their community, meeting in the hall that was ostensibly built for their use, died.

And, as Damas put it, "The donor ... doesn't see it." The buildings continue to stand. Somewhere, perhaps, in Canada or the United States or Britain, someone claps a friend on the back and describes the community hall they built in Tanzania.

Yet we can find water seeping through the cracks in the buildings, filling the holes left by poor planning, flowing into spaces where no structures have yet been set. Perhaps it makes one wonder: How many more donors will come, asking for buildings, before the flood breaks through and sweeps the structures away?

Chapter
Five
Fluid
(Re)mapping

Before modern maps and modern boundaries, the world was limitless. Movement was free. Mobility was a way of life.—Sabelo J. Ndlovu-Gatsheni, *Epistemic Freedom in Africa*

I wonder what the community hall at the Little Community would look like if it were unbound from restriction on who might use it, and for what cost. What kind of meetings would be held there? Would people come and go, simply to see who was around? Perhaps some would stop by on their walk or motorcycle ride to the next village just to greet whomever happened to be there. Would the hall ever be empty, or would it act as a constantly-engaged nexus of rotating bodies and relational connections?

The only time I witnessed the community hall in use was when the medical students held one of their field clinics there (see chapter 1). Within an hour of opening, the hall was filled with people, and it stayed packed until nightfall. With its decorations still in place from a wedding the weekend prior, I got a sense on that bustling day of what the hall could look like on the night of a special event. But I was left wondering what kinds of relations and meetings might occur if it was open all of the time, and not only for those willing and able to pay for its use.

The community hall was caught between (neo)colonial epistemologies of land as individual property and Indigenous epistemologies of land as communal ground.[1] In the first set of logics, the community hall had to be rented out in order to recuperate funds required for its upkeep and staffing. In the second, the community hall was a place of connection that should be open to all, imbued with the stories, thoughts, emotions, and relations of Mikoda's people. What it meant when the community hall stood empty depended on one's relationship to land. The Tanzanian cultural history that predates colonial land relations still encodes in law that customary use relations of land, where one is entitled to land based on having used it for an extended period of time, are valid grounds for claiming that land as one's own.[2] If there is a correspondence between use and claim, and the community hall was ostensibly for the benefit of the community, should they not have had its use?

Being told they needed to rent the community hall presented a dilemma for the Tanzanian villagers, as well as for Mama Isaak and Peter, who acted as its caretakers:

> MAMA ISAAK: When he built this community hall, Mr. Giles said it was for the school and citizens to use. Now, the problem came after this, when the budget became shaky. We started to lease the community hall. Now, what happened is a lot of people started to think that we were taking their money for ourselves. They would say, "Why? Isn't the community hall for us?" They agreed to pay rent for it, but not peaceably, for how is the hall built for us and called ours if you're charging us? And they started to have ideas, saying, "If we have to pay to use the hall, then that money should be returned to the village, right? It shouldn't go elsewhere." So we told them, "No, the money should go back to the orphanage. If there are problems there, it helps the children. It shouldn't go back to the village office." . . . Some of them understood, but others didn't.
>
> PETER: And another thing . . . some of this money went to making the community hall better, like here you can see there weren't any curtains or other things. But we put up curtains, we put up beautiful textiles. . . . Again, many people did not understand. They didn't understand.

Mama Isaak and Peter were forced to deny community members use of their own hall. And the community didn't understand. Its lack of understanding demonstrates an epistemological divide between the Western donors and leadership at the nongovernmental organization (NGO) and the Tanzanian community it serves. The villagers saw the hall as a communal space, one they had a right to use. Why else was the hall built, if not to be used? But under Western logics, the hall figured as property, a bounded place, separate from the rest of the village. It had been bought and paid for—and was in need of further funds for maintenance.

Mama Isaak and Peter thus found themselves caught between (neo)colonial epistemologies of landownership and Indigenous epistemologies of land usage. But the struggle was not waged on equal ground. Under coloniality, land relations exist within contexts of epistemic injustice. Sabelo Ndlovu-Gatsheni locates epistemic injustice in "the reality of continued entrapment of knowledge production in Africa within Euro-North American colonial matrices of power."[3] Mama Isaak and Peter clearly struggled with whether or not to allow the community access to the community hall without payment. But doing so would have put them at risk of running afoul of the NGO leadership (maybe costing them their jobs) or even the Western donors (maybe costing the organization further funding). Trapped by Western hegemony, they received the treatment that befalls many bearers of bad news. As Mama Isaak noted sadly, "When we refused, now we were the ones who looked bad. . . . It looked like we were acting badly toward the community."

We might think of the community hall as a microcosm of the Little Community itself. And the ramifications that fell hardest on Mama Isaak and Peter are representative of the burden placed on the Tanzanian NGO workers more generally. Tanzanians are not always or only trapped within epistemologies of coloniality, however. Instead, this chapter will also show how Tanzanian community members and NGO workers engaged in fluid responses to epistemological conflict through (re)mapping practices that counter (neo)colonial epistemologies—without necessarily confronting them directly.

Land in the Context of Epistemological Injustice

I examine the clash between different epistemologies of land relations in the intercultural context of the NGO and how this simultaneously left the NGO workers in a bind and engendered fluid attempts at (re)mapping. Through the particular cases of Mr. Giles and a pair of donors, Esther and Gail, I will explore how Western epistemologies of landownership provoked shifting means of Indigenous (re)mapping that often functioned surreptitiously and ambivalently in relation to (neo)colonial structures.

Conflicting Epistemologies

Through Mr. Giles and Esther and Gail's relations to land, the logics of solidity from chapter 4 make a reprise. Here I trace them further back, however, examining where these logics stem from. That is, the logics of solidity seen in chapter 4 are outgrowths of Western epistemologies of relation, and particularly relation to land.

It is almost inevitable that Western understandings of land would run into problems in Tanzania. According to the Land Act of 1999, which laid out much of the contemporary legalities of land claims in Tanzania, foreigners cannot own land. They may be granted leaseholds for rights of occupancy on the land for up to ninety-nine years, but cannot actually own it. Leaseholds for foreigners are also contingent on development. For Mr. Giles, who was granted land for both his tourist business and the NGO, his leasehold presumably fell under the jurisdiction of the village council in Mikoda, under the Village Land Act of 1999.[4]

Yet one would not say that these legal logics are strictly Indigenous, either. Enacted as Tanzania shifted from the socialism of President Julius Nyerere to ever-increasing neoliberalization under the watchful eye of international bodies such as the International Monetary Fund, Tanzania's land acts demonstrate a mixture of appreciation for Indigenous relations to land and a desire to solidify those into legal parcels that can be documented and controlled. As such, Indigenous relations of communal responsibility and customary use are often relegated within both postcolonial land law and neocolonial ideologies of relationship to land in Tanzania.

Prior to colonization, "one could not talk of a right to land as a private property," and in fact, "commoditization of land was almost a sacrilege, because there was no buying or selling of land."[5] Land was part of the communal relations, something to be stewarded. Many African traditions and customs "see the human and more-than-human world as interconnected and constitutive,"[6] meaning engagement with land is a form of relation rather than ownership. In precolonial Tanzania, people were seen as having claims over only the land that they related to—that they worked on, built on, and used. Any land that was unused was therefore open for someone else—as long as the community agreed to it. One could never lay claim to land that one did not use.

There is a clear disconnect between this logic of ecological interconnection with land—underlaid by communal consent, consistent presence, and respectful relations—and how Western colonial or postcolonial actors engage with land as individual property. Indigenous scholar Mishuana Goeman describes a similar disconnect in North American contexts. Goeman locates "the most vivid place" of her childhood as a place caught between colonial logics and her own Indigenous ones: "Twelve Corners, while it was marked as individual property by state authorities, was more than a piece of land owned or occupied." Rather than a distinct and bounded location, Goeman viewed the land not as "just a surface we crossed, but a place built through intersecting histories, longings, and belongings."[7] Although Tanzanian epistemologies are not equivalent to those of Indigenous peoples in the Americas, Goeman's experience can help us locate the colonial assumptions that are at play in both settler colonial North American contexts and postcolonial Tanzanian contexts. Specifically, she narrates how colonial logics bound land as "individual property."

In Western conceptualizations of land as property, an individual has claim to a limited area with strict physical boundaries, whether or not the individual uses it or even indeed occupies it at all. Property then functions as a locus of control, as well as a tool to be used for the benefit of the individual who owns it. Understanding land as property depends not only on the liberal human subject as unitary individual but also on the ability to individualize and separate parcels of land themselves.[8] Logics of individuality thus underlay how land is something that may be cut up, differentiated, and sold. Rather than locating it as the sum or even nexus of relational histories, land in a Western sense is separable from relations—an object that exists individually, external to the meetings and relations that take place on it.

(Re)mapping for Epistemic Justice

When Western epistemologies that locate land as individual property meet Tanzanian epistemological legacies of communal decision-making and customary use rights in relation to land, the resulting conflict denigrates Indigenous epistemologies and forces Tanzanians to engage in fluid practices of resistant (re)mapping.[9] Following Joëlle Cruz and Chigozirim Utah Sodeke, I use the term *fluid* here rather than *liquid*, as liquidity describes means of organizing, whereas fluidity "refers to the process of adaptation shaping liquidity differently in situ."[10] Fluidity thus encompasses not only alternative organizing practices but also the awareness of and attunement to alternative rationalities; it can be seen as epistemological because it describes the attunement to perspectives that make liquid organizing processes intelligible and actionable.

As we saw in chapter 4, fluidity and liquidity are not only products of marginalization wrought by epistemic injustice but also alternative epistemologies of organizing and relation that can help to combat the very conditions that made such fluid responses necessary in the first place. In short, fluid (re)mapping is necessary because of the context of epistemic injustice, but it also acts as a means of challenging Western epistemological dominance. Goeman defines (re)mapping as "the labor [that] Native ... communities ... undertake, in the simultaneously metaphoric and material capacities of map making, to generate new possibilities" for life against, beyond, and outside Western colonial structures.[11] For Goeman, "(re)mapping is about acknowledging the power of Native epistemologies in defining our moves toward spatial decolonization," as they resist what Chamoru scholar Tiara Na'puti terms *"colonial cartographic violence."*[12] Yet as Western property logics hold dominance not only through the context of coloniality but also the legitimacy provided to colonial legacies through Tanzanian land law's enshrinement of individual property claims, Tanzanians cannot simply endorse Indigenous epistemologies without facing repercussions. Fluidity then offers a means of engaging with (re)mapping in ways that respond to specific conditions of marginalization without directly challenging systems of power.

(Re)mapping is not a simple return, however. There is no "pure" Indigenous Tanzanian epistemology to return to; nor, in fact, would it resolve contemporary epistemological injustices if there were. Goeman writes, "Even if we were to recover the historical and legal dimensions of territory, for instance, I am not so sure that this alone would unsettle colonialism."[13] Ngũgĩ wa Thiong'o demonstrates that the epistemic injustice of coloniality is much deeper than what is found encoded in law, training Africans to venerate Western epistemologies above their own.[14] As a result, for Africans, epistemic injustice structures "what it is that we are free to express and on whose terms."[15] Fluid (re)mapping engages Indigenous logics in the emergent and shifting contexts of the (neo)colonial present in ways that activate new epistemic and material possibilities.

In this manner, we might think about Tanzanian (re)mapping as "convivial" or "ambivalent."[16] Rather than acting or speaking in a manner that can be recognized as fully resistant within (neo)colonial epistemologies, or fully succumbing to Western domination, the Tanzanian NGO workers and community members hold "the ability to engage in baroque practices fundamentally ambiguous, fluid, and modifiable even where there are clear, written, precise rules."[17] Through emergent responses to conflicts over land and epistemologies of its value, Tanzanian staff members engage in "everyday practices of resistance and survival that draw on dominant (colonial) cultural codes" and reframe them in alternative ways.[18] In contexts of epistemic injustice, Tanzanian actions are simultaneously bound up in and emergent against neocolonial control, making them radically contingent, rarely predictable, and often unrecognizable in typical Western narratives. In this way, fluid (re)mapping is both a response to and a rethinking of (neo)colonial logics of organization and relation. In chapter 6, I will define the accessing of fluid (re)mapping and liquid organizing as forms of what I term liquid agency and explore how the NGO leadership used liquid agency to engender decolonial possibility as the NGO fell apart.

In the analysis that follows, I examine the beginnings of the impending collapse and argue that the Little Community became caught between (neo)colonial and Indigenous logics in two relational contexts: Mr. Giles's leveraging of land as property against villagers' (re)mapping according to use, and Esther and Gail's individualistic assumptions of land's separability against NGO workers' (re)mapping around relational interconnection and responsibility. Although fluid (re)mapping opens new conditions of possibility, it is not an unencumbered process. Cruz and Sodeke remind us that "marginal organizational actors resort to fluidity involuntarily to escape hostile conditions and make a livelihood."[19] Even for those unaffiliated with the NGO, global pressures on Tanzania have resulted in laws that marginalize Indigenous relations to land. For the Little Community and those who work there, being caught in between has consequences. In particular, the destructive community relations resulting from Mr. Giles's control of land placed the Little Community in physical danger. In addition, when the NGO workers pushed back against Esther and Gail's disconnected plan to build a new trade school, it led to financial precarity for the NGO.

Fluid (re)mapping is both a response to unjust (neo)colonial epistemologies that leave Tanzanians with few obvious options and a means of recalibrating through differential epistemological bases. As such, I argue that the ambivalent positioning of the NGO, even though it results in negative material consequences in the short term, is also what allows for its ability to enact liquid agency and move toward epistemic justice in the long term. When the NGO workers refuse to support solid Western structures and instead engage in fluid (re)mapping antithetical to Western epistemologies, they demonstrate that the systems wrought by coloniality are not as immutable as they might seem. And when the systems begin to crack and break, decolonial ways of relating are released, flowing out through the fissures.

Mapping and (Re)mapping

In this section, I examine two conflicts over land relations within contexts of epistemic injustice. The two examples of Tanzanian-Western relations presented here each highlight one particular facet of (neo)colonial epistemologies of land and how the community works to (re)map along different epistemological grounds. In the first case, Mr. Giles and his conflicts with the community demonstrate how colonial logics of land as property are met with multiple attempts to (re)map the land through logics of customary use. In the second, the donors Esther and Gail and their tensions with NGO workers demonstrate how neocolonial logics of separability are met with (re)mapping based in communal responsibility and interconnection.

Land Ownership and (Re)mapping for Use

MR. GILES'S PROPERTY LOGICS

Mr. Giles was a confounding part of the Little Community structure for the people who worked there. He was the one who provided land for the NGO, but he did not financially donate to its management. He sat as the head of its board of directors, but it was unclear how the board, populated almost entirely by Mr. Giles's family members and Tanzanians who worked directly under his authority at his tourist lodge, related to the management structure of the NGO. What they did know was that Mr. Giles often attempted to control NGO operations, and particularly micromanaged when Sarah and Tim were away visiting family in North America.

As Damas summed it up, "The *mzee* is one of the very biggest challenges in the running of this orphanage."[20] In the following pages, I connect Mr. Giles's fervent displays of control to epistemologies encoding land as property that must be strictly managed to display independent ownership. To Mr. Giles, the land that the NGO occupied was his property just as much as his expatriate retreat lodge and farm across the valley were.

That Mr. Giles viewed the NGO as his personal property could be seen in his controlling behavior toward the leadership. For one, he would often show up at the NGO and issue multiple commands at one time. As Arnold mentioned, "One challenge, for example, is that Mr. Giles gives many orders at once . . . so it can be difficult to accomplish everything he requests." In addition, his style of leadership did not sit well with some Tanzanian workers:

> FADHILI: He thinks this way because of his life in the past. You remember those who were born a long time ago, they got used to—what kind of leadership?[21]
> JENNA: European?
> FADHILI: Colonial. Mm-hmm. That is, the style of dictators.
> JENNA: Aha.
> FADHILI: That is, like commands.

Fadhili later added, "The old man is a person who rants and raves," saying things like "Who is the idiot, you or me?" and implying that the only acceptable answer from Mr. Giles's perspective was the former.

In order to demonstrate that he had the ability to command obedience at the NGO, Mr. Giles would sometimes go so far as to force NGO employees to do work that was not their responsibility. For instance, Fadhili described one point where he and another Viongozi Wa Shirika member, Deo, were forced to pull weeds in the Little Community garden:

> *Eeh*,[22] but the old man can be very harsh when he comes here.... For example, one day when he came, he met me and Deo and he grabbed us and told us, "You, Fadhili and Deo, let's go over there." He continued, "Do you see what's here?" There were long grasses, I don't know what, but that was the gardener's work ... to pull out the grasses up and down there. Mr. Giles said, "You, Fadhili, because your workshop is next to here, why haven't you done this work?" I said, "This falls under another department." He said, "No it doesn't. You're nearby, it's necessary you do this work." He made us go up there and uproot plants, and he supervised us. He told us, "Until you're finished." When we finished the work, he said, "Thank you very much," and left in his car.

Mr. Giles not only forced two leaders in the NGO to do menial labor that fell under the jurisdiction of another Viongozi Wa Shirika member, Sofia, and her department, but also stood and watched over them until they finished. Here his control extended past issuing instructions about NGO management and finances to overseeing particular relations to the land. Presumably, Mr. Giles stood over the two men to exert dominance, encoding the land through property in two ways: by using it as an intermediary tool through which to enact a colonial relation of overseer to forced laborers, and through an end goal of land beautification that situated the land as his personal responsibility to manage—though in colonial fashion, through the labor of others.

When Sarah and Tim were on an unexpectedly long stay in the United States after a medical emergency, Mr. Giles tightened his grip over the NGO and its operations. He took control of all NGO finances, making the staff ask him for money for every budgetary need. Damas explained how Mr. Giles's complete jurisdiction over the Little Community finances resulted in problems for the Tanzanian workers:

> Everything you tell him, he responds with, "I'm the chairman and I have final say." So if he says, maybe, "Go build something at Mabolo," *basi*,[23] it will happen. He's already sent craftspeople there many times without telling us. The craftsperson finishes their work and goes there [to Mr. Giles] and is told they can get their money at the NGO. They arrive here and

are told, "Why the hell didn't we know about this work?[24] We won't give you money." Now, when Tim and Sarah weren't here, the money all stayed at the bank. So they dished it out there [at Mr. Giles's lodge], and we were just given reconciliations that they paid for this and this and this. While we're on a fixed budget! So our budget for the month was already ruined. We couldn't finish the month because that craftsperson had already taken money without it being budgeted for.

The departments of the Little Community were not able to buy or do everything for which they budgeted because Mr. Giles unilaterally decided to spend money without concern for the department leadership or their budgets. He even ran a surprise audit of the NGO. Without informing Sarah, Tim, or any of the Tanzanian staff, he arrived one day with an accountant and reviewed all the NGO's financial records. Fadhili described it like this: "We workers, we all really hated the Giles regime when they came here to harass us this time and that time.... He comes over, 'I would like to see your notebooks. I'd like this thing, this thing, this thing. You haven't prepared—what are you?' *Basi*. A few times, a certain person would come, his son [David Giles] would come ... a total harasser. We said, 'What is it they want us to do? Do they want us to leave, or do what?'" According to Mr. Giles, the audit revealed "serious theft." According to Sarah, he found that one of the staff was buying gas in the village where the price was significantly higher than what Mr. Giles's staff paid buying gas in town. Mr. Giles wanted this employee fired, but Sarah and Tim refused to fire them. It is not inconsequential that the audits apparently included Mr. Giles's son David (see chapter 2, where a volunteer described how David believed that Tanzania needed to be returned to British colonial control in order to be managed properly). It's no wonder that the audit left the NGO employees feeling unappreciated and offended. Mr. Giles's understanding of the NGO as part of his property led to (neo)colonial enactments of control over the NGO land, its finances, and the people who work there.

(RE)MAPPING FOR USE

Conceptualizing land as property also placed Mr. Giles at odds with the community. The land encompassing both the Giles lodge and the NGO was quite a large area, and seemed particularly wasteful as unclaimed land grew scarce in Mikoda and the surrounding villages. Unable to find land to farm under codified processes of documented leaseholds, many villagers turned to (re)mapping as circumstances—and survival—required. One example of this is the community members who began subsistence farming on land technically leased by the Gileses but left unused.

The land of the Little Community is located between the lodge and an empty patch of land leased by the Gileses' business. As part of a plan to generate more interest in and revenue for the lodge, the Giles family planned to use the land on the far side of the NGO as an airstrip. They started building the airstrip but ran out of money and put the construction on pause until more money could be obtained. Time passed, and the land sat unused. Laws and epistemologies encoding land as property left little available for long-term leases in the Mikoda area. And many families were too poor to afford such purchases and processes of documentation, even if there was land to be had. This context created a need for fluid (re)mapping, and the unused space around the airstrip offered the perfect place to actualize it.

Families began to surreptitiously use the land for subsistence farming. After a while, as their farming continued uninterrupted, plots began to trade hands under the table as well. Some who had begun farming were either no longer able to or thought that it would be more beneficial to their families to gain money by selling their plot. Using renegade subsistence farming, the villagers (re)mapped the land through logics stemming from customary law traditions wherein use of land constitutes a fair claim to it.[25] In present day conditions of capitalist-produced scarcity, they employed customary use traditions in an ambivalent fashion that simultaneously commodified land for economic exchange. The villagers took up some aspects of colonial land epistemologies, but utilized them against Mr. Giles's claims to individual property.

Sofia noted that this caused problems in two ways for the NGO:

SOFIA: Challenges exist, such as, *bwana*,[26] at first we farmed really well, but now we're constricted because other people came and are farming.
JENNA: Uh-huh. So, the problem is knowing what land is whose?
SOFIA: *Eeh.* I see they're talking about borders. We sat with Sarah, and she claimed that Giles didn't show them the borders of the NGO. They don't know where the borders of the NGO lie.
JENNA: Uh-huh. So knowing which parts are the Gileses'—like the Gileses' lodge—and which are the NGO's is a problem?
SOFIA: Yes. *Eeh.*

Situated between the airstrip and the Gileses' lodge land, the NGO began to lose ground as subsistence farmers extended their use claims. But perhaps the larger problem was that the threats to Mr. Giles's property rights, in this example and the example below, led to him grasping control of his land even more tightly. Mr. Giles wanted clearly delineated answers to where the borders of each property lay. While Sarah and Tim were gone, he insisted the primary NGO vehicle be kept at the lodge. During that time, his son David used the car to survey the exact borders of the Giles land without informing the NGO staff that he was doing so. The rough terrain caused damage to the car, leaving it inoperable. Faced with the impending visit from a volunteer dentist who needed transportation, Mr. Giles had the vehicle fixed at great expense—and charged the damage to the NGO.

Facing a legal land threat in the village as well, Mr. Giles decided to make the newly mapped boundaries of his land clear to everyone encroaching on it—including the people who were continuing to farm on the otherwise unused airstrip land. But since the money for the airstrip project never materialized, he could not do it by actually putting the land to use himself. Instead he ordered Sarah to have the NGO use it, suggesting that the children living in the Little Community should take over the villagers' farms. She refused, recognizing that doing so would place the Little Community in direct conflict with the larger Mikoda community. The Giles family ordered the people off the land themselves. Yet as the land still stood unused, the question remained as to how long the command would hold sway against further fluid (re)mapping.

A second example of contention between Mr. Giles and the Mikoda community over usage of land took the form of a legal challenge. Maurus Nomba, a local villager, sued Mr. Giles on the ground that some parts of the land should never have been sold to him and that it should be returned to Mr. Nomba as its Indigenous owner. Mr. Nomba claimed preexisting customary right to the land based on ancestral use.

Concomitant to his suit against the Gileses, Mr. Nomba ran for chairman of the village council. According to Sarah, he campaigned on a platform of "taking back what is ours." In part, this action included taking back the areas of land under dispute, but it also included the NGO. Specifically, he referenced two programs that the NGO had begun but let lapse as part of what the villagers needed to "take back": providing porridge to primary school students and the salary of a kindergarten teacher. Mr. Nomba argued that as village coucil chairman he would push for the villagers' rights to programs such as these. According to Sarah, he had a rally where he yelled, "We need to take back what is ours! If we don't get our kindergarten teacher and porridge program back, blood will be spilled!" The NGO was again caught in the struggles between Mr. Giles and the villagers over epistemologies of land.

After his campaign to become chairman of the village council failed, Mr. Nomba took up other tactics. He started a committee named the Claw of the Eagle and began writing letters to the village government about the Gileses and the NGO. Regina described the Claw of the Eagle and how it causes problems for the Little Community:

JENNA: Claw of the Eagle. How did that come about?

REGINA: This letter was written from the Claw of the Eagle. It was read in a government meeting. So, it's like people sat somewhere to write that they wanted their rights. That is, that there's land Giles took without the government knowing. That it was sold by one lone man, and not recognized by the government. Yes.

JENNA: So, does this cause problems?

REGINA: Yes. . . . Their goal is to find out why this land ended up in Giles's hands. Yes.

JENNA: So, what do you think? Who is correct here?

REGINA: From my perspective, I can say that Giles is correct because he has paperwork and it was written along with certain clans . . . but the government was not involved. That means that [the] family used a hurried process to write the bill of sale without involving the government.

JENNA: Why did they do this?

REGINA: The children sold it after their parent died; at least that's what I heard. Yes.

JENNA: So this person, Claw of the Eagle . . . what is his quarrel with Giles?

REGINA: From what I heard about the meeting, his problem is that the land way back when wasn't Giles's, no. And in the map it looks some drawings weren't there. Later they found that the map was added to. So they want to know if the map is correct or not.

JENNA: And right now they're still looking, right?

REGINA: Yes.

JENNA: Uh-huh. So, what do you think of community members? How do they see the Claw of the Eagle or Mr. Giles?

REGINA: From what I can see, the community members don't really have a good read of Giles. . . . Some of the people still haven't seen very deeply into it, of—what is it this person helps? And why does he do it? So I've been thinking their goal should be to get arbitration so that this matter can be finished, over how this area came to be this way. Was it really sold to the elder? And if it was sold, *basi*, the government should go with the flow and help. Yes. Because when they generalize it's [a problem] for the children who are here because they're involved with that man who built [this place].

Through Regina's explanation, the politics of (re)mapping come to the fore. Mr. Giles ordered a comprehensive map done of his property in order to stand up against the claims made by Mr. Nomba, that the land should not have been sold to him in the first place. Under colonial logics, the answer to such a challenge is to solidify one's claim by producing documentation that clearly delineates the boundaries of the property and proves ownership. In doing so with the NGO car, Mr. Giles again made clear that he considered the NGO as property under his jurisdiction.

Mr. Nomba's challenge, however, (re)mapped the land claimed by Giles through Indigenous logics of customary use. By claiming that his family's use of the land predated Mr. Giles's purchase—which according to Regina was rushed through without proper authorization—Mr. Nomba attempted to leverage the law against Mr. Giles's claims to property. Notably, Mr. Nomba did not stop at one tactic, but rather continued to respond to emergent contexts with additional attempts at (re)mapping, demonstrating a fluid relation continually flowing around and through whatever constraints it met. He ran for office, filed a lawsuit, and petitioned the community leadership. None of it succeeded, however.

When all else failed, Mr. Nomba gathered sympathetic community members and set fires around the Giles lodge—and the NGO. Once again the Little Community was caught in the middle, leaving staff members feeling frightened for their lives and those of the children under their care. But in relation to Mr. Giles, the Claw of the Eagle found its target: the fires acted as a material (re)mapping that threatened Mr. Giles's property.

Land Disconnection and (Re)mapping for Communal Responsibility

ESTHER AND GAIL'S LOGICS OF SEPARABILITY

Esther and Gail were introduced to the NGO through the Gileses' lodge. As guests who ran their own charity, they were interested when Mr. Giles asked if they wanted to tour the Little Community. The pair eventually pledged funding from their organization to the NGO of C$100,000 a year for ten years. In 2015, donations from Esther and Gail's organization made up 41 percent of the NGO's annual budget, making their financial contributions vital to the organization's daily operations and survival. Perhaps the money was given more along the lines of investment than donation, as along with it came expectations for how it would be used.

Building on the donor logics of solidity from chapter 4, here I examine how Esther and Gail's building projects stemmed from understandings of land as separable, both in terms of signaling distinct areas and in relation to community life. That is, Esther and Gail demonstrated an epistemology that perceived land as differentiated locations detachable from community relations. Esther and Gail's individualistically oriented ways of maneuvering and understanding land were particularly problematic for the NGO leadership, as their donations made up nearly half of the NGO budget.

The weight of interacting with Esther and Gail primarily fell on Sarah and Tim. Even though Esther and Gail came to visit the NGO for a month every year, they could not speak Swahili and did not spend much time building relationships with the Viongozi Wa Shirika. When I asked Damas, who is an excellent English speaker and often spends time with foreign guests, he said they did not have much of a relationship to speak of:

JENNA: Um, okay, what kind of relationship do you have with donors like Esther and Gail?
DAMAS: Ah, not a very close relationship.
JENNA: But they do come for a month every year?
DAMAS: Yes. But, for example, Esther and Gail I've only seen once. And when they come, they stay—they don't come to many meetings. And they spend all their time in the village. So they came to the office only once. And they . . . it's like they only want to spend their money on what they want. They ask, maybe, "Why hasn't this thing been done?" You tell them there isn't money for it. That we haven't done that thing because the budget for this month is too small. . . . But [they say] we gave you money to do only this thing. You see? So it's a problem when they want us to do—it's a little different than, say, maybe the US organization. They [the US organization] ask us, maybe. They give their ideas and then they ask us, "What should we do?" So we sit together. When they come we sit together and discuss.

Damas described how his relationship with Esther and Gail was particularly thin, even when compared to donors from other countries. I view this as emblematic of Esther and Gail's epistemology, wherein places are separable from relations. They were constantly traveling to the various sites where their donations are put to use, but not concerned with building the type of connections to the staff or community that might help them to understand the embodied impact or experiential meaning of the places they had built on.

Sarah or Tim often accompanied Esther and Gail on their tours, providing at least some connection to the NGO staff and their understanding of how the projects the donors funded were received by the community. Yet when the pair visited during the period that Sarah and Tim were in the United States unexpectedly, they simply drove themselves around to check on their projects—and to implement more. Damas described how this created problems when Esther and Gail handed out money for projects in the village without consulting anyone at the NGO:

> DAMAS: They didn't know how the process of construction goes here. We still don't know today what Esther and Gail were told when they went there.... We don't know what they were told by the people at Lulongu about us that made Esther and Gail decide to put money straight into their hands so that they would be the ones to lead the project.
> JENNA: How much money?
> DAMAS: They [at the school] were given 1,300,000 [Tanzanian shillings].... They [Esther and Gail] went there with it, and gave it to someone, and the head teacher didn't know. Even now we're still looking for it, because Esther and Gail want to know how the money was used. Now they ask us, and we don't even know who was given the money. And we've asked the head teacher... "What did the money do?" They say, "Even me, myself, I don't know." We went the first time and they told us the money was used to build a shelf... and they gave the money straight to the carpenter.... Later, when we asked, "Why was so much money used here? How much are boards? How much was the carpentry?," *kumbe*, they say the money was also used to put on roofing. So they bought new tin roofing sheets. *Basi*, give us the sums: "How much money was the roofing? How much did you use for the shelf?" We still don't have what they know.
>
> So when they [Esther and Gail] give money, they don't let us into how much they gave or for what. But they come to tell us that we should be following how the money is used and for what... the whole process from start to finish was rotten.

If places are conceptualized as separable and distinct, perhaps it would make sense to hand someone money at the precise location where one wants something done. This, however, fails to account for the intricate—and sometimes fragile—relational networks that the NGO built within the community, how these networks created certain relations to certain places, and the processes that should be followed to maintain them. In addition, Damas described the two donors as making unilateral decisions—acting, perhaps, as if investing money in certain places gave them claim over it. That is, Esther and Gail engaged in logics of individual property ownership as if their investment of capital was in itself indicative of some sort of property right. They then reinforced this perceived right of individual decision-making and control by expecting the NGO staff to follow up on the donation that they made, without explanation or warning.

The Viongozi Wa Shirika was stymied. It could not simply tell Esther and Gail no. First, it needed the money. Second, Esther and Gail never asked for the opinion of the Viongozi Wa Shirika. And finally, even if the Tanzanian leadership spoke out anyway, its ideas were not taken seriously. As Damas put it, "They don't like to listen to us." So when the NGO was in need of money to support its current projects, rather than add new buildings, it had to get creative in order to be heard.

(RE)MAPPING FOR COMMUNAL RESPONSIBILITY

While I was staying in the Little Community, Sarah and Tim received an email explaining that Esther and Gail were courting another wealthy Canadian who wished to donate a large sum of money to the Little Community. The donors suggested that a trade school at the NGO might catch his interest, and told Sarah and Tim to start developing a plan for what that would look like. Instead the managers brought the issue up for discussion at the monthly Viongozi Wa Shirika meeting, to see what the Tanzanian leadership would like to do with such a large sum of money.

It was a beautiful July day, warm enough for us to sit in a circle outside the office building, while a group of high school volunteers painted and sealed the office. All of the departments were represented, with the exception of Health and Medicine, as Mustafa had patients who needed attention at the clinic. After voicing different options, and discussing the merits of each, the committee voted nearly unanimously: the Tanzanian leadership would use the money to purchase land.

The NGO was located in an area of dense pine and eucalyptus forests. For many families in the area, financial stability comes from owning acres of land and planting trees that can be harvested for lumber. Pine tree lumber from this area is in high demand, and ten-year-old trees fetch a handsome sum. Trees can also be sold at seven years, if need be—and it often is. Many families purchase a plot of land to plant trees when a child is born so that seven years later they will have the money necessary for school fees and educational expenses. For the NGO staff, land was the clear answer to donor trouble. Regina put it succinctly in her advice for the NGO "to find a large area of land to grow trees so that later, if donors have nothing left to contribute, if we grow a plot of trees we can sell them to continue to help the children and sick people in the village." If the NGO owned its own land, and planted trees in a ten-plot rotation such that some acreage could be harvested each year, it could function independently of donor funds.

For many staff members, the most pressing issue at the NGO was not opening a trade school, or funding more kindergarten programs, but ensuring the financial stability of the NGO itself. Peter was concerned about this in his interview, saying, "My advice to keep going well is, if there comes a time when we have a lot of donors, for them to at least get us the things we need to maintain. The things we need to maintain so that even if the donors don't continue to give money there, it can keep the organization going." Having witnessed the capriciousness of donors, the staff decided that the NGO needed to own its own land. Then, if the donors stopped donating, they would still be able to feed and care for the children and sick.

The Viongozi Wa Shirika's plan to purchase land can be seen as an ambivalent form of fluid (re)mapping. Arising in response to the unexpected possibility of having a large, lump-sum donation, the Tanzanian leadership was given a chance to think beyond the day-to-day concerns of keeping the NGO afloat. Although it landed on a plan to purchase land, something that could be read as in line with colonial logics of land commodification and ownership, the NGO engaged this method through alternative logics.[27] Instead of desiring land as property, it envisioned land as a sort of communal trust. The point of purchasing land, ultimately, was to ensure the financial means to continue to provide health care, education, and care for vulnerable children. The Viongozi Wa Shirika responded to Esther and Gail's epistemologies that disconnected land from relationship by (re)mapping land at the center of communal responsibility and possibilities to engender community health, welfare, and perhaps even abundance.

Another ambivalent aspect of the (re)mapping included making the NGO's plan palatable to the donors. The Viongozi Wa Shirika put together an intricate scheme to connect the land purchase to the trade school, thus seeming to be following donor instructions while stealthily (re)mapping all the while. They argued that one of the largest trades in the area was woodworking, and being trained in woodworking would be a useful skill for the trade school to teach local people. In order to train people in woodworking, the school would need a constant supply of wood, and the best way to have a constant supply of wood was to purchase land and grow trees. As Damas asserted, "We still need to entice donors. If the donors are persuaded and agree, it's a blessing, but if they refuse, we will still continue to have the very same challenges. But we can't say we refuse, because we need the money. So I think the biggest path forward is to convince them to leave the NGO to manage all the funds." The idea was to participate enough within donor logics of building on a separable plot of land that the NGO could slip in community-oriented (re)mapping without notice.

The logic was not as convincing to the Canadian donors or Mr. Giles as the NGO leadership had hoped it would be, however. In fact, when Sarah and Tim emailed Esther, Gail, and Mr. Giles about the tentative plan, the latter's immediate reaction was anger—specifically, anger that Tanzanian staff had been consulted and that members of the Tanzanian staff were part of the email exchange itself. For Mr. Giles, this took the form of exclamations that Sarah and Tim were the managers, not the Tanzanians, and that the Viongozi Wa Shirika should not be included in decision-making. Esther and Gail, on the other hand, saw it as an issue of protecting the interests of the donor. They said the land is a great idea for the *future*, but that the donor had a dream of building a technical school, and they didn't want to scare him off with such complicated plans.

When I returned to the NGO a few years later, I found a new trade school, another quiet building on another quiet hill. But there were no trees, and no new land.

The Material Effects of Epistemic Injustice

In the end, both Mr. Nomba's Claw of the Eagle and the Viongozi Wa Shirika's dreams of purchasing land to sustain the NGO came to naught. The fluid (re)mappings made by both groups demonstrated sophisticated understanding of both (neo)colonial epistemologies and how they might be turned inside out, using (re)mapping as a means of responding in the moment to shifts and changes in context. Under conditions of epistemic injustice, (neo)colonial logics maintained the upper hand, however, and the Little Community faced the consequences.

In part this was because the NGO was not understood as different from the Giles business by many in the community. Peter and Mama Isaak explained how they thought the NGO was wealthy until coming to work for it:

PETER: For example, when you see this NGO as it is, you could possibly think ... Mr. Giles probably has lots of money to keep it going, *kumbe*, later when I started working here ... you realize, *kumbe*, the work that keeps it going comes from donor money. Certain people volunteer to help. This helped me to understand that, *kumbe*, this NGO depends on donors.

MAMA ISAAK: And not on Mr. Wallet.

PETER: Not on Mr. Wallet directly, no.

JENNA: Even you didn't know Mr. Giles doesn't put in any money at all.

PETER: Yes [*laughter*]. So the community thinks it is Mr. Giles.

JENNA: Him and his money.

PETER: Because we work inside, we understand.

MAMA ISAAK: We understand truly, but the community doesn't understand that there is someone who worries over this like Sarah and Tim. They're distressed when they're away, when someone else here has to deal with an insecure budget, maybe of the children there, they are the ones that carry the heavy burden, truly. They have heavy thoughts about, "What should we do?" But the community here outside doesn't understand that there's a problem over there. They think there's lots of money there to be distributed, but we who are inside know totally that the context is hard.

Given this context, it's not surprising that Mr. Nomba brought together demands for Mr. Giles to return land and demands for the NGO to restart the porridge program. Without context regarding donors and funding structures, the NGO seemed like a venue for Mr. Giles's financial overflow. As Regina explained, "It's a problem. Because when the community and Giles live differently, it becomes a problem for the children who are raised here. Because we can't know what the community is discussing about all this land."

The perceived equivalence with the Gileses' lodge had material impacts on the lives of NGO workers. The Little Community faced three forest fires, deliberately set, in areas that threatened the safety of their people and structures. One was in the heat of the day, the next in late afternoon, and the final, terrifyingly, in the morning before many people had awoken. Each time, the NGO emptied, as all hands went to fight the fires—including the children under guardianship there. Fighting fires in rural Tanzania is no easy task; water comes from rivers and storage tanks, so buckets must be carried from the nearest source to douse the flames. Other people grab branches or sticks to beat them out. The work is long, slow, and arduous. The early morning fire in particular left many NGO workers shaken.

Sarah also described how women workers at the NGO faced harassment on their way to and from work at the times when Mr. Nomba's conflict with Mr. Giles was at its most tense. Employees began to leave immediately after work ended rather than lingering to socialize as they had in the past. They feared to walk home at twilight or after dark.

Things only intensified for the NGO workers after the village leadership decided in favor of Mr. Giles's claim to the land. They dismissed the suit on one condition: that Mr. Giles fulfill the promise he initially made to the village when purchasing the land by building a clinic in Mikoda proper, near the community hall. The NGO was thus drawn further into the conflict, as chapter 6 explains.

Although Esther and Gail did not directly involve the NGO in material injury, the fear of losing their funding hung heavily over many NGO staff. Many staff members expressed worries regarding what would happen to them if they were no longer able to work for the NGO. Upendo explained, "But truthfully . . . even if I stop working right now, this very minute, truly there is nothing I have that can take care of me. That is, I have no savings at all. So, I'm working, but I'm just staying here. I work and work, and my salary is only enough to buy what I need for supper." Peter and Mama Isaak put this in bleak perspective, comparing their future postwork lives to returning from prison:

> PETER: If you reach the end of working, you have no life savings.
> MAMA ISAAK: You just return.
> PETER: You return . . . it's like a person who is released from prison or the hospital. You just return and nothing's changed.
> MAMA ISAAK: Like you'd been a prisoner.

Nearly all NGO employees expressed a fear for a future without enough donor funding, whether it was for themselves personally or on behalf of the community.

Caught in the middle of contradictory logics of individual property and communal responsibility, what was the Little Community to do? Its association with Mr. Giles left it vulnerable to the ire of the larger Mikoda community, even as the foremost thought of every staff member was for supporting the villagers around them. Meanwhile, the Tanzanian staff struggled against donor control over funds and projects, activating liquid organizing and fluid (re)mapping to get community members what they needed when they needed it, even against donor wishes. But running into walls over and over again is exhausting,[28] regardless of how prepared one is for the walls' resistance or how fluidly one recuperates from the impact.

The NGO workers repeatedly collided with structures that were not created with them or their context in mind. It wore on them. But it wore on the structures as well.

Approaching Collapse

What happens when a solid structure is consistently battered by liquid movement? Things that seem impermeable begin to wear away. Cracks widen, become fissures, and eventually water bursts through. A trickle can become a river as things fall apart. And the walls that once made some thoughts and actions seem impossible no longer bound the imagination.

In chapter 6, I examine the decolonial possibilities that emerge from organizational collapse through the lens of liquid agency, which describes actions that emerge from and are made possible by refusing the epistemologies of coloniality and the choices they offer, opting instead for fluid forms of relation that allow for emergent responses to marginalization and for transformative action. Liquid agency is often opaque in Western systems of thought, allowing for subversive acts that may destabilize (neo)colonial power relations.

The inequitable contact zone where epistemic systems meet both produces the need for and allows for the emergence of liquid agency. The Little Community, trapped by (neo)colonial walls both physical and metaphorical, is forced to respond in fluid ways in order to struggle for epistemological justice and the material ways such justice would enable it to transform the community around it. And eventually that fluidity will wear down the very walls that made it necessary. There is decolonial potential within and emerging from such collapse.

In this manner, the fluid (re)mapping and liquid organizing that Tanzanians enact to counter (neo)colonial epistemologies demonstrate that the continuation of imperialism, "the 'rot' that remains,"[29] is not only destructive to Indigenous ways of life. Rather, land relations in the Little Community demonstrate "how people refuse *to be* ruined, while surrounded by processes of ruination."[30] The story of the NGO is one of liquid agency, of what can flow forth as the structures that contained it are razed to the ground. Liquid relations to processes of ruination create pathways through and out, and they re-form networks in transformative ways in the aftermath of the collapse.

Chapter Six
Things Fall Apart

Caring is anxious—to be full of care, to be careful, is to take care of things by becoming anxious about their future, whether the future is embodied in the fragility of an object whose persistence matters. Our care would pick up the pieces of a shattered pot. Our care would not turn the thing into a memorial, but value each piece; shattering as the beginning of another story.—Sara Ahmed, *Living a Feminist Life*

We had spoken the unspeakable, almost as if we had called for the end of the world.
—Ngũgĩ we Thiong'o, *Globalectics*

Leaving my Peace Corps village for the final time in 2009, I still could not escape Mbuji. As the Land Rover slowly climbed the treacherous mountain road up and out of the valley, it turned a corner to reveal Mbuji majestically positioned over the landscape. The man next to me spied my camera and instructed me to take a picture of the impressive stone. I tried to demur, but he was insistent—he would not let me leave the valley without a picture of Mbuji. It was a unique aspect of the valley that I needed to remember. I could not explain to him that it was already burned into my brain. I gave in; the button sank with a soft click.

I don't have the photograph. I never actually saw it developed. A few days later, my camera was stolen along with the rest of my luggage—all that physically remained of two years of my life. I was left with only my memories and a clay bowl that had been given to me by a student the night before I left. It was too fragile to pack and had to be carried by hand in a basket. When the rest of my things were stolen, the clay bowl was all I had left. It contained the ghosts of all my stolen possessions. *My possessions*, I say, as if those possessions didn't emerge from histories of theft. How were they ever *mine*, the clothes, carvings, and images of the Hagati Valley, enabled by the routes of capture established by colonialism so long ago and continuing today? And yet, many of the things were given by friends, (host) family and students, reflecting the meaningfulness and depth of our relationships to one another. Can relationships undo what (neo)colonialism has wrought? The clay bowl was my only gift, my only possession, left. The clay bowl reminded me of all these things; the clay bowl contained multitudes.

For about a decade I kept the bowl in a prominent location wherever I lived. Then, one evening, I walked past it a little too fast, brushing it with my shoulder enough to destabilize it from its position on the mantle. It fell, shattering; another shattering fall.

The pieces remain there, above the fireplace. The pieces of the clay bowl still carry multitudes, though perhaps now they are uncontained.

This chapter examines the decolonial potential unleashed by things falling apart, the rhetorical agency enabled by liquidity as it bursts through the solid structures of the nongovernmental organization (NGO) I call the Little Community. It follows the flow of relationships as they create the bases for liquid forms of agency, and asks what relation their fluid epistemologies have to decolonial possibility. I start with the conversation that initiated the end of the Little Community as I knew it. Circling back through time, I contextualize this conversation within the history of fluidity in the NGO, centering the concept of liquid agency. The conclusion to the book then follows how liquid agency produced the dissolution of the Little Community as I knew it. I search for the decolonial potential in the ruins, concluding with the possibilities liquidity opens when it pushes through structures and into futures beyond imagining.

The Beginning of the End

In the end, it was the community hall that did it. It really is an impressive structure, one of the largest buildings in the area, one able to hold so many people. When value is measured in size, imposition on the landscape, and technological advancement, the building is amazing. But those who measure it this way rarely stay long enough to see how and when the building is filled, hear laughter or music echo through its space, or blow the dust off of the computers and switch them on.

In the end, another donor is impressed by the community hall. In the end, they pledge the money to build yet another structure. In the end, the NGO staff is done with structures—with buildings that stand empty, money that is never enough for the work that Westerners cannot put their names on; with the expectations imposed that come attached to strings stretching across continents; with constantly butting up against a system that refuses to change; with the solidity of (neo)colonial hegemony and the epistemologies it engenders.

In the end, things fall apart. And when the walls no longer stand tall, constraining action and thought, new systems become possible.

On February 5, 2017, I received an unexpected phone call from Sarah. She said that she and Tim really needed to talk with me about a communication issue at the NGO. I was in the middle of breakfast, and asked if she could call back later. While eating, I tried to think of what could be so important as to call, when it was usually easier for us to connect via email given the time difference.

It turned out that Mr. Giles, the chairman of the board of the Little Community, had crossed a line this time. Over the past two days, Sarah and Tim had played host to a wealthy Belgian donor under the impression that he was willing to contribute substantially to the NGO. Tim took him on a three-hour tour of the Little Community grounds, Sarah met him for tea, and then the following day Sarah and Tim spent four hours taking him on a tour of their projects in various villages. The final stop was the community hall. There Mr. Giles and the donor walked around the building by themselves and emerged from their jaunt shaking hands and clapping each other on the back. Mr. Giles announced to Sarah and Tim that the donor had agreed to fund the project of building the new clinic in Mikoda—and that the NGO would be managing the project. He then called his son David and asked him to have the clinic plans ready so that he and the donor could talk them over as soon as they returned to the Gileses' lodge.

Sarah and Tim were stunned. Not only was this another building project foisted onto the NGO without input or even consent from any of the Little Community workers, and one that would be particularly expensive to maintain, but it was also a project that tied the NGO even closer in the public eye to the Giles expatriate lodge and business. Building the clinic in Mikoda was Mr. Giles's personal responsibility—the condition on which the land suit against him had been dropped. If the project was funded by a donor and managed by the

NGO, it would take the entire burden off of the Gileses' business and place it squarely on the Little Community in a manner that did not seem ethical.

Sarah and Tim sent Mr. Giles a message saying that they had some reservations about this plan and would like to speak with him about it. He pushed for more explanation, and they responded that they were "hurt and discouraged" by the quick turnaround of the project from the business's responsibility to the NGO's responsibility, and how the decision was made with no consultation from them. Mr. Giles was incensed, and demanded that they clear their schedules for the following day so that they could meet to discuss it.

Sarah and Tim called me the evening before the meeting, because they did not know what to do. Sarah explained,

> We have a meeting with him at ten, and this is my purpose.... I need an outside person who knows the history of the NGO to give us—if there's a different perspective we need to think about, um, is there something, like—Tim right now is feeling really down, and is like, "Well, why should we even bother fighting, the decision is done." I'm kind of in the boat of, like, I want to at least try to convince Mr. Giles that he's making a bad decision. Even if I lose that battle, at least I've tried. So, we need to hear: What does Madam Communication think?

The responsibility to give a carefully thought-out and useful response weighed heavily. I walked us through a few different paths, first considering how, if their use of personal feelings and "*I* statements" had not worked in their original explanation to Mr. Giles, perhaps the use of seemingly objective evidence would have better results:

> Okay, so here's what I see as being a route to avoid emotion in this, and to hopefully stifle his anger a little bit, is um, if you've got things in writing that you can just point to and be, like, "Well, we're confused because here's what it says in the village notes." In the interview that you guys did with him—when you said, "What is the financial relationship between the business and the NGO?" He said, "Absolutely none. There's absolutely no relationship."... So, you can point back to that, like, "Hey, we had this conversation where you said that there's no financial relationship between the business and the NGO. And you know, we feel like this is a contradiction, and that this project needs to come from the business."

Sarah responded that she was concerned about that approach, because she felt like facts were not a stable ground on which to challenge Mr. Giles:

So, like, Jenna . . . he's like [then president Donald] Trump, as David [Giles] is to [Steve] Bannon, as his Tanzanian counterpart is to Sean [Spicer]. So, uh, like, we sort of feel like we're being *alternative fact-ed* over here a lot. 'Cause all of them have convinced themselves, like, "Why are you guys making such a big deal out of this? Isn't this a *good* thing? Aren't you guys going to be looked so well at? Like, the NGO is going to make even a bigger splash!" Where I really and truly think that *they don't have the money that they promised for this*. I think that is the heart of the issue: because their business is going under, they cannot make good on their promise, and so because this magical donor appeared, it's saving their ass.

Sarah was concerned that providing factual evidence would be an attempt to solve the wrong problem. And she was correct. At the time, I didn't have a grasp on what made speaking to Mr. Giles directly about their concerns about buildings in general, let alone this particular building, so difficult. But looking back, the problem is clearly epistemological: Mr. Giles was operating in a colonial mindset, looking for the most expedient way to provide the structure that would legitimate his ownership of the land. And after a decade of working with the Tanzanian staff of the NGO in ways that attempted to refuse neocolonial relations, Sarah and Tim had adopted more fluid ways of thinking about the world. As many of the staff members put it, "Tumewazoea kabisa" (We have gotten completely comfortable with them). In every interview, Tanzanian staff spoke about how working with Sarah and Tim was easy, because "tumekaa pamoja" (we have stayed together) and "tumewazoea" (we have become comfortable with each other). These uses of the verbs *kukaa* (to stay/sit) and *kuzoea* (to become comfortable) register the type of understanding that comes from long-term relationships built across power lines, the "deep connections along lines of difference [that] are a transformative source."[1] As I wrote in chapter 3, it is impossible for any Western subject's understanding to be totally divorced from coloniality, but Sarah and Tim were engaging in the types of relational labor necessary to transform subjective and epistemological perspectives. The more this process worked, the more pronounced their tensions with Mr. Giles became.

Here they finally came to an impasse. If the Gileses were willing to have a donor pay for what should have been a penalty to the business, and to funnel money through the NGO to do so, without bothering to speak to even the Western managers before finalizing the decision, how could they be reasoned with in terms that would make sense under the logics of the staff? We talked through multiple strategies that might assist with convincing Mr. Giles not to impose the clinic project onto the NGO but slowly began to realize that, in all likelihood, nothing would work.

> JENNA: What happens if you simply refuse to do it?
> SARAH: Yeah. I'm—I mean, I'm there. I'm adamant. Like, no. My answer is no. Are you going to fire me? Fine. That's fine with me. Like, let us go. . . . If you want to find another person to do this, [go ahead]. But when I go, that means Tim goes. That means [the US NGO] go[es]. That means Peace Corps leaves.[2] [The long-term volunteer dentist] has said, "If you go, I go." [The long-term volunteer pediatrician] has said that same thing. You've just kicked yourself in the ass.

The clash of epistemological perspectives that had always existed at the heart of the NGO—between (neo)colonial and decolonial relations, solidity and liquidity, individual control and communal responsibility—had finally come to a head. There would be no crashing against a solid wall this time. This time the wall was coming down.

Sarah and Tim finally admitted that the Little Community could not continue with Mr. Giles at the helm. They had known that for a long time, at least since my fieldwork at the NGO in 2015, but it took years for the knowledge to turn into action. In a conversation with a nearby missionary couple a few days after my initial arrival at the NGO, Sarah and Tim described all of the problems of working with Mr. Giles and Western donors. The conversation began to redirect from complaint to conceptualizing action:

> MR. JENSEN: The system is unlikely to change. And so, really the question—the question is *not* asking yourself, Can *we* and our children find a way of *adapting* and living in this system? If you ask yourself that question—
> SARAH: No, I don't—
> MR. JENSEN: —you're putting yourselves in a bad way.
> SARAH: I agree with that.
> MR. JENSEN: I think the question is, If we know that the system will not change, what do we have to do to move the NGO into a *different* system?

The Jensens are older than Sarah and Tim, and functioned as mentors who helped them process the neocolonial implications of doing aid work as white Westerners in Tanzania. Originally from the United States, the Jensens had spent decades in Africa, first in the Democratic Republic of the Congo and then in Tanzania. They had started their own aid organization after working for too many missions that relied on neocolonial dynamics and hierarchies.

The Jensens started the organization for which they now worked, but had long ago turned the leadership over to a Tanzanian board and continued on simply as employees. They knew well the feelings of working within a clearly neocolonial organization, and had encouraged Sarah and Tim to start thinking about how to shift directions two years earlier.

The Tanzanian staff had also long recognized the need to eventually move away from Mr. Giles. As the quote from Damas in chapter 5 made clear, "The *mzee* is one of the very biggest challenges in the running of this orphanage." Similarly, Fadhili passionately argued,

> If the NGO wants to continue here, the primary thing I would like—we should get rid of the word "Giles." . . . We should not depend on saying, "Giles, Giles." Because of the villagers' hatred . . . he should hand over the land to us. Once he has given us the land . . . a new [NGO] board should be started. We shall continue. *Eeh.*[3] . . . There was a day when he told us here, "Leave, Leave, leave all of you! I want to build a certain thing here. Leave, all of you and take your children with you to the village!" You see? So, we must first make a plan for ourselves.

In a fit of rage, Mr. Giles had at some point told the NGO staff to leave and take the vulnerable children with them, as he wanted to build on the land. Fadhili knew then that the Little Community did not stand on solid ground; at any point Mr. Giles could show up and order them off the land, and then what would become of them? It was necessary, he insisted, to plan for this eventuality. For marginalized subjects, solidity cannot be trusted. Solidity is often an outgrowth of coloniality, serving the interests of maintaining neocolonial dominance. Thus, "in postcolonial contexts . . . intersections of colonialism, capitalism, and neoliberalism fuel extreme liquidities."[4]

When I caught up with Sarah again, two weeks later, she told me that as she and Tim walked out of the meeting with the Giles family, they looked at each other and agreed it was time to leave.

Sarah and Tim described their actions as "staging a coup." They outlined a variety of steps to remove the NGO from Mr. Giles's control, each of which included activating long-standing relational connections in order to respond to the emergent context in innovative ways. Sarah and Tim's plan depended on liquid action.

They decided to contact the donors and affiliated nonprofits that support the organization but were not connected to the Giles family. Sarah and Tim had a pretty good idea of who would trust them and the Tanzanian leadership over Mr. Giles and the NGO board. They created a plan to register a new nonprofit organization in Tanzania, co-led by the two of them and two Tanzanian partners, Musa and Faraji. By reaching out to donors, nonprofits, and NGO staff one by one, they would activate the relational networks necessary to engage in drastic liquid action: to take most of the NGO's current donors and staff in one fell swoop, leaving to start a new and different organization away from the (neo)colonial structures that had bound this one. The only problem was where to operate. So they decided to begin covertly raising money through the US organization to attempt to make an offer on the Little Community land. Whether or not they were able to buy the land, however, Sarah was convinced that Little Community's work would continue—separate from the Giles family.

In her second phone call, Sarah sounded almost giddy. Once the pressure of attempting to hold the current system together was relieved, she realized how little they needed it. The Little Community ultimately did not depend on its property or buildings, but on the relations built within the organization:

> Nuru, we could build her an office on her own land. . . . We can give her the laminating machine, and all of the school supplies. . . . So, like, "We will continue to pay your salary . . . we will still help provide you with school fees of children, and we will help you implement classrooms." We think that we could take all of the kids, guardians that we employ right now, and we bring them to the [district-level] social welfare office and we say, "We would like all of these women that have had ten-plus years' experience of being a housemother to be registered as fit families," and then we talk to the housemothers and say, "We want you guys to all leave, and we will continue paying your salaries, but now you will be raising these children in your own homes." And we will help supplement family income. . . . And, you know, like, we will have Arnold employed to continue following them to make sure these kids are being cared for. So we will go ahead with the team that we believe in. . . . We could even live in [the city, and] then, like, once a week we travel out to Mikoda and we say, "Hey Tanzanians, who we love and who are managing these projects, we think you're doing a great job. Do you have any problems that we need to know about? Or any government meetings that we need to attend while we're there?" And this also lets, I feel like, Tanzanian ownership of the programs that they have technically started and run—like, it's this project that we have always—you know, this is where we're supposed to be headed!

Only by dismantling the NGO would the managers and staff be able to have the Tanzanian-run organization they desired. The collapse of the Little Community both enabled—and was enabled by—liquidity.

Liquid Agency

I use the concept of liquid agency to make sense of how the Little Community staff enacted fluidity in ways simultaneously "reactive and proactive to threats,"[5] both reacting to coloniality and at the same time enabling alternative possibilities constructed outside its logics. As defined in this book's introduction, liquid agency comprises actions and relations that delink from (neo)colonial epistemologies through contextual responses based in relational connections. In my first draft of this chapter, I initially labeled the NGO's actions as "fugitive," but I struggled with ways the concept did not quite fit, as explained in the introduction. Liquid agency better figures the fluid and emergent relations in African contexts based in relational connections that are not necessarily hidden but simply unintelligible to Western epistemological structures.

Fugitivity often moves through refusal, but liquidity might be said to engage in redirection. Refusal, for the fugitive, is "not an abdication of contention and struggle; it is a reorientation toward freedom in movement, against the limits of colonial knowing and sensing. It seeks to limn the margins of land, culture and consciousness for potential exits, for creative spaces of departure and renewal."[6] Liquidity offers reorientation as well, but it does not necessarily seek exit but instead seeks shifting contexts and interpretations in ways that channel thought and action in different directions. Refusal directly challenges hegemonic systems, whereas liquidity works ambivalently and discreetly. As I described in chapter 5, fluid epistemologies operate "both within and against" Western systems of understanding in order to redirect understanding, energies, and relations.[7] Because of this, liquid agency might be more constrained than fugitive action. If fugitivity is "constantly in flight, marked by multiplicity, unbounded, and contingent,"[8] liquidity can sometimes face the constraints of viscosity. Liquid agency thus endeavors to act discreetly in order to engender flow that "dissolves quickly and enters the social fabric inconspicuously." When it becomes "conspicuous," however, liquid action "dissolves slowly and cannot enter the social fabric; it is viscous. Viscosity complicates escape attempts."[9] Fugitivity and liquidity both work outside the boundaries of Western systems, but where the fugitive is seen as "criminal" under coloniality,[10] the liquid actor instead often fails to register Western notice at all when it succeeds, dissolving into the surrounding context. Searching for possibility on the margins, at the edge of chaos,[11] where the world is unpredictable and may be refashioned anew, is a capacity of both fugitivity and liquidity that produces possibilities for agency that had been unthinkable within the confines of the system.

Liquid agency is thus inherently connected to epistemic justice. The freedom in movement sought by fugitivity and liquidity both relies on and creates the ability to think outside the confines of coloniality—particularly since according to coloniality there is no African knowledge to find, as Africans are considered unable to produce it: "Denial of being automatically denies epistemic virtue. This is simply because non-humans do not produce knowledge."[12] Enacting liquid agency requires perceiving possibilities outside Western epistemological structures and activating their potential—which in turn creates new possibilities that might previously have seemed impossible.

If fugitivity produces "fragments,"[13] what does liquidity produce as it flows around structures or pressures them until they give way? Perhaps there are fragments, pieces of the collapsing structures lying there in wait to be picked up and pieced together in radical new ways. But liquidity also creates new pathways and trajectories that did not exist before. It brings together emergence from the confines of systems and the relational interdependence that created the conditions for alternative paths. It operates outside Western logics, but not necessarily or only against them. Rather, it refigures the ways that people, contexts, and places interrelate in illegible terms.[14]

What Sarah and Tim initially termed as a "coup" could perhaps better be termed liquidity in action, at least in hindsight. The structure of the NGO did not end up being overthrown; instead it burst open. Rather than simply instituting new leadership into the same NGO system, actors in the NGO chose new directions based on relational conditions and emergent contexts, moving together to enable new possibilities. And as parts of the NGO that were assumed to be solid by Westerners started acting in liquid ways, the entire structure of the organization was put into question. We know what happens when a load-bearing wall is removed from a building: the building collapses, or at least radically shifts its position, materials, and heft. It is profoundly reshaped. The liquid agency of the Viongozi Wa Shirika, Sarah, Tim, and other NGO staff both transformed the shape of the Little Community, and brought forth unimaginable possibilities for future aid work. Here I highlight three particular ways that the Little Community staff engaged in liquid agency: redirection, collectivity, and ruination.

Liquid Agency in Redirection

It sounded almost nonsensical to refuse. On the surface, the Little Community had been asked to spearhead a project that would make medical care more readily available in an underresourced village area. There was a donor lined up and prepared to provide all of the funds for the construction of the clinic, and he had already sealed the deal with a handshake. Even the project of building the clinic would enable some community members to have work for a few months who might not otherwise. How could they possibly say no to the project secured by Mr. Giles?

Fluid epistemologies placed the decision within a long-standing relational context that recognized the problems with suggesting solid solutions to emergent issues. Mikoda needed better medical care. But simply building a new structure would not ensure that the villagers received the types of care they needed, nor would it ensure that such care was continued for as long as it was necessary. Even if the building itself was indispensable, who would build it, and how, registered meaningfully in relation to how community members would relate to it and use it. The Little Community had long found itself caught in the middle of Mr. Giles's problems with the village—many of which stemmed from projects that donors began but for which they did not provide the money to keep running. Mr. Nomba's fervent call for the porridge program to be returned to the village "or else blood will be spilled" comes to mind.

Yet even though it might have been very satisfying to simply say no and march out of the NGO forever, that is not what Sarah and Tim did, though it is important to note that they could have. Unlike the Tanzanian staff, who were more tightly constrained by neocolonial power structures—which could result in lack of savings, inability to find other work, Western expectations of deference, and the like—Sarah and Tim had the power to say no and to return to North America. In part, this is why fugitivity does not quite fit as a descriptor for the actions of the NGO staff. Sarah and Tim would not be taking flight but simply activating the privileged ability to relocate—what I have elsewhere termed the "white right to migrate."[15] Instead, after a decade of living and working at the NGO, Sarah ended up thinking more fluidly.

Sarah recognized that direct confrontation would not be the best strategy if they wanted to maintain the relational networks of the Little Community and shift them into new, Tanzanian-controlled forms. Instead her plan signaled redirection. Sarah conceptualized a number of redirectional steps with liquid contingencies. First, she envisioned tapping into relational networks to secure enough funds to purchase the NGO's leasehold from Mr. Giles. But she also recognized that he might not agree to such a deal. She then detailed how each Little Community department could continue to do its work even without such a solid basis as land. The children's guardians could be labeled "fit families" by the government to care for children in their homes. Nuru and Arnold could continue their work with children in the village. The labor of the NGO could shift direction, turn a corner, and still continue to provide the services the community needed.

With redirection comes a little misdirection. Instead of directly telling Mr. Giles that they would not be building the clinic, thus instigating tension and distrust, they needed Mr. Giles to continue focusing on his clinic plans so that he didn't notice what they were up to. We have seen in chapter 5 how Mr. Giles tended toward micromanagement when he didn't trust that decisions would be made to his satisfaction: he stood over Fadhili and Deo as they pulled weeds, and arranged a surprise audit of the NGO finances when Sarah and Tim left the Viongozi Wa Shirika in charge. Sarah and Tim needed to act inconspicuously, fluidly dissolving into the background, in order to put their plan into action.

Sarah and Tim planned liquid actions and reactions activating their relational connections across both Tanzanian and international networks. Liquidity provides access to new forms of agency that were previously obscured. Sarah and Tim's choices before were circumscribed by the maintenance of the NGO: they needed to sustain a good relationship with Mr. Giles in order to continue their work, they needed to bend a little to donor desires in order not to lose the funding in the future, and they needed to host unskilled volunteer groups in order to not lose the opportunity to host skilled volunteers in the future. When their actions were no longer contained by the need to maintain this status quo, potentialities and possibilities for alternative NGO structures emerged.

But this is not the first example of redirection that we have seen in the Little Community. Redirection is also a means of interpreting the ways that the Viongozi Wa Shirika attempted to change the terms proffered by donors to redirect funds toward NGO sustainability. In chapter 5, when the donor wanted to give money for a trade school, the Viongozi Wa Shirika attempted to shift the plan toward providing money to purchase land and plant trees. This liquid redirection attempted to discreetly transform the logics and outcomes of the donor's plan, but without tipping them off to the resistance. Although the liquid movement turned out to be more viscous than the Viongozi Wa Shirika desired and was recaptured by donor logics, the Viongozi Wa Shirika redirected energy toward local Tanzanian leadership and communal responsibility. It set different terms for the conversation—and for conversations to come.

Liquid Agency in Collectivity

Sarah's plan to redirect and re-form the NGO also required collective understanding and networks of trust.[16] As we examined in chapter 4, liquid organizing and agency emerge from trust and connection with other NGO employees and community members. Sarah's flights of future fancy highlighted how the Little Community was an embodied collective more than a place or organization. She described how even if the land was taken away, even if the physical organization itself no longer existed, the staff of the NGO could continue their work by moving down paths opened by liquid reactions within contexts. Liquid agency moves around static manifestations of power, locating agency in ephemeral spaces of relation. Focusing on the collective relations of the NGO demonstrates how the perceived need for the current organizational structure is a fiction. Why work to maintain a NGO where someone like Mr. Giles makes decisions that benefit him personally without consulting any Little Community leaders? Why maintain an organization that compromises the staff's ability to make collective decisions on behalf of the local community?

In addition, Sarah brought international donor networks into the fold. Sarah and Tim's connections with those in the West and the ability to expand the Little Community's relational network was understood as an important facet of their work. In my interviews with the Viongozi Wa Shirika members, many emphasized that most of the work at the Little Community could be led by Tanzanians, except for securing international donors and funding. As Fadhili put it succinctly, "I don't have any friends there outside [Tanzania]." He added, "This NGO, without the skills of Sarah and Tim, you could find that the children have to leave or to go back to the village. It comes from Sarah and Tim's ability to ask for aid from many people outside so that it can come here to help the children eat and do other things." Deo similarly emphasized that "it would be very difficult to say the NGO would be able to work without them [Sarah and Tim]," because "they find donors and have connections with many people across the world." This is a large part of the reason why the Viongozi Wa Shirika worked to make the NGO financially self-sufficient—to bring the collective networks necessary to run the Little Community into a tighter range that Tanzanians could reasonably manage *without* Western interference or the need to rely on Sarah and Tim to secure funding.

Conversely, many staff responded that it would be difficult to find other Westerners to replace Sarah and Tim should they choose to leave. Mama Isaak was suspicious of the idea that anyone could take their place, saying it would only be possible "if Sarah knows this person and Tim knows this person ... because they have gotten extremely used to us. They would need to bring the person, *basi*,[17] to stay with us for a long time." Here we see again the importance of *kuzoea* and *kukaa* (to get used to or comfortable with, and to stay together) in order to build the relational understanding necessary for a Westerner with access to Western donor networks to do an adequate job working with the Tanzanians on the ground. Fadhili accentuated that Sarah and Tim would need to "explain to this person very clearly how we live here" and that the person "would need to stay with us for at least six months" at first. Liquid agency is not and cannot be individual. It is a collective form of agency and organizing that requires intimate connections with both people and context in order to work.

Damas also demonstrated how collectivity was central to the Little Community's work with the village. He described how, early in his work at the NGO, he found in conversations with people in the village that they did not trust Deo, the Viongozi Wa Shirika member in charge of administration who often worked closely with village leaders:

> DAMAS: I moved to the village. I started to get comfortable [*kuzoea*] with the people in the village and they started to tell me stories about this place. They say, *bwana*, Deo is like one, two, three.... So already maybe the people of the village had built a certain animosity.
> JENNA: Why?
> DAMAS: I think it's a person's attitude. When I arrived, I got used to [*kuzoea*] Deo, we built a friendship. *Basi*. So we went to the village especially to sit [*kukaa*] with the person who told me the things [about Deo]. Now I wanted to show them, why is it that I see him so differently than how you do? *Basi*, we sat [*kukaa*] and traded stories. Every evening we met with various people until now at this point I see that the original atmosphere is gone.

After Damas brought Deo to sit and trade stories every evening—to build relationships—with the people in the village, he found that the atmosphere of animosity that had infused talk about Deo and the Little Community had dissipated. Here we see that creating collective understanding between the Little Community and the larger community shifts the conditions under which the NGO is working. Instead of finding resistance from village leadership, it was met with understanding and cooperation because of the relational labor the NGO had put in. In addition, creating those connections in the village was integral in dissociating the Tanzanian NGO workers and the NGO itself from Mr. Giles in the minds of the community members.

On the surface it would seem that all NGOs should center collectivity. They are supposed to exist for the benefit of the people in a given community, whether that be local, national, or global. But the maintenance of the organization—keeping donors happy, attracting new funds, demonstrating success to Western overseers—often begins to take on more importance than the work itself.[18] Liquid agency uses different epistemological structures from those underlying neocolonialism and neoliberal individualism, turning away from notions of the autonomous subject who considers themself master of their domain. As seen throughout *The Center Cannot Hold*, a collective politics of relationality is integral to challenging neocolonialism and working toward decoloniality. Neocolonial dynamics infuse the decision-making, reinforcing global hierarchies that call for a fidelity to Western donors over Tanzanian villagers or staff members. To act in liquid ways that deny logics of coloniality, attention must be drawn to the *politics of relation*,[19] to the way networks of communication and decision-making in the NGO are intimately neocolonial and racialized, and to re-forming them in a redistributive manner. This collective action holds no responsibility to maintain a typical organizational form; liquid agency may in fact require its dissolution.

Liquid Agency in Ruination

Colonialism has been described as "the 'rot' that 'remains.'"[20] Within the Little Community, we can see this rot infusing relations with land, volunteer action, and even Western subjectivities in a process of ruination. Ruination "allocates imperial debris differentially."[21] If some types of rot slowly eat away at ecosystems, local organizing, or Indigenous epistemologies, other types eat away at the ethics of those made dominant by neocolonial systems, eroding their senses of relational connection, ethical responsibility, and empathy across difference.[22]

Yet liquids seeping into solid structures also cause rot. Liquidity also produces ruination, but it is a type of ruination that combats the seeming solidity of hegemony, the monoliths that stand tall and firm. Liquidity can seep into the cracks in the structures, silently and slowly taxing them from the inside. Waves can batter from the outside, seemingly innocuous one at a time, but year after year they wear structures down. Liquid agency, as a form of ambivalence that uses systems against themselves,[23] activates ruination as a means of tearing down (neo)colonial structures. Such ruination is not simply destructive. Tearing down structures allows for alternative ways of thinking and being to emerge. Organizational ruination figures the possibility for decolonial transformation.

As I have written elsewhere, "from a postcolonial perspective, the *existence of the organization itself* must be problematized" in order to decolonize NGO aid work.[24] Ruins do not only emerge from the rotting destruction of (neo)colonialism; they can also be caused by turning (neo)colonial rot against itself. As I noted in the introduction, what waits on the other side of ruination is the possibility of justice.

Sarah and Tim knew that they had reached a juncture where the NGO could no longer continue holding the tensions that it had managed to keep contained for many years. The meeting of liquid agency and solid structure was beginning to tear it apart. But they had been preparing for this inevitability. In 2015 Tim knew they were approaching the end of their time at the NGO: "I think it's kind of like final phase—it's kind of relieving. It's not gonna be that fun, but I think our final stage at this organization is taking a really good crack at those up above us, and getting that organized, and getting a vision that everyone is aware of, to start with, and is on board with." So much became possible once the people of the Little Community no longer directed their labor toward the NGO's structural coherence. As Sarah had explained, the housemothers and -fathers did not need the organization to get paid for their guardian services; they could do so within their own homes if they desired. With Nuru's skill and training, she could open a school anywhere. The Little Community itself could continue, detached from the NGO structure that was holding it back. Sarah and Tim had long described their vision of the NGO's path: they wanted to train a Tanzanian counterpart in each of their management positions and then turn the leadership over to them, remaining available as consultants if needed. But as the chairman of the NGO board, Mr. Giles would never have allowed that transition to take place.

Freed of the bounds of the NGO, the possibility of Tanzanian leadership could be revived. Sarah and Tim began to imagine starting a new organization afresh, with Tanzanian managers, and putting in place policies from the beginning that would explicitly prevent donors or volunteers from dictating how money was spent, what projects the organization undertook, or how the organization was run. Yet the organizational structure was not the only aspect of the current NGO that restricts agency; the physical location also played a role. Untethered from the Gileses' land, the Little Community would also be released from the land politics described in chapter 5. The land provided a place in which the Mikoda villagers could protest the context of ruination. But the NGO was caught in the middle; any use of the land included simultaneous and opposing pulls—toward ruination and decolonization, toward Mr. Giles and toward the village community—forces that the Little Community could no longer cumulatively resist.

The dissolution of the NGO was brought about not simply by liquid action but by the recuperative responses that sought to shore up the neocolonial system in place rather than give in to the decolonial potential of its demise. At the Little Community, things fell apart because the organizational center could not continue to hold the contradictions between decolonial and neocolonial forces. The NGO did not fall apart because Mr. Giles decided to use donor money to fund a clinic. It did not fall apart because Sarah and Tim refused to support that decision. The NGO fell apart because, year after year, it was placed under increasing contradictory pressures: pressure to increase donor funding and simultaneously increase Tanzanian decision-making power; pressure for the NGO to represent Mr. Giles's legacy and at the same time represent collective community growth; pressure to serve as a playground for white volunteer fantasies of personally saving the world and yet as a place where those fantasies were challenged and Western subjectivities destabilized. Eventually the pressure burst through the organizational container.

The Little Community shattered.

The End of the Beginning

In August 2019, I watched the tea fields pass by out the window as I accompanied Sarah, Tim, and their children to their first return to the Little Community in over a year. There are two paths to the NGO grounds; we took the one that ran through the Gileses' business. The entrance is unmistakable: jacaranda trees line the path, rising above the road to create a brilliant purple gateway when in bloom. They were not in bloom now. It was not the season for blooming.

We were let into the grounds by Maasai guards. After exchanging greetings and news, Sarah asked them if Mr. Giles was awake or "taking his notes"—his code for an afternoon nap. They said that he was awake and ready for a visit. As we pulled up in front of their home, the Gileses stood out front facing away from us, looking at their view of the beautiful valley below. They turned and came to greet us, laughing like grandparents would at seeing their beloved grandchildren, even asking the children to come give their *babu* (grandfather) and *bibi* (grandmother) a hug. They then invited us in for tea.

Their house seemed very nice, though I only saw the entrance and the sitting room where they served us tea and cake. It struck me that it was the least Tanzanian house in which I had ever been in Tanzania. Even the Westerners often have *kitenge* decorations or furniture, carvings and stools, African art. But the Giles had only one or two carved items, out of place among the British-looking decorations throughout the rest of the room. In the corner sat Mr. Giles's father's pith helmet, from when he was a colonial official in Uganda. The house was designed based on a plan of an old English cottage that they loved, and the furniture was Mr. Giles's mother's; it all came over in a container from Britain. From inside you would never have known that we were in Tanzania.

After getting updates on the family from Tim, the Gileses spoke about how the children were doing at the Little Community. There was obvious care and concern in the way they described how things were going, and they knew the condition of various children. Yet I noticed that the ones they named were all the most dire cases: Bakari, with cerebral palsy; Upendo, the young woman with cognitive disabilities and epilepsy who had fallen into a fire and scarred her face; Dani, who had surgery as an infant to repair a hole in his heart. They turned to Sarah's role in Dani's heart surgery. The way Mr. Giles explained it to us was that Sarah had yelled and screamed and cried to convince the doctor to give Dani heart surgery. At first the doctor would not do it, because he said the chance of success was too slim. Mr. Giles made it sound like Sarah had thrown a temper tantrum to get her way. He then said that Dani "owes [her] his life," a comment that struck me. There were many ways to say that she was integral in making the surgery happen, or even simply to celebrate that the surgery itself was successful and Dani was living happily and healthily. That it instead became about him owing his life to Sarah says a lot about the way the Gileses think about the *wazungu* here at the NGO—the ones that the children owe their lives to. The saviors.

Conversation then moved to how the NGO itself was continuing. The Gileses shook their heads sadly and said that they only had enough money to keep the NGO running through the rest of the year. Donations, they said, had dried up. Mr. Giles added that this was a "global" occurrence and that he had heard the same from a friend who ran another NGO. I was surprised that the Gileses didn't connect the lack of funding to Sarah and Tim leaving and no longer contributing their efforts to fundraising. Their tone was doom and gloom, through and through.

We spent the night in the Little Community, beginning the next day with a tour of the garden. We walked through paths that used to be well trodden and well kept, now having to pick our way through the underbrush, sometimes getting caught on thorny branches. I tore my skirt in multiple places, the thorns cutting through to my skin as well. I bled. We passed by multiple hives that used to house bees but now lay silent. Hearing no telltale hum, I doubted the bees were alive. The land that used to be planted with various greens, beans, pumpkins, squash, and peas was overgrown instead with weeds, and frost had burned the tips of the corn stalks. Hillsides that were once green were barren. One small plot remained well tended. The new greenhouse, which had been planned as a place to have a variety of vegetables grow year around, some to use and some to sell, had been planted only with Chinese cabbage. Why it was planted with only one crop I'm not sure. Perhaps it was the only seed they could get.

The Gileses were not exaggerating when they described the financial situation of the NGO with a dire tone of voice. The cows and chickens were gone—all sold to people in the village. The children no longer had a steady supply of milk and eggs; those things now had to be bought, and I did not think I needed to ask to find out that money often was not enough to do so. When the Viongozi Wa Shirika refused donor terms one too many times, Esther and Gail pulled their support from the NGO. Although they tried to find other donors to fill in the financial hole that Esther and Gail left, Sarah and Tim were unable to gather enough funding.

Without Esther and Gail's money, Sarah and Tim had to lay off a number of the NGO staff before they left, including Viongozi Wa Shirika members such as Deo. Deo, however, ended up being just fine. Building off his experience at the Little Community, he opened his own kindergarten in the village. Damas grew tired of the financial instability of the NGO and left for a position at a for-profit institution. His wife, a member of the NGO's household staff, went with him. Idda, the translator and teacher at the kindergarten, got married and moved to Mwanza. Several women who had been household workers at the NGO left to study hospitality management at the nearby professional school. A teacher funded by the NGO in the local school district left and was replaced by another at the school's expense. Similarly, a librarian hired to work in the donor-funded library was let go, and the school hired someone with a college degree in library science to replace him. The Home-Based Care program was shut down, but as the AIDS crisis had been attenuated by steady access to antiretroviral drugs in the village the importance of it had lessened. The NGO could no longer afford to pay the salaries of medical officers at the nearby HIV Care and Treatment Center, but since the positions were so important, the center had easily found another, more well-funded, organization that agreed to take over the financial responsibility. A porridge program similar to the one that Mr. Nomba lamented was turned over to the school's control and continued under its auspices. And the NGO leaders finally turned the community hall over to local government management and it was now used regularly for a variety of village activities.

Although the Gileses regard the Little Community's situation as dire, there was something freeing about its falling apart. Decolonial potential exists in the ruins. Running out of money led to a situation where control was forced out of Western hands: without the means to fund projects through donors, the Western managers and the chairman of the board had to turn over control to the local government or to other organizations. In many instances, the NGO running out of funds had led to increased community control of projects. The community hall, *uji* (porridge) program, school library, and village kindergarten were now run for Tanzanians by Tanzanians.

Even the NGO itself was turned over to Tanzanian leadership. Ironically, the contradiction between neocolonial and decolonial futures that caused Sarah and Tim to leave the NGO was ultimately solved by their departure. By leaving, Sarah and Tim brought about the decolonial transition to Tanzanian management for which they had tried to fight and failed. The circumstances forced Mr. Giles's hand, whether he liked it or not. When they left, Mr. Giles could not find other Westerners to take over management of the organization. He tried for a time, but was eventually forced to hire Musa as the new NGO manager, who worked together with Arnold, promoted to head of human resources, and Micah, a college graduate who had returned to the village, to run the Little Community.

The NGO may no longer have steady funding or control over all the projects that it started, but those, perhaps, are goals written for NGOs by coloniality. The organization continues to serve the community, led by Tanzanian men, two of whom grew up in Mikoda, and the projects the Little Community began continue to grow in the villagers' capable hands. The Little Community, as I knew it, fell apart. And what remains in the ruins may be less stable and certain, but it is also more connected to the community and its desires.

Liquidity breaks through structures and systems, revealing decolonial possibilities on the other side. This is not to say that neocolonialism is simply removed through liquid agency or productive ruination but that it becomes possible to imagine futures where neocolonialism is undone. Mr. Giles remains at the head of the Little Community board, continuing to cause tension and ire. For instance, Musa did not remain the Little Community's manager for long. A few months into his tenure, the Gileses performed another audit of the NGO finances and accused Musa of stealing from the organization. According to Musa, the accusations stemmed from his use of an NGO vehicle to drive a villager to the hospital two hours away in an emergency. He was placed on administrative leave until they concluded their investigation. Musa was devastated; serving the village was his dream, and it is no small thing to be accused of theft in Tanzania. Yet, even so, Arnold and Micah remain. And Musa eventually decided that he did not need to wait for the results of the investigation. Instead he redirected. Working together with Faraji, Sarah, and Tim, Musa started a new organization. He is now the manager of Youth Leaders Tanzania. Neocolonialism cannot simply be removed, but neither can the dream of decolonial futures once their possibility becomes imaginable.

Liquid Futures

One could say that the future of the Little Community is in the air, but I prefer to think of it as flowing through the ruins. There are cracks and holes where they did not used to be, places where darkness holds the secret of something new, growing where nothing previously grew, pieces that have landed in unfamiliar places where they may be used to build different structures than they were part of before. Liquidity, like fugitivity, flows in and through "new modes of being," which are necessarily something that cannot be known or expected in advance.[25] Liquid agency recognizes "that the path to reach spaces unknown is necessarily unpredictable."[26] The unpredictability of liquid actions carries the potential for decolonial futures.

Coloniality attempts to foreclose future possibility, circumscribing what can be thought, fought for, and thus brought into being.[27] Liquid futures, by navigating around structures and breaching solidities, exceed what coloniality allows us to imagine possible. As Samuel Gerald Collins argues, it is only the "utterly unanticipated . . . the context of surprise and shock" that can deconstruct the oppositions between self and other that ground not only aid work but also research into it as well.[28] From a perspective grounded in coloniality, no one could have predicted that losing funding is what would bring meaningful change to the leadership structures of the NGO. Losing funding is the ultimate fear of NGO existence, to the point where more effort is placed on protecting donors and donations—protecting the existence of the organization itself—than on making sure the work being done by the organization is substantive and useful.[29] From the stance of coloniality, running out of money could only mean the demise of the organization—and thus, it was assumed, the projects benefiting the community. Similarly, fear of the NGO falling apart, of losing coherence, kept Sarah and Tim from seeing that their departure is all that stood between the Little Community and Tanzanian management. Coloniality keeps tight restrictions on imagination. But when the future is viewed through alternative epistemologies, we find more possibilities, opportunities that are illegible to hegemony. We redraw the map, and its pieces fit together in new ways. What once appeared as madness now seems tenable. And the demise of the organization does not seem so bad, because we recognize that the NGO is not the only means of improving community life. Far from it; running out of money allowed for control to be pried from Western hands and Tanzanian community members to claim leadership over their own initiatives. Sarah and Tim's departure finally turned management of the NGO over to the local people. Liquid agency, what looks like madness from the perspective of the normative, can make the impossible—"a present future beyond the imaginative and territorial bounds of colonialism"[30]—possible.

Decoloniality is the end of the world as we—a certain "we"—know it. As Ngũgĩ wa Thiong'o describes in the epigraph at the start of this chapter, speaking "the unspeakable" initiates the end of the world as coloniality understands it.[31] As Maya Berry, Claudia Chávez Argüelles, Shanya Cordis, Sarah Ihmoud, and Elizabeth Velásquez Estrada argue, a call for the "dismantling of [(neo)colonial and patriarchal] violence is, after all, a call for the end of the world."[32] The end of the world always figures what is ending from a particular perspective, attuned to threats to a particular way of life. For those who have the power to define their world as universal, the end of the world feels totalizing. For those epistemologies relegated to particularity, the end of the world is liberating; it is not the end of *the* world, but of *a* world. And it is the beginning of something new. As Alexis Pauline Gumbs movingly demonstrates in her "speculative documentary" *M Archive: After the End of the World*, people continue after the end of the world. People survive—and thrive.[33] They just may not look like "people" as defined under the racial-colonial contours of liberal bourgeois humanity.[34] From there we may find that what happens "after the end of the world as we know it. After the ways we have been knowing the world" holds within it the seeds of decoloniality.[35]

Liquid futures imagine the impossible, and in doing so create the groundwork to make it real. To dream new futures, then, we must learn decolonial epistemologies that can help us to imagine the end of the world. We must follow the paths that liquid agency opens to us, into the unthinkable. The Little Community, as "we" knew it, as I and other Westerners knew it, needed to fall apart for new worlds to be possible. It needed to fall apart to pry open epistemological foreclosures and bare their effects, so that other choices would be possible, so that Tanzanians were no longer figured only or primarily through epistemologies viewing them as unable to develop and enact their own futures.[36] It needed to fall apart to produce the potential for an *Africanfuturism* of development.[37]

Conclusion
Rivulets in the Ruins

When something breaks, something greater often emerges from the cracks.
—Nnedi Okafor, *Broken Places, Outer Spaces*

After the end of the world as we know it. After the ways we have been knowing the world.
—Alexis Pauline Gumbs, *M Archive*

I yawned. Not out of boredom, for I was focusing as hard as I could on the process unfolding before me. But it was 2:00 a.m., and I was eleven time zones away from where my body had been acclimated. I reached over and patted Sarah on the back, breaking her concentration for a moment as she looked up from the notebook where she was writing fervently. We smiled at each other. The warmth of the smiles mixed with the heat of the fire and the sparkle of laughter from Musa, Faraji, and Tim filling the room. Electric. Something new had begun.

While they were writing, I examined the area. I sat in a mauve armchair near the fireplace centered in the expansive, open room. In the future, it could be used as a meeting room for Tanzanian student groups, perhaps, or a place where the leaders stayed and had their meetings at the end of the day. But I was getting ahead of myself. Shelves lined large portions of the walls, nearly filled with books left behind from the previous owners. A piano cordoned off a small nook on one side of the room, which apparently had been used as a "shop" in the past, according to a remaining sign. On the other side of the room, a table with six chairs flanked the doorway that led to the kitchen in the back. Hallways extending behind the fireplace led to two bedrooms, each with its own bathroom. Sarah, Tim, and their children were staying here. Musa, Faraji, and I were staying in another house on the property. There was land to build more houses as well, if they needed it: sixty acres of land.

We took a tour the next day. Like when we toured the Little Community garden, I made the mistake of wearing a long, flowing skirt that caught on all the flora. This skirt was stronger than the other, however; *kitenge* rather than silk. It did not tear, and I did not bleed. As we traipsed through acres of pine trees and muddy fire lines separating them, I gathered the material of my skirt, knotting it between my legs to create the impression of loose pants. My gait was not unhindered, but walking was no longer as much trouble as before. We walked for miles around the acres of pine forest, the campsites where Western volunteer groups had slept, the farmland growing a variety of crops for both staff and organizational use, and the staff housing. Sarah and Tim had found the land for sale through one of their expatriate contacts. When the Giles family refused to sell them the Little Community land, they had sent out feelers in the nearby expatriate community to see if any other land was available. Luckily, the previous owners of this particular plot wanted to move back to California and were willing to sell the property with all furniture, appliances, and animals included. Meanwhile, Musa and Faraji drew up the paperwork to register a new nongovernmental organization (NGO). The process was long, and required multiple follow-up trips to the registration bureau to push the application through, but it was finally successful.

Welcome to Youth Leaders Tanzania. Sitting around the fire that first night, I asked Musa, Faraji, Sarah, and Tim to write out the strengths they saw in each other, and in themselves, and how those strengths could be utilized in the new organization. We moved around the circle, celebrating each of the new leaders one by one, starting with Musa. Faraji shared first, about how Musa had a strong moral compass, and was not afraid to stand up to those doing wrong. Sarah continued, describing Musa's impressive ability to take any situation and make something good out of it. Tim described Musa as a "promoter," enthusiastically making jokes and raising the energy in the room, but able to funnel that energy into serious subjects and tasks. Everyone agreed that he would make a great manager of the new organization. The sharing went well into the night, showing the strength of the relationships these four had already built through their years at the Little Community. The mood was joyous, with laughter flowing throughout the room, carving paths through the debris and leading to something new.

I had been invited to join this formative meeting as a facilitator, to assist the four leaders in developing an organization that bucked coloniality from the outset—or attempted to, at any rate. From the leadership structure to donor relations to the mission and projects, I assisted them in discussing the future of the organization. Youth Leaders Tanzania was nothing but what they wanted it to be, nothing but what they could imagine. Among the sixty acres of pines—pine trees that spoke to previous plans, previous impossible imaginings now realized—they dreamed. They dreamed of a place where poor Tanzanian youth from challenging backgrounds would come and learn the skills necessary to plan, activate, and organize change in their home communities; where youth would gather every school break from O-Level through university to learn entrepreneurship,[1] leadership, and organizational management; where youth would imagine their own impossible futures, and learn to make them real; where Tanzanian youth would leave with the skills necessary to create their own NGOs and transform their own communities—without Western aid.

Youth Leaders Tanzania did not emerge from nowhere. It grew in and through the ruination of the Little Community. Tensions between the colonial and decolonial that fractured and split the Little Community into pieces created the space and seeds out of which this new organization could grow. The liquid agency of the NGO workers galvanized new epistemological approaches to aid, new ways of thinking about what aid could be and how it could be done. As Alexis Pauline Gumbs says, it is not only the world that must sometimes end to make way for liberatory futures, but the ways that we have been knowing it.[2]

Nongovernmental organizations often act to preclude the ability to imagine futures without them in it by constraining epistemologies of aid. How we understand and enact aid is fettered by Western subjectivities that rely on helping for our own self-understanding, by organizational structures that place the survival of the NGO above quality of work, and by a global financial order that normalizes African dependence on aid by obfuscating the neocolonial violence that makes it seem necessary.[3] More abstractly, epistemologies of aid are bound by the corporate futures industry that squelches radical imagination in order to maintain global control. On the one hand, corporate control makes the imagination seem extraneous. As Samuel Gerald Collins explains, "We don't need to speculate on what the future may bring when the answer is on the next page of the catalog."[4] On the other hand, corporations employ their own teams of speculative specialists, meant to delineate potential futures within certain parameters, and then make their handpicked futures seem as if they are the only possible options. In this way, corporations engineer a "subtle oscillation between prediction and control... in which successful or powerful descriptions of the future have an increasing ability to draw us towards them, to command us to make them flesh."[5] Corporate visions of the future may at first seem unrelated to the nonprofit world of NGOs and aid. But both depend on the maintenance of a certain vision of Africa. To bring corporations and NGO aid into the future undisturbed, Africa must be figured as "the zone of the absolute dystopia."[6]

Teju Cole ties corporate global domination to aid and Western subjectivity through his concept of the "white savior industrial complex." Aid, and Western subjectivities predicated on helping and saving, act as "a valve for releasing the unbearable pressures that build in a system built on pillage."[7] That is, aid and Western saviors are the embodiment of global capitalism's excess, created to gloss over corporate contradiction—Africa is poor and needs our help (silenced: because we have taken and continue to take from Africans). Thus, contemporary configurations of both NGOs and Western subjectivities depend on imagining Africa as the space of lack, Africa as in need of aid, and Africans as unable to help themselves. Achille Mbembe describes how the West uses Africa as an empty signifier through which to claim its humanity in opposition.[8] Western subjectivities thus are built out of a continual labor to relegate African subjects to a place without agency in order to declare their agency in opposition. Under coloniality, Black African bodies are used as a medium, a tool through which white Western subjectivity may be constructed.[9] What is left of the Westerner when the medium of abject Blackness is taken back? Decolonial futures require the dissolution of the contemporary Western subject and a radical rethinking of aid as we know it.

The Center Cannot Hold has traced how one possible opening for decolonial futures of aid came about through concomitant processes of ruination: the falling apart of Western subjectivities and the collapse of an NGO. Neither reflexive Western subjects nor the Little Community itself could maintain the tensions between coloniality and decoloniality fighting within. Both fell apart. Part I followed the tension and dissolution of Western subjectivities. In chapter 1, the US medical students who came to the NGO engaged in differential relations with Tanzanian translators and patients, in ways that both bolstered and challenged neocolonial white masculinity and the subjectivities it enables. Chapter 2 then addressed how (de)colonial tensions structure US American subjectivities themselves, and how volunteers handle the contradictory situation by simultaneously refusing and embracing white savior fantasies. Chapter 3 concluded part I by theorizing a type of reflexivity that repeatedly seizes Western subjects in the grips of their own contradictions in order to re-create them. Through haunted reflexivity, Western subjects are faced with their own complicity in histories, presents, and futures of violence and must choose to turn from fictions of innocence and reckon in a way that undoes and redoes subjectivity. Here, as anywhere, (de)colonial tensions cannot be escaped, but they can always be handled otherwise, and more justly.

Part II then examined how similar tensions within the NGO itself led to a collapse of the current structures that enabled future possibilities. In particular, it demonstrated how the Western subjectivities described in part I used (neo)colonial epistemologies that often failed to understand or notice Tanzanian logics of organizing and action. Chapter 4 analyzed interviews with Tanzanian NGO staff to highlight the ways that they often engaged in liquid organizing that ran contrary to donor desires for buildings and control, and how donor misunderstanding reinforced the need for liquid organizing to redress the problems created. Chapter 5 then continued the focus on fluid epistemologies, examining how the Mikoda community members and NGO staff used fluid means to (re)map colonial and neocolonial relations to land in ways that instead emphasized use value and collectivity. Finally, the epistemological injustice constantly hampering Tanzanian thought and action came to a head in chapter 6, when the Little Community fell apart. Chapter 6 detailed liquid agency in the NGO, showing how the Little Community falling apart enabled decolonial potential by centering Tanzanian leadership and desires.

When the center cannot hold, when things fall apart, what is loosed upon the world?

One answer, the one I will focus on here, is decolonial dreamwork. The corporate futures industry has created an imagination gap that differentially distributes not only future possibilities according to the contours of racialization and coloniality but also training in *imagining*.[10] Creating and practicing decolonial dreamwork can help to break the hold of the white savior industrial complex, reconfiguring both NGOs and Western subjects. Decolonial dreamwork intersects with the liquid, the ambivalent, and the radical to "imagine futures unbound by ideologies and structures designed to delimit black lives."[11]

Decolonial dreamwork emerges from the gaps revealed when things fall apart, from the holes in hegemony, the spaces elided by "common sense." As such, there is an element of the fictive in decolonial dreaming. To imagine outside the lines of coloniality requires dabbling in the impossible, that which the corporate futures industry tells us cannot be. Visions of the future developed out of African epistemologies, radically situated within specific African material realities and circumstances, have the potential to refigure aid and the Western subjectivities it organizes.[12] Nnedi Okorafor calls these visions "Africanfuturism." She defines Africanfuturism as "somewhat similar to Afrofuturism, but ... specifically and more directly rooted in African culture, history, mythology, and perspectives where the center is non-Western."[13] Elsewhere she notes that "Africanfuturism is concerned with visions of the future, is interested in technology, leaves the earth, skews optimistic, is centered on and predominantly written by people of African descent (black people) and it is rooted first and foremost in Africa. It's less concerned with 'what could have been' and more concerned with 'what is and can/will be.' It acknowledges, grapples with and carries 'what has been.'"[14] Although Okorafor is specifically writing about the place of African thought in speculative fiction, her premises have direct impact on the world of aid. What happens to white saviorism when Africans write their own futures? What is the place of aid when the "optimistic" futures are premised on African technologies and epistemologies? What does development look like within African dreams of their own futures—or does it appear at all? Where do aid and its Western subjects fit within Africanfutures?

I do not and cannot know. It is not for me to decide. To activate liberatory futures, we must stage a "chronopolitical intervention" in the corporate futures industry, constructing and magnifying alternate timelines that pull us toward justice.[15] But the burden of doing so falls differentially along and through power lines.[16] White Western scholars such as myself should not be the primary drivers of imaginative creation, but neither should we sit idly by; we should know by now that both speaking *for* and refusing to speak *with* are means of avoiding the labor of making the world more just.[17]

And decolonial dreamwork is labor. Just as the process of constructing subjects is laborious, something we invest time and energy into whether we do so in ways that challenge or uphold coloniality, the process of constituting futures is work. We are either throwing our energy into drawing decolonial future visions into life, or we are using our imaginations to reiterate and support contemporary systems of power.

Our futures are just as haunted as our pasts. The revenant always returns, and we cannot have done with ghosts. As Okorafor recognizes, even our boldest futures must acknowledge, grapple with, and carry what has been. For myself and other Western scholars, the primary task may be to continually engage with reflexive reckoning, repeating cycles of confrontation with our ghosts, learning over and over to more quickly and fervently refuse innocence, attempting to understand more and more each time how our violent pasts have constrained our conceptualizations of the future. For NGOs we might keep in mind that the "transduction of one organization of things into another, however rapidly or gradually that occurs, involves an entanglement with existing matter(s)."[18] Decolonial struggle, and the process of falling apart, are not elided through liquid organizing or action. Nor should they be.

One of the last nights I spent at the Little Community, the Giles family invited us up to the lodge for a picnic on the lake to watch the sunset. We sat on blankets by the water, drinking beer and watching the children play with puppies on the shore. That morning, Sarah and Tim had taken me, Prisca, Mama Anita, and other Tanzanian friends of their children to visit a beautiful escarpment overlooking miles and miles of valley stretching below. I felt Musa's absence. He awaited us at the new NGO grounds, unable to return to the Little Community. To reach the escarpment, Mr. Giles had provided us a hand-drawn map with directions. He had labeled one of the dams we passed while driving "The Great Mistake." I inquired as to why. Mr. Giles's eyes lit up, and it was clear that he was about to put on his storyteller cap.

He told us: There was once a British colonial governor, replete with safari hat and long blonde curvy mustache, who was told to build a dam to stock with fish. Mr. Giles imitated the governor, twirling his imaginary mustache and adding an accent, saying, "That would be a great mistake." The governor believed that all the nearby villagers would steal the fish and the reservoir would be worthless after a few months. Yet, after the dam opened, they found that it was in the perfect position for fish to fall into it from a lake they hadn't known existed.

He continued: Once upon a time, a colonial official had driven out to see construction of a dam and parked his car on top of it. Getting out to look around, he tossed his keys to a Tanzanian man and said, "You look like a chauffeur; you can drive my car. But if it falls in, I will cut your bollocks off." The official turned around to go examine the dam, and behind him heard a great splash.

Mr. Giles laughed. He described how the colonial official had gone home for Christmas that year and printed woodblock images on Christmas cards of him chasing a Black man with a machete. He laughed harder.

As his laughter surrounded us, attempting to engulf us, I heard instead the rushing of water—the power that liquid movements can hold. What if we told the stories this way: how the flows into the dams acted beyond Western predictions and upended certainty, how bodies of water engulfed colonial vehicles, disrupted colonial plans, and incited colonial anger. Water flows unexpectedly, bringing unrecognized bounty. Water surrounds things, swallows them, drowns them. With both the movement and depth of water, things may be transformed. Water takes us into futures unimagined.

I heard: Once there was a British colonial governor who did not notice that water moved on its own, had its own plans. He tried to control the water, and failed. In this failure, he was lucky, because the water carried with it gifts he knew how to recognize and understand.

I heard: Once there was a colonial official who did not notice the depths held by water, the space to affect the world within it. He lost something to the water, and projected his own responsibility for what he lost onto Blackness, reacting with violence.

Mr. Giles did not notice the water. He just laughed.

Turning away, I caught a glimpse of a different future. Anita, the daughter of Sarah's good friend, stood on the shore of the lake, looking defiantly at the sunset. Mr. Giles's laughter must have reached her, but she showed no signs of it affecting her as she stood gazing over the water, past the setting sun, and into tomorrow. Mr. Giles's laughter echoed through the remnants of the Little Community, forming part of the context for both the people who stayed and those who left. Although we drove away two days later knowing that Tanzanians were in charge of managing the organization, Mr. Giles was—and remains—the chairman of the NGO's board. Even for those such as Musa and Faraji, who created Youth Leaders Tanzania out of the ruins, memories of working under Mr. Giles hold strong. Musa refuses to speak about the Gileses, after being accused of stealing money and being ousted from leadership of the Little Community. Such a traumatic experience cannot simply be escaped.

And yet. Youth Leaders Tanzania has the potential to decolonize organizational structures, volunteer and donor relations to staff, and decision-making processes precisely because it emerged from the tensions of the Little Community and its sparring between racist, neocolonial plans and decolonial imaginings. Part of decolonial dreamwork is recognizing and delinking from coloniality.[19] Part of creating radical futures is putting fungible structures in place that foil neocolonial machinations. Many of the conversations we had while building the new NGO from the ground up, out of the remnants, centered on how to avoid the racial-colonial problems that all had experienced at the Little Community. We spent time talking about how to address the possible problem of Sarah and Tim acting like sole managers, or that Musa and Faraji might turn to them as final authority out of habit. We brainstormed how to ensure that donors could not take control of projects. We discussed if, when, and what kind of volunteers might be welcome and under what conditions. My favorite part was listening to Musa and Faraji detail what they imagined when they saw this new land: futures where Tanzanian students are trained to envision creative projects and return home to put them into action. In their dream, the NGO acts as a catalyst for ideas they cannot even begin to imagine—ideas that are contingent on the young leaders brought into the organization, their own contextualized experiences, and the limits of *their* imaginations. The NGO's leadership training is meant to teach the youth it sponsors to dream, to create innovative solutions to community problems and not be held back by what is expected or thought possible. Youth Leaders Tanzania is the product of decolonial dreamwork, and it desires a future where the spark of decolonial dreamwork lights innumerable fires—fires that catch, spread, and change the face of the future.

Radical futures, futures that break the epistemological strictures of coloniality, must seem illogical to the status quo. Perhaps that is why W. B. Yeats saw the failure of the center's integrity as loosing "mere anarchy" upon the world—something I would not call "mere," as it resonates with the liquid actions of the NGO as well.[20] Liquidity is confusing for, incomprehensible to, or even utterly unnoticed by the normative. Chaotic. Unmoored. The decolonial futures that await on the horizon urge us to think differently, impossibly.

When the center cannot hold, when things falls apart, what is loosed on the world is much more than mere anarchy, after all. It is the potential for a decolonial future, if we have the imagination to create it.

NOTES

INTRODUCTION

1 I will use the shortened name, Tanzania, throughout the book. The Tanzanian education system begins with two years of preprimary school, or what is usually translated to kindergarten, and continues into seven years of primary school. At the time I was teaching there, students had to pass a national examination before they could advance to Ordinary Level (O-Level) secondary school. If they completed four years of O-Level education and passed another round of national exams, students would then move on to Advanced Level (A-Level) secondary school for two years.
2 Here I am drawing from Gumbs, *M Archive*, xi.
3 As Cruz, "Introduction," 102, puts it, "To think that African contexts can teach us [in the West] anything is provocative on many levels."
4 Little Community and Mikoda are pseudonyms to protect anonymity, as are all the names in this book that are related to the NGO and its operations.
5 Madison, "The Labor of Reflexivity."
6 Eshun, "Further Considerations," 291. Although Eshun is describing the power of the corporate futures industry to subvert the radical imagination, I also believe it is possible to invest decolonial visions of the future with similar power to captivate.
7 Easterly, *The White Man's Burden*; Moyo, *Dead Aid*.
8 As Spivak, *A Critique of Postcolonial Reason*, 6, puts it, "As the North continues ostensibly to 'aid' the South—as formerly imperialism 'civilized' the New World—the South's crucial assistance to the North in keeping up its resource-hungry lifestyle is forever foreclosed." Ahmed, *The Cultural Politics of Emotion*, 22, similarly notes that "the West gives to others only insofar as it is forgotten what the West has already taken in its very *capacity* to give in the first place." See also Mamdani, *Citizen and Subject*; Rodney, *How Europe Underdeveloped Africa*; and Timberg and Halperin, *Tinderbox*.
9 Bell, "'A Delicious Way'"; Hanchey, "Agency beyond Agents."
10 Richey and Ponte, *Brand Aid*; Baaz, *The Paternalism of Partnership*; Ferguson, *Global Shadows*.

11 Beck, *How Development Projects Persist*, 14.
12 Biruk, *Cooking Data*; Smith, *Bewitching Development*; Hunt, *A Colonial Lexicon*; Shaw, *Colonial Inscriptions*.
13 For critiques of the lack of scholarship attendant to race in anthropology, see Beliso-De Jesús and Pierre, "Introduction"; Berry et al., "Toward a Fugitive Anthropology"; Harrison, "Anthropology as an Agent of Transformation," 3, 9; D'Amico-Samuels, "Undoing Fieldwork," 124; Hale, "Introduction," 20; Pierre, "Activist Groundings," 115–35. For an excellent examination of how racialization is tied to histories of colonialism, see Lowe, *The Intimacies of Four Continents*. Alexander Weheliye's work also speaks to these connected processes; see, for example, Weheliye, *Habeas Viscus*.
14 Ahmed, *The Cultural Politics of Emotion*; Carrillo Rowe, *Power Lines*; Lugones, *Pilgrimages/Peregrinajes*.
15 Behar, *The Vulnerable Observer*; Berry et al., "Toward a Fugitive Anthropology"; Ritchie, "An Autoethnography."
16 Kleinman and Fitz-Henry, "The Experiential Basis of Subjectivity," 52.
17 Biehl, Good, and Arthur Kleinman, "Introduction," 13.
18 Beliso-De Jesús and Pierre, "Introduction," 66, describe how "mainstream anthropology continues to steer clear of analysis that centers race and processes of racialization" but also note that even those studies that do focus on processes of racialization fail to link to broader global structures of white supremacy. They advocate that anthropologists "must therefore situate the inter-connected local and global histories of race and racialization in relation to global and local forms of white supremacy."
19 Cole, "White-Savior Industrial Complex"; Hanchey, "Constructing 'American Exceptionalism.'" Pratt, *Imperial Eyes*, 7, defines contact zones as "social spaces where disparate cultures meet, clash, and grapple with each other, often in highly asymmetrical relations of domination and subordination—such as colonialism and slavery, or their aftermaths as they are lives out across the globe today."
20 Stoler, "Introduction," 7.
21 Stoler, "Preface," x.
22 Gilliam, "Militarism and Accumulation," 183.
23 Stoler, "Introduction," 29.
24 Dichter, *Despite Good Intentions*; Hanchey, "Reworking Resistance," 285.
25 Dempsey, "NGOs, Communicative Labor"; Dempsey, "Negotiating Accountability."
26 Beck, *How Development Projects Persist*, 20, 23. Similarly, Smith, *Bewitching Development*, 10, sees the concept of development itself as necessarily encapsulating a tension between the universal ideal and particular reality, thus "creat[ing] all kinds of paradoxes" in aid work.
27 Hanchey, "Reworking Resistance."
28 As Ahmed, *Living a Feminist Life*, 94, puts it, "If we are not exterior to the problem under investigation, we too are the problem under investigation."

29 Here I draw my understanding of subjectivity from Judith Butler's and Gayatri Chakravorty Spivak's work on Lacanian theories that consider subjects as inherently based in foreclosures. Unlike Jacques Lacan, I read these foreclosures as political. That is, I see subjects as unable to recognize the politics of their own construction without iterative reflexivity leading to subjective transformation.
30 Saks, *The Center Cannot Hold*.
31 As James Baldwin writes in Peck, *I Am Not Your Negro*, "Someone once said to me that people in general cannot bear very much reality. He meant by this that they prefer fantasy to a truthful re-creation of their experience" (69). As Baldwin further explains, the reality that white people in the United States cannot bear to examine is their own violence against Black and Indigenous peoples, instead projecting their own violence onto Blackness and Indigeneity. In doing so, Baldwin explains, those invested in whiteness and coloniality become "moral monsters" who "have deluded themselves for so long that they really don't think I'm human" (39). Haunted reflexivity seeks to redress this moral monstrosity.
32 For example, Harrison, "Anthropology as an Agent of Transformation," 9, notes that the discipline is "preoccupied with constructions and representations of Otherness."
33 Although many anthropologists maintain a focus on "the other," there has always been a contingent that focuses on the nuance of contact zones; see, for example, Shaw, *Colonial Inscriptions*. Yet comparatively few have turned their attention primarily to aid workers who are Westerners. For notable exceptions, see Baaz, *The Paternalism of Partnership*; and Malkki, *The Need to Help*.
34 Wanzer, "Delinking Rhetoric," 652.
35 Ndlovu-Gatsheni, *Epistemic Freedom in Africa*, 3, defines epistemic freedom as "the right to think, theorize, interpret the world, develop own methodologies and write from where one is located and unencumbered by Eurocentrism"; it is a product of the struggle for epistemic justice, the "liberation of reason itself from coloniality." See also Mignolo "Delinking"; Ngũgĩ, *Globalectics*; Ogone, "Epistemic Injustice"; and Wanzer-Serrano, *The New York Young Lords*. "Man" is a term that Wynter, "Unsettling the Coloniality of Being," uses to describe a particular Western colonial-rational ontology of being human that overrepresents itself as if it were equivalent to the human itself. See also Maldonado-Torres, "On the Coloniality of Being"; and Towns, "Black 'Matter' Lives."
36 For an overview of and responses to this dynamic within communication studies, see Asante and Hanchey, "African Communication Studies."
37 Grosfoguel, "The Epistemic Decolonial Turn," 212, emphasis in the original.
38 Mignolo, "Delinking," 463; Ngũgĩ, *Globalectics*, 8.
39 Cruz and Sodeke, "Debunking Eurocentrism," 536.
40 Cruz and Sodeke, "Debunking Eurocentrism," 529, 532, 542.
41 Lowe, *The Intimacies of Four Continents*; Wynter, "Unsettling the Coloniality of Being."
42 Cruz, "Reimagining Feminist Organizing," 31.
43 Cruz and Sodeke, "Debunking Eurocentrism," 540.

44 Ndlovu-Gatsheni, *Epistemic Freedom in Africa*. Throughout the book, I use the term *fluid* to refer to the epistemological perspectives that allow for liquid motion, organizing, and action.

45 Gumbs, *Spill*.

46 Harrison, "Anthropology as an Agent of Transformation," 9, questions "whether anthropology can continue to be preoccupied with constructions and representations of Otherness if the discipline is to undergo a thorough process of decolonization," implying that the discipline must be undone, in some ways, to truly decolonize its work. Similarly, Hale, "Introduction," 14, introduces his collection of activist scholarship by arguing that "central to [an] agenda for institutional change ... is to challenge and unlearn the deeply embedded unearned privileges of social science and humanities research." That is, social sciences and humanities must unlearn their disciplinary norms, must undiscipline, in order to work toward (decolonial) justice. In rhetoric particularly, Wanzer, "Delinking Rhetoric," 648, argues that rhetoricians must grapple with "epistemic coloniality (not merely colonialism as an economic-political system)," which requires undisciplining ourselves of the very logics that undergird rhetorical scholarship.

47 As Behar, "Ethnography and the Book That Was Lost," 15–16, notes, if ethnography "has its origins in the flagrant colonial inequalities from which modernity was born and in the arrogant assumptions that its privileged intellectual class made about who has the right to tell stories about whom" we must necessarily ask, "What can be salvaged from the original vision of ethnography to make it a project of emancipation?" Many anthropologists recognize that the field's colonial legacies often spur an unjust relationship to otherness; see, for example, Shaw, *Colonial Inscriptions*; Harrison, *Outsider Within*, 7, 44; Holsey, *Routes of Remembrance*; Das and Kleinman, "Introduction"; D'Amico-Samuels, "Undoing Fieldwork," 68; Jones, "Epilogue," 195. In rhetoric, the field's focus on publics and counterpublics has long centered the nation-state, to the exclusion of other understandings of civic life, and even those who extend beyond the nation-state primarily do so to investigate issues of immigration and the politics of citizenship—thus, still locating the nation-state as central to political and civic demands. See, for example, Asen and Brouwer, *Counterpublics and the State*; and Brouwer and Asen, *Public Modalities*. A few notable authors, however, question the centrality of citizenship narratives to the discipline. See, for example, Chávez, "Beyond Inclusion"; Chávez, *Queer Migration Politics*; Chevrette, "Assembling Global (Non) belongings"; Lechuga, "An Anticolonial Future"; and Na'puti, "Archipelagic Rhetoric."

48 Some authors have made moves to center interculturality and/or the West itself in anthropology, and global networks in rhetoric. In anthropology, see Baaz, *The Paternalism of Partnership*; Malkki, *The Need to Help*; Shaw, *Colonial Inscriptions*; and Gilliam, "Militarism and Accumulation," 170. For rhetoric, see Brouwer and Paulesc, "Counterpublic Theory," 83–86; Colpean and Dingo, "Beyond Drive-By Race Scholarship"; and Na'puti, "Speaking of Indigeneity."

49 Beliso-De Jesús and Pierre, "Introduction," 66, 65.

50 Regarding representations of Africa and Africans, see Bell, "'A Delicious Way'"; Hanchey, "Agency beyond Agents"; Hanchey, "Reframing the Present"; and Steeves, "Commodifying Africa." On white saviorism and American exceptionalism, see Cloud, "'To Veil the Threat of Terror'"; Kelly, "Neocolonialism and the Global Prison"; Harris and Hanchey, "(De)stabilizing Sexual Violence Discourse"; Bell, "Raising Africa?"; and Schwartz-DuPre, "Portraying the Political." Regarding the investigation of intersectional complexities, see Chávez, *Queer Migration Politics*; Chevrette, "Assembling Global (Non)belongings"; Corrigan, *Prison Power*; Mack and Na'puti, "'Our Bodies are Not Terra Nullius'"; McCann, *The Mark of Criminality*; Hoerl, *The Bad Sixties*; and Kelly, *Food Television and Otherness*.
51 For exceptions, see Cram, *Violent Inheritance*; de Onís, *Energy Islands*; Lechuga, "An Anticolonial Future"; Na'puti, "Archipelagic Rhetoric"; Na'puti, "From Guåhan and Back"; and Wanzer-Serrano, *The New York Young Lords*.
52 See, for example, Cloud, *We Are the Union*; McKinnon et al., *Text + Field*; Middleton et al., *Participatory Critical Rhetoric*; and Pezzullo, *Toxic Tourism*.
53 As Chávez, "Beyond Inclusion," 163, argued on the centennial anniversary of the foremost journal in the field, "From traditional studies of public address, to an array of social movement studies, to analyses of democratic deliberation and the public sphere, Rhetoric scholars are concerned almost exclusively with citizen discourses, mostly from white men in *public*" (emphasis in the original).
54 Beck, *How Development Projects Persist*, 4.
55 Na'puti, "Speaking of Indigeneity," 496.
56 Berry et al., "Toward a Fugitive Anthropology," 538.
57 Hanchey, "Toward a Relational Politics of Representation," 265.
58 Hanchey, "Toward a Relational Politics of Representation," 266, referencing Wynter, "Unsettling the Coloniality of Being."
59 Berry et al., "Toward a Fugitive Anthropology," 539, write that "the notion of engaging in fieldwork is often approached by activist anthropologists in a gender-neutral way, one that still assumes an unencumbered male subject with racial privilege." And as Bourgois, "Confronting the Ethics of Ethnography," 115, candidly puts it, "We have chosen to study the wretched of the earth."
60 Ticktin, *Casualties of Care*; see also Ahmed, *The Cultural Politics of Emotion*, 192.
61 See, for example, Collins, *All Tomorrow's Cultures*, 115, who notes, "Reviving a more activist anthropology . . . means returning to the image of an anthropology that can change the world"; and Philippe Bourgois, "Confronting the Ethics of Ethnography," 115: "Although as uninvited outsiders it might be naïve and arrogant for us to think we have anything definitive to offer, we can still recognize the ethical challenge. Why do we avoid it?" More difficult to parse, perhaps, is the challenge issued by in Goldstein, "Laying the Body on the Line," 839: "Like those we study, activist anthropology requires us to lay our bodies on the line." Goldstein calls the act of living by this requirement "a fundamentally different way of being physically in the world." Although in some ways this is laudable, Goldstein frames the bodily vulnerability of activism as "fundamentally different" than that of normal circumstances, and as a *choice* that the researcher has—whether or not to lay his

body on the line (gendering intended). As Berry et al., in "Toward a Fugitive Anthropology," and other Women of Color anthropologists have intimately related, their bodies are never not "on the line" in fieldwork or at home. For Women of Color, laying their bodies on the line is neither a choice, nor is it a "different way of being" confined to fieldwork. In short, comments such as these reveal how the assumed researcher in activist work often lines up with the expectations of Man.

62 Asante, "'Queerly Ambivalent.'"
63 Cruz and Sodeke, "Debunking Eurocentrism," 529; Gumbs, *Spill*.
64 As Pindi, "Promoting African Knowledge," 332–33, explains, using the context of feminist theory,

> In the case of Africa in particular, the problem of feminist theorization is not only white, but also Western. In fact, an African critique of Western feminism cannot solely be limited to white feminism. . . . For instance, whereas Black feminist frameworks such as BFT [Black Feminist Thought] can speak to the lived experiences of African women as Black women of African descent, such frameworks, which stand as "Western" vis-à-vis African feminisms and their usage, must ultimately be revised within the context of African culture. Failing to do so can result in problematic Western-centric interpretations and representations of African realities. Ultimately, this calls attention to how the historical legacy of Western/white perspectives has played a role in the erasure of African perspectives.

Pindi and other African scholars helped me to understand that by importing a concept such as "fugitivity" into an African space without retheorization, I was participating in the erasure of African perspectives on their own contexts and resistance.

65 Ndlovu-Gatsheni, *Epistemic Freedom in Africa*, 3, argues that coloniality "reduced some human beings to a sub-human category with no knowledge." If Western epistemologies are based on rendering Africa as a site devoid of knowledge, per Mbembe, *On the Postcolony*, 2–3, then such epistemological structures make it inherently impossible to recognize African knowledge as such. This leads Atieno-Odhiambo, "Democracy and the Emergent Present," 31, to wonder, "Need African epistemes be intelligible to the West?"
66 See, for example, Baaz, *The Paternalism of Partnership*.
67 Asante, "Glocalized Whiteness"; Mbembe, *Critique of Black Reason*; Ndlovu-Gatsheni, *Epistemic Freedom in Africa*.
68 Aminzade, "Dialectic of Nation-Building," 336.
69 Shivji, Yahya-Othman, and Kamata, *Development as Rebellion*, 1:250.
70 "Non-racialism" is the way that the authors of the biography of Julius Nyerere describe Nyerere's refusal to make racial difference the basis for policy, even when it may have been used to redress historical inequities. The three-volume set, though following Nyerere's life, also offers an intimate and powerful overview of Tanzanian politics from late colonization to Nyerere's death in 1999; see Shivji, Yahya-Othman, and Kamata, *Development as Rebellion*.

71 For more information, see Shivji, Yahya-Othman, and Kamata, *Development as Rebellion*, vol. 3.
72 Berry et al., "Toward a Fugitive Anthropology," 560, 539.
73 Berry et al., "Toward a Fugitive Anthropology"; Rosaldo, "Imperialist Nostalgia."
74 Corrigan, "Decolonizing Philosophy," 166.
75 Puri, "Finding the Field," 38.
76 Keeling, *Queer Times, Black Futures*, 12–13, recognizes the ambivalence of interdisciplinarity but also its potential to build liberatory futures. Although "the logics and methods of interdisciplinarity do not guarantee, nor do they inherently express, liberatory or radically transformative knowledges . . . interdisciplinary knowledge—that is, knowledge that transforms the disciplines while creating other forms of knowledge—might still be fashioned into a weapon directed against the [corporate] investment in interdisciplinarity as a strategy of control," widening our possible futures.
77 Cruz and Sodeke, "Debunking Eurocentrism," 536.
78 Cruz and Sodeke, "Debunking Eurocentrism," 531.
79 Ndlovu-Gatsheni, *Epistemic Freedom in Africa*.
80 Lowe, *The Intimacies of Four Continents*.
81 Davis and Baliff, "Extrahuman Rhetorical Relations."
82 Barnett and DeLuca, "Conditions That Form Us," Keeling, "Of Turning and Tropes"; Gordon, Lind, and Kutnicki, "A Rhetorical Bestiary"; May, "The Orator-Machine."
83 Hanchey, "Toward a Relational Politics of Representation."
84 Carrillo Rowe, *Power Lines*.
85 Here I draw from the work of Natalia Molina and Lisa Lowe, both of whom argue that processes of coloniality and racialization can only be understood through relating a variety of historical groups and formations; see Molina, *How Race Is Made*; and Lowe, *The Intimacies of Four Continents*.
86 As Ndlovu-Gatsheni, *Epistemic Freedom in Africa*, 80, argues, "Epistemic freedom has the potential to create new political consciousness and new economic thought necessary for creating African futures."
87 Hanchey, "Reframing the Present," 322.
88 Hanchey, "Reframing the Present," 322.

CHAPTER ONE. DOCTORS WITH(OUT) BURDENS

This chapter is derived in part from the article "Doctors without Burdens: The Neocolonial Ambivalence of White Masculinity in International Medical Aid," in *Women's Studies in Communication* 42, no. 1 (2019): 39–59, https://www.tandfonline.com/doi/abs/10.1080/07491409.2019.1576084.

1 Johnson, "The Art of Masculine Victimhood"; Johnson, "Walter White(ness) Lashes Out"; Kelly, "The Man-pocalypse"; Kelly, "The Wounded Man"; King, "It Cuts Both Ways."
2 Bandini et al., "Student and Faculty Reflections," 57.

3   Inui, *A Flag in the Wind*, 19.
4   Ashcraft and Flores, "'Slaves with White Collars,'" 2.
5   Bandini et al., "Student and Faculty Reflections"; Underman and Hirschfield, "Detached Concern?"
6   Bandini et al., "Student and Faculty Reflections."
7   Johnson, "The Art of Masculine Victimhood"; Johnson, "Walter White(ness) Lashes Out"; Kelly, "The Man-pocalypse"; Kelly, "The Wounded Man"; King, "It Cuts Both Ways"; King, "The Man Inside."
8   McClintock, *Imperial Leather*.
9   Johnson, "Walter White(ness) Lashes Out."
10 Kelly, "The Man-pocalypse," 96.
11 Johnson, "The Art of Masculine Victimhood"; Ahmed, *The Cultural Politics of Emotion*, 42–61.
12 Underman and Hirschfield, "Detached Concern?," 96.
13 Johnson, "The Subtleties of Blatant Sexism"; Johnson, "The Art of Masculine Victimhood"; Johnson, "Walter White(ness) Lashes Out"; Kelly, "The Wounded Man."
14 The idea that religion, masculinity, democracy, and/or capitalism can be made better by starting over and trying again on someone else's land has been part and parcel of colonialism throughout history. See Grandin, "Empire's Ruins," 125–26.
15 Johnson, "Walter White(ness) Lashes Out," 18; Kelly, "The Man-pocalypse," 110.
16 Kelly, "The Wounded Man," 165.
17 See, for instance, Ahmed, *The Cultural Politics of Emotion*, 2–3; Mbembe, *On the Postcolony*, 1–23; Mbembe, *Critique of Black Reason*, 103–28.
18 Molina, *How Race Is Made*, 6, 7.
19 Hall, "The Whites of Their Eyes."
20 McClintock, *Imperial Leather*, 23.
21 Hall, "The Whites of Their Eyes," 91.
22 Gunn, "Father Trouble," 16.
23 Cole, "The White-Savior Industrial Complex."
24 Ahmed, *Cultural Politics of Emotion*, 3, notes that this threat also entails "moving backwards in time, such that one would come to resemble a more primitive form of social life, or a 'lower and animal like condition.'" Approaching the medical mission "frontier" thus threatens white masculinity with "going native," or becoming too much like the other, receding backward in time, if too much care and vulnerability is shown.
25 Butler, "Gender Is Burning," 383.
26 Dutta, "Hunger as Health," 368; see also Dutta and Basu, "Meanings of Health."
27 Davis, *Inessential Solidarity*. For a politicizing of the relational perspective on subjectivity, see Carrillo Rowe, *Power Lines*.
28 This number is drawn from surveys commissioned by the organization, and was reported to me in 2015.
29 Here I purposefully do not specify the tribal language in order to maintain anonymity of the NGO, the village, and its location.

30 Gunn, "Father Trouble."
31 Hanchey, "Constructing 'American Exceptionalism.'"
32 Until 2010 in Tanzania, pregnant women were expelled from school and not allowed to continue their studies at a public school after giving birth. Although the law had been changed at the time this conversation was held, stigma continued to have much the same effect as the law, so much so that President John Magufuli reinstituted the ban in 2017. Bébien, "Education—Tanzania"; "JPM Closes Debate on Teen Mothers."
33 Different understandings of time and tempos of social life have baffled not only Western volunteers but also many scholars. Yet, as Rosaldo, "Ilongot Visiting," 256, reflects, this is a problem not with other cultures but with the Western inability to conceptualize social grace in variable terms:

> In my view, optionality, variability, and unpredictability produce positive qualities of social being rather than negative zones of analytically empty randomness. Far from being devoid of positive content (presumably because of not being rule-governed), indeterminacy enables a culturally valued quality of human relations where one can follow impulses, change directions, and coordinate with other people. In other words, social unpredictability has its distinctive tempo, and it permits people to develop timing, coordination, and a knack for responding to contingencies. These qualities constitute social grace, which in turn enables an attentive and gifted person to enjoy and be effective in the interpersonal politics of everyday life.

34 Ndlovu-Gatsheni, *Epistemic Freedom in Africa*.
35 Hanchey, "A Postcolonial Analysis," 88–92.
36 Sullivan, "International Clinical Volunteering in Tanzania," 310–24.
37 Kelly, "The Man-pocalypse," 110.
38 King, "It Cuts Both Ways."
39 Ndlovu-Gatsheni, *Epistemic Freedom in Africa*, 87–88.
40 Carrillo Rowe, *Power Lines*, 4.
41 McClintock, *Imperial Leather*.
42 Kelly, "Women's Rhetorical Agency," 227.

CHAPTER TWO. ALL OF US PHANTASMIC SAVIORS

This chapter builds on the article "All of Us Phantasmic Saviors," in *Communication and Critical/Cultural Studies* 15, no. 2 (2018): 144–49, https://www.tandfonline.com/doi/abs/10.1080/14791420.2018.1454969.

1 The electricity at the NGO was only on from approximately 5:00 a.m. to 8:00 a.m. and 7:00 p.m. to 11:00 p.m. These times were chosen for the children living at the Little Community: in the morning, so they could get ready for school, and at night so they could have light to do their homework.
2 Hunt, *A Colonial Lexicon*, 322, describes soap and papers as "debris from colonial life," noting, "Since soap and papers emerged from a culture of domination, their

positional meanings remain magnified ... giving them their capacity to condense meaning and crystallize history."
3 Lacan, "The Subversion of the Subject."
4 Butler, "Changing the Subject," 332.
5 Lacan, "The Subversion of the Subject," 679.
6 Butler, "Changing the Subject," 333.
7 Gunn, "Refitting Fantasy," 19.
8 Gunn, "Refitting Fantasy," 8, 10.
9 Spivak, *A Critique of Postcolonial Reason*, 6.
10 Hanchey, "Constructing 'American Exceptionalism.'"
11 Cole, "The White-Savior Industrial Complex."
12 Spivak, *Critique of Postcolonial Reason*, 6; Hanchey, "Constructing 'American Exceptionalism.'"
13 Cole, "The White-Savior Industrial Complex."
14 Carrillo Rowe, *Power Lines*, 15–16.
15 Mama, *Beyond the Masks*, 114.
16 Asante, "Glocalized Whiteness," 92.
17 Butler, "Changing the Subject," 333.
18 Cloud, "The Irony Bribe," 416.
19 Carrillo Rowe, *Power Lines*, 4, 10.
20 Endres and Gould, "'I Am Also in the Position,'" 419.
21 See, for instance, SAIH Norway, "Africa for Norway"; Humanitarians of Tinder, website; and Barbie Savior, Instagram page.
22 Gunnarsdottir and Mathers, "'Doing Good' in an Age of Parody."
23 Endres and Gould, "I Am Also in the Position."
24 Cloud, "The Irony Bribe," 415, emphasis in the original.
25 Cloud, "The Irony Bribe," 416.
26 Hanchey, "A Postcolonial Analysis," 75–107.
27 Lavelle, *Whitewashing the South*, 189, emphasis in the original.
28 The trip manager had told Sarah that one of her staff members had agreed to host the group, but when the staff member later sent her a screenshot of the conversation, it was clear she had said "You have to ask Sarah about the group" rather than just agreed to it.
29 Mama, *Beyond the Masks*, 6.
30 In case the reader is left wondering, baby Siva was eventually able to get on antiretroviral medications. By being fed through an eyedropper for weeks, she regained strength enough to live for another year. Sadly, she then succumbed to an opportunistic infection and died.
31 Cloud, "The Irony Bribe," 416, quoting Kenneth Burke, emphasis in the original.
32 Hartman, *Lose Your Mother*, 84–100.
33 I and other scholars have written about similar demonstrations of exceptionalism in and through lack of skill; see, for example, Hanchey, *A Postcolonial Analysis*; and Sullivan, "International Clinical Volunteering."
34 Cole, "The White-Savior Industrial Complex."

35 Constance Gordon, personal communication with the author, February 20, 2017. I also reflect on this in a forum piece on identity in ethnographic work; see Jensen et al., "Pushing beyond Positionalities."
36 Madison, "The Labor of Reflexivity."
37 Rosaldo, "Imperialist Nostalgia," 108.
38 Rosaldo, "Imperialist Nostalgia," 120.
39 Talton and Mills, "Race and Gender in Research," 4.
40 Rosaldo, "Imperialist Nostalgia," 120.
41 Behar, "Ethnography and the Book That Was Lost," 36, emphasis in the original. As Schieffelin, "Performance and Cultural Construction," 270, explains, "It is not an uncommon experience for an ethnographer toward the end of the second year of fieldwork to realize suddenly that some issue or activity, long since thought to be thoroughly understood and laid to rest in his or her fieldnotes, had an unsuspected dimension that required its significance to be entirely reexamined." Extending this realization, I argue that the pattern continues, that there is always something that seems settled waiting to be undone and reexamined.
42 As Berry et al., "Toward a Fugitive Anthropology," 538, write, "Activist research that does not pursue epistemological decolonization will . . . inevitably reproduce the very hierarchies of power that it seeks to help dismantle."
43 Ahmed, *The Cultural Politics of Emotion*, 147.

CHAPTER THREE. HAUNTED REFLEXIVITY

1 Colpean and Tully, "Not Just a Joke," 162, examine white feminist comics' use of racial jokes, terming it "weak reflexivity": "Weak reflexivity is a form of weak intersectionality that allows white feminist comedians to joke about their whiteness without critically examining it, ultimately reproducing dominant racial ideologies rather than working to dismantle them." Weak reflexivity is similar to what Lugones, *Pilgrimages/Peregrinajes*, 77–100, terms a "noninteractive" engagement with difference, where people from more dominant groups do not allow encounters with difference to substantively change or transform them or their ideological perspectives. Berry et al., "Toward a Fugitive Anthropology," 539, call out this tendency particularly in activist anthropology, noting that "dominant strands of activist anthropology replicate that which they critique, by silencing the racialized, gendered researcher's embodied experience or by inscribing it in new colonial narratives."
2 As Ahmed, *The Cultural Politics of Emotion*, 183, notes, "Capacity is not something we simply have, as if it were an inherent quality of this or that body."
3 Gordon, *Ghostly Matters*, 19, explains that "in haunting, organized forces and systemic structures that appear removed from us make their impact felt in everyday life in a way that confounds our analytic separations and confound the social separations themselves." They are the things that haunt influence and impact our theories and research experiences, yet cannot be reduced to the theoretical

constructs by which we operate as scholars. There is an excess to haunting, a not-yet-understood remainder that needs to be addressed.
4. Morris, "(Self)-Portrait," 33.
5. Behar, "Believing in Anthropology," 107.
6. For examples of those who engage substantively with reflexivity, see Rosaldo, *The Day of Shelly's Death*; Behar, *The Vulnerable Observer*; Visweswaran, *Fictions of Feminist Ethnography*; Hegde, "Fragments and Interruptions"; and Madison, "The Labor of Reflexivity," 130.
7. See Ndlovu-Gatsheni, *Epistemic Freedom in Africa*; Ngũgĩ, *Decolonising the Mind*; and Na'puti, "Archipelagic Rhetoric."
8. Lowe, *The Intimacies of Four Continents*; Towns, "Black 'Matter' Lives"; Wynter, "Unsettling the Coloniality of Being."
9. For a detailed examination of the politics of representation in rhetoric, see Hanchey, "Toward a Relational Politics of Representation."
10. Carrillo Rowe, *Power Lines*, 189.
11. Madison, "The Labor of Reflexivity," 130.
12. See, for example, Behar, "Ethnography and the Book That Was Lost," 36; Castillo and Puri, "Introduction," 7; Loperena, "A Divided Community," 335; Hegde, "Fragments and Interruptions," 291; Garrett, "Tied to a Tree"; and Broadfoot and Munshi, "Diverse Voices."
13. Carrillo Rowe, *Power Lines*, 5, emphasis in the original.
14. Ono, *Contemporary Media Culture*, 4. See also Harrison, *Outsider Within*, 45; Hoerl, *The Bad Sixties*, 10; Bergland, *The National Uncanny*; and Harney and Moten, *The Undercommons*, 17.
15. As Ahmed, *Cultural Politics of Emotion*, 160, notes, "To preserve an attachment is not to make an external other internal, *but to keep one's impressions alive*, as aspects of one's self that are both oneself and more than oneself, as a sign of one's debt to others."
16. Das and Kleinman, "Introduction," 2. As Kleinman, "Violence of Everyday Life," 228, further explains, violence affects subjects of all social locations, though differentially: "Structural violence occurs in a variety of ways that affect people throughout the social order. I do not contest that social force grinds most brutally on the poor. Yet the violence consequences of social power also affect other social groups in ways that are often not so visible, perhaps because they are also not so direct and also, not surprisingly, less likely to be labeled 'violence.'"
17. On violence in relation to subject and researcher, see Das et al., *Violence and Subjectivity*; Das et al., *Remaking a World*; Scheper-Hughes, *Death without Weeping*; Scheper-Hughes, "A Talent for Life"; Berry et al., "Toward a Fugitive Anthropology"; Rosaldo, *The Day of Shelly's Death*; and Petray, "A Walk in the Park."
18. James Baldwin, in Peck, *I Am Not Your Negro*, 39, refers to this as "moral apathy" or "death of the heart" that comes from having "deluded themselves for so long that they really don't think I'm human. . . . And this means that they have become in themselves moral monsters."
19. Ahmed, *The Cultural Politics of Emotion*, 33. Young, "America's Transient Mental Illness," 157, describes the "self-traumatized perpetrator" as "a victim in a double

sense: he not only suffers, but his suffering is somehow unjust." The self-traumatized perpetrator theory is helpful in that it recognizes that perpetrators of violence also experience effects of trauma; however, the theory ignores systemic power relations by equating the feelings of the oppressor with the trauma of the oppressed. Such theories engage in the type of "melancholia, compassion, and pity," that Stoler, "Introduction," 14, describes as "nourish[ing] imperial sensibilities of destruction and the redemptive satisfaction of chronicling loss."

20 Das, "The Act of Witnessing," 207, describes how what "is too terrible to behold" is the very injustice of the social order itself, the social order that we all have internalized in order to become subjects, that which allows for our being. Drawing from Jacques Lacan's work on Antigone, Das explains, "For Lacan, the unbearable truth that Antigone speaks is too terrible to behold. For, in questioning the legitimacy of a rule that would completely efface the uniqueness of a being even in death, she shows the criminality of the social order itself."

21 Ahmed, *The Cultural Politics of Emotion*, 36, emphasis in the original.

22 Calafell, "Monstrous Femininity."

23 Fellows and Razack, "The Race to Innocence," 335–36, describe the way that feminists, even those critical of gendered oppression, still attempt to "race to innocence": "the process through which a woman comes to believe that her own claim of subordination is the most urgent and that she is unimplicated in the subordination of other women." By claiming my encounters with reflexivity *as* trauma, I put forth my experiences of reflexivity as most urgent, subtly subverting the very reflexive engagement to which I thought I was attending. Similarly, Tuck and Yang, "Decolonization Is Not a Metaphor," 1, write about "settler moves to innocence" as the ways in which settler-colonists obscure their own continued participation in the violences of occupation.

24 Cacho, "The Presumption of White Innocence," 1086–87; Harris, "Whiteness as Property," 1707–91.

25 As Ahmed, *Living a Feminist Life*, 141, notes, those who call out problems of injustice are often labeled *as* the problem.

26 Ritchie, "Feeling for the State."

27 Caruth, *Unclaimed Experience*, 11.

28 I am indebted to the readers of this manuscript, who pushed me to face what I was still covering over—the ways that my own emotional reaction to reflexivity was another way of attempting to secure innocence.

29 DiAngelo, "White Fragility," 65.

30 National Communication Association, "2019 NCA Organizational Communication Division Top Paper Panel Account"; National Communication Association, "Distinguished Scholars." In the summer of 2019, the National Communication Association decided to change the selection process for its Distinguished Scholars. The previous selection process had depended solely on votes from *current* Distinguished Scholars to choose new members from the nominees. In addition, any nominee not ranked in the top five by at least 50 percent of the current Distinguished Scholars would be dropped from consideration. From 2008 to 2018,

69 percent of those selected were men, and only one was a Person of Color. There were no Women of Color selected until the process was changed.

31 Johnson, "The Art of Masculine Victimhood"; Johnson, "Walter White(ness) Lashes Out"; Kelly, "The Man-pocalypse"; Kelly, "The Wounded Man"; King, "It Cuts Both Ways."
32 Caruth, "Trauma and Experience," 4–5.
33 Lowe, *The Intimacies of Four Continents*; Towns, "Black 'Matter' Lives"; Wynter, "Unsettling the Coloniality of Being."
34 Saks, *The Center Cannot Hold*, 32, emphasis in the original.
35 Davis, *Inessential Solidarity*.
36 As I have written elsewhere,

> I mean responsibility not in the paternalistic manner of the white savior in aid (Cole, 2012; Hanchey, 2018), but rather the responsibility of the politics of relation, which sees "subject formation as a function of belonging" (Carrillo Rowe, 2008, p. 6). When we see our very selves as dependent on our relations with those around us—and how those relations are steeped in racial-colonial politics—we find we are responsible to others as a part of their *becoming*. Thinking through a politics of relation provides a means to escape the "politics of difference" that Mbembe (2017) articulated as based in "guilt, resentment, or pity" by providing avenues to see ourselves as intimately connected to the social processes that constrain and oppress us and those around us (p. 50). The responsibility that comes out of such awareness is a responsibility that aims toward justice—the responsibility not of the savior, but of the ally.

Although I would now use "accomplice" rather than "ally," the primary point stands. See Hanchey, "Reframing the Present," 326.

37 Behar, "Ethnography and the Book That Was Lost," 16.
38 As Speed, *Rights in Rebellion*, 14, explains,

> I want to suggest . . . that the researchers' engaging in a politics of reflexivity, while vitally important rendering visible the power dynamics at work in the anthropological research, is nevertheless not enough to move the discipline beyond the neocolonial framework it is bound by. A critical engagement with our research subjects, which makes them part of the process of knowledge production itself, is a vital component of a decolonized anthropology. The tension between political commitment and critical reflection will always exist to one extent or another. Activist research has the benefit of bringing that tension to the fore, maintaining it under scrutiny as part of the project, and thus potentially transforming it into a productive tension.

39 Berry et al., "Toward a Fugitive Anthropology," 538.
40 Here I take the notion of "spill" from another beautifully haunting work on violence against Women of Color, and the potential for liberatory fugitivity. See Gumbs, *Spill*.
41 Berry et al., "Toward a Fugitive Anthropology," 560.

42 See Sandoval, *Methodology of the Oppressed*.
43 As Spivak, *Critique of Postcolonial Reason*, 37, 130, puts it, "there is something Eurocentric about assuming that imperialism began with Europe." In thinking that I could possibly understand the ramifications of colonialism in total, bring the other's experience into resonance with my own, I reinforce a kind of imperialism: "No perspective *critical* of imperialism can turn the other into a self, because the project of imperialism has always already historically refracted what might have been an incommensurable and discontinuous other into a domesticated other that consolidates the imperialist self."
44 Madison, "The Labor of Reflexivity," 129.
45 Derrida, "Signature, Event, Context," 6, 10.
46 Hanchey, "Toward a Relational Politics of Representation."
47 Fellows and Razack, "The Race to Innocence."
48 Visweswaran, *Fictions of Feminist Ethnography*, 99–100.
49 Carrillo Rowe, *Power Lines*, 53.
50 The abbreviation WWOOF stands for World Wide Opportunities on Organic Farms. Through this organization, volunteers work on organic farms in exchange for room and board. More information may be found at World Wide Opportunities on Organic Farms International, "Welcome to WWOOF."
51 Hunt, "An Acoustic Register," 55.
52 Ahmed, *The Cultural Politics of Emotion*, 93.
53 Caruth, *Unclaimed Experience*, 100 (citing Freud), 106, 111.
54 Freud, "The Uncanny."
55 Rosaldo, "Imperialist Nostalgia," 121.
56 Gordon, *Ghostly Matters*, 49–50, 51–52, 190, 60.
57 Derrida, *Specters of Marx*, 11. Derrida argues that ethics and justice are not possible without recognizing ghosts since they depend on relationships to people and things *not present*: "It is necessary to speak *of the* ghost, indeed *to the* ghost and with it, from the moment that no ethics, no politics, whether revolutionary or not, seems possible and thinkable and *just* that does not recognize in its principle the respect for those others who are no longer or for those others who are not yet *there*, presently living, whether they are already dead or not yet born" (xviii, emphasis in the original).
58 Derrida, *Specters of Marx*, 5–6, 46. Undecidability is the key to ethics for Derrida. In this perspective, if one faces a situation for which there is a preordained answer, one is not really *deciding* but simply following orders or instructions. Taking a decision means facing the infinite responsibilities inherent in a situation, knowing it is impossible to meet them all, and deciding what to do anyway. Derrida, "'Eating Well,'" 167.
59 Oliver, *Witnessing*, 17.
60 Gordon, *Ghostly Matters*, 190.
61 Gordon, *Ghostly Matters*, 190.
62 Carrillo Rowe, *Power Lines*.
63 Sandoval, *Methodology of the Oppressed*, 32.

64 On differential historical relations to coloniality, see Lowe, *The Intimacies of Four Continents*. On white women and "niceness above all else," see Talley, "White Women Doing White Supremacy."
65 Visweswaran, *Fictions of Feminist Ethnography*, 77.
66 Cho, *Haunting the Korean Diaspora*.
67 Caruth, *Unclaimed Experience*, 71.
68 Bell, "'Wildest Dreams.'"
69 Oliver, *Witnessing*, 86.
70 Caruth, *Unclaimed Experience*, 106, 111.
71 Gordon, *Ghostly Matters*, 139, referring to slavery and its resonances during Reconstruction.
72 Komba, "The Search for Magical Mbuji."
73 "Incredible Mbuji Rock & Tourism Attraction in Mbinga Tanzania."
74 Mukiva Online, "Magic Stone in Tanzania."
75 Ndlovu-Gatsheni, *Epistemic Freedom in Africa*, 7–8, 80. See also Macharia, "On Being Area Studied," 183–90.
76 Ndlovu-Gatsheni, *Epistemic Freedom in Africa*, 24.
77 Derrida, *Specters of Marx*, 224, 123.
78 Valencia, *Gore Capitalism*.

CHAPTER FOUR. WATER IN THE CRACKS

1 *Basi* implies "the end," "that's enough," or "full stop," and *bwana* is a general way to refer to a person without using their name—similar to "man" or "dude," except ungendered.
2 Ndlovu-Gatsheni, *Epistemic Freedom in Africa*, 7–8, describes how Africans are allowed to register as "native informants" in the Western collection and analysis of data but not as producers of knowledge themselves. The knowledge produced in the West is then fed back to the continent for African consumption: "A long-standing asymmetrical division of intellectual labor sustains epistemic hegemony. In this context African scholars have largely functioned as 'hunter-gatherers' of raw data as well as 'native informants.' Europe and North America have remained sites of processing raw data into concepts and theories. These concepts and theories are then consumed in Africa. Africa remains a large laboratory for testing of concepts and theories."
3 Cruz and Sodeke, "Debunking Eurocentrism," 529.
4 Imas, Wilson, and Weston, "Barefoot Entrepreneurs," 568.
5 Cruz, "Reimagining Feminist Organizing," 31.
6 Cruz and Sodeke, "Debunking Eurocentrism," 532.
7 Hanchey and Berkelaar, "Context Matters"; Imas, Wilson, and Weston, "Barefoot Entrepreneurs."
8 Cruz and Sodeke, "Debunking Eurocentrism," 536, 538, 540.
9 Mumby and Stohl, "Disciplining Organizational Communication Studies," 59.
10 Broadfoot and Munshi, "Diverse Voices."

11 Jensen, "'People Can't Believe We Exist!'"
12 See, for example, Dempsey, "Negotiating Accountability"; Dempsey, "NGOs, Communicative Labor"; Ganesh, "Organizational Narcissism; Gill and Wells, "Welcome to the Hunger Games"; and Hanchey, "Reworking Resistance."
13 Jones, "The Multiple Sources of Mission Drift," 306. See also Weisbrod, "The Pitfalls of Profits."
14 Ndlovu-Gatsheni, *Epistemic Freedom in Africa*, 3.
15 Cruz, "Africa as Negative Space of Organization."
16 Jensen, "'We Help Who HUD Tells Us to Help.'"
17 Mignolo, "Delinking," 499.
18 *Kumbe* is a word marking surprise, something unexpected, or a moment of realization.
19 Cruz, "Reimagining Feminist Organizing," 31.
20 Here Arnold is using a Swahili pedagogical style of using tag questions to prompt correct fill-in-the-blank responses.
21 *Eeh* is a means of emphasizing a point or agreeing with what someone else has said.
22 Cruz and Sodeke, "Debunking Eurocentrism," 539–40.
23 *Jamani* is an ungendered word that can be used similarly to "man" in the sense of "aw, man" or "c'mon, man," and often connotes frustration or resignation.

CHAPTER FIVE. FLUID (RE)MAPPING

1 Nyerere, *Ujamaa*, 7; Rwegasira, *Land as a Human Right*, 30–31.
2 Rwegasira, *Land as a Human Right*, 88, relays how the Court of Appeal in Tanzania came to the decision to grant legal protection to customary land rights by saying that if they refused, "most of the inhabitants of Tanzania mainland are no better than squatters in their own country." Recognizing the danger should this become precedent, they instead concluded "that customary or deemed rights in land, though by their nature are nothing but rights to occupy and use the land, are nevertheless real property protected by . . . the Constitution."
3 Ndlovu-Gatsheni, *Epistemic Freedom in Africa*, 8.
4 Rwegasira, *Land as a Human Right*, 100, 104.
5 Rwegasira, *Land as a Human Right*, 30, 31.
6 Karikari, Castro-Sotomayor, and Asante, "Illegal Mining," 246.
7 Goeman, *Mark My Words*, 8.
8 As Goeman, *Mark My Words*, 15, puts it, "the settler state . . . rests on the individual." For more on the humanist individual and how it undergirds racial and colonial structures, see Lowe, *The Intimacies of Four Continents*.
9 Gardner, *Selling the Serengeti*, examines this struggle through discourses of conservation in the Serengeti, but his study similarly demonstrates that "in places . . . where property rights have remained somewhat flexible, as well as contested, neoliberalization encouraged efforts to clarify and codify property relationships. This new policy context created openings to appropriate land rights vulnerable to market-based dispossession" (152).

10 Cruz and Sodeke, "Debunking Eurocentrism," 532.
11 Goeman, *Mark My Words*, 3.
12 Goeman, *Mark My Words*, 4; Na'puti, "Archipelagic Rhetoric," 6.
13 Goeman, *Mark My Words*, 3, also explains that "(re)mapping is not just about regaining that which was lost and returning to an original and pure point in history but instead understanding the processes that have defined our current spatialities in order to sustain vibrant Native futures."
14 Ngũgĩ, *Decolonising the Mind*.
15 Ndlovu-Gatsheni, *Epistemic Freedom in Africa*, 4.
16 Mbembe, *On the Postcolony*, 104; Asante, "'Queerly Ambivalent.'"
17 Mbembe, *On the Postcolony*, 129.
18 Asante, "Queerly Ambivalent," 166.
19 Cruz and Sodeke, "Debunking Eurocentrism," 532.
20 The term used here to refer to Mr. Giles, *mzee*, simply means "elder." And even though "elder Giles" maintains the gender neutrality and respectful connotations of typical uses of the term, when referring to him in English the typical wording was "Mr. Giles." I use "Mr. Giles" throughout in order to maintain consistency. In addition, although Maurus Nomba was not referred to with an honorific in conversation, I similarly refer to him as Mr. Nomba so that my naming practices are not subtly reinforcing neocolonial hierarchies.
21 Fadhili is using a pedagogical question to which I am supposed to fill in the answer.
22 *Eeh* is a sound connoting emphasis or agreement.
23 *Basi* implies "the end," "that's enough," or "full stop."
24 "Why the hell" is not a literal translation, but it is the closest approximation in English to the *mbona* form of "why" rather than the more regular *kwa nini*, as *mbona* also connotes outrage or disbelief.
25 Rwegasira, *Land as a Human Right*, 88.
26 *Bwana* is a general way to refer to a person without using their name, similar to "man" or "dude," except ungendered.
27 For a similar example of using colonial structures against colonial logics, see Hanchey and Asante, "'How to Save the World from Aliens.'"
28 Ahmed, *Living a Feminist Life*, 135–60.
29 Stoler, "Introduction," 2.
30 Chari, "Detritus in Durban," 133.

CHAPTER SIX. THINGS FALL APART

1 Carrillo Rowe, *Power Lines*, 8.
2 Sarah and Tim had, through the years, gotten various US Peace Corps volunteers to extend their service for an extra year working with the organization.
3 *Eeh* is a sound connoting emphasis or agreement.
4 Cruz and Sodeke, "Debunking Eurocentrism," 532.
5 Cruz and Sodeke, "Debunking Eurocentrism," 532.

6 Martineau and Ritskes, "Fugitive Indigeneity," iv.
7 Asante, "'Queerly Ambivalent,'" 166.
8 Wanzer-Serrano, *The New York Young Lords*, 177.
9 Cruz and Sodeke, "Debunking Eurocentrism," 543.
10 Harney and Moten, *The Undercommons*; Rosas, "Fugitive Work."
11 I was exposed to the notion of "the edge of chaos" at a panel discussion in 2019 at WisCon, the feminist science fiction and fantasy convention. Andrea Hairston spoke about how the edges of the normative where the system begins to break down and trend toward chaos seem frightening to those ensconced in hegemonic power but liberating to those marginalized within it. At the edges of chaos, anything becomes possible—even liberation. The world must be built anew, and that is challenging. But building the world anew holds the potential for building the world differently, more justly, and better.
12 Ndlovu-Gatsheni, *Epistemic Freedom*, 80.
13 Houdek, "Racial Sedimentation," 296–97.
14 For example, Westerners often map African subjectivities onto a binary that opposes them to Western subjectivities: collective versus individual. But this is an oversimplification that attempts to make Western sense of subjective understandings that exceed Western terminology. Gyekye, *An Essay on African Philosophical Thought*, uses the metaphor of "amphibious" to try to explain Akan subjectivities, comparing them to two-headed crocodile iconography. In this understanding, individualism and communalism are both fully operative in African subjectivities in ways that cannot be made sense of under logics of coloniality.
15 Hanchey, "Catastrophe Colonialism," 2–3.
16 Cruz, "Reimagining Feminist Organizing," 31, describes collectivities based in trust as a key part of African, and particularly African feminist, organizing.
17 *Basi* implies "the end," "that's enough," or "full stop."
18 Dempsey, "NGOs, Communicative Labor"; Dempsey, "Negotiating Accountability."
19 Carrillo Rowe, *Power Lines*.
20 Stoler, "Preface," x.
21 Stoler, "Introduction," 7.
22 James Baldwin, in Peck, *I Am Not Your Negro*, 39.
23 Asante, "'Queerly Ambivalent.'"
24 Hanchey, "Reworking Resistance," 285, emphasis in the original.
25 Rosas, "Fugitive Work."
26 Berry et al., "Toward a Fugitive Anthropology," 560.
27 As I address more extensively in the conclusion, although imagination is conditioned by coloniality, by imagining differently we can bring decolonial futures into being. Eshun, "Further Considerations of Afrofuturism," 290, 292, makes the argument that the predictions of science fiction are working predominantly to imagine white, Western technocapitalist futures—and thus subtly calling us to actualize them, to bring them into being. Such control over what we imagine the future can possibly be has only tightened in the Western world. Keeling, *Queer*

Times, Black Futures, uses Shell Oil in Nigeria as a contemporary example of how corporations keep their fists tightly wound around the power of imagination in an attempt to erase the possibility that a future might exist without their corporation in it. I believe similar arguments could be made about the neocolonial work of NGOs; the very structure of the organizations do not allow for imagining a future without them in it, and we need new ways of conceptualizing them.

28 Collins, *All Tomorrow's Cultures*, 11.
29 Dempsey, "NGOs, Communicative Labor"; Dempsey, "Negotiating Accountability"; Hanchey, "Reworking Resistance," 285; Dichter, *Despite Good Intentions*.
30 Martineau and Ritskes, "Fugitive Indigeneity," IV.
31 When Ngũgĩ wa Thiong'o and two other colleagues called for the "abolition" of the Department of English at the University of Nairobi in 1967 in favor of recognizing a multiplicity of linguistic and cultural centers, their actions were nearly incomprehensible: "We had spoken the unspeakable, almost as if we had called for the end of the world." See Ngũgĩ, *Globalectics*, 9.
32 Berry et al., "Toward a Fugitive Anthropology," 560.
33 Gumbs, *M Archive*, xi.
34 See Wynter, "Unsettling the Coloniality of Being"; and Towns, "Black 'Matter' Lives."
35 Gumbs, *M Archive*, xi.
36 Ndlovu-Gatsheni, *Epistemic Freedom in Africa*.
37 *Africanfuturism* is a term coined by Nnedi Okorafor to describe her African-based science fiction work and to differentiate it from Afrofuturism. For an expanded explanation, see the conclusion to this book. See also Okorafor, "Africanfuturism Defined."

CONCLUSION

1 Here I mean entrepreneurship not in the neoliberal fashion idealized in the West, but more in the sense that is explored in Imas, Wilson, and Weston, "Barefoot Entrepreneurs": a more communal, fluid, and survival-oriented idea of entrepreneurship.
2 Gumbs, *M Archive*, xi. See also Keeling, *Queer Times, Black Futures*, 214.
3 Dempsey, "NGOs, Communicative Labor"; Dempsey, "Negotiating Accountability"; Dichter, *Despite Good Intentions*; Hanchey, "Reworking Resistance," 285; Spivak, *A Critique of Postcolonial Reason*, 6; Ahmed, *The Cultural Politics of Emotion*, 22. See also Mamdani, *Citizen and Subject*; Rodney, *How Europe Underdeveloped Africa*; and Timberg and Halperin, *Tinderbox*. Regarding aid and notions of self-understanding, see chapters 2 and 3 of this book; and Malkki, *The Need to Help*.
4 Collins, *All Tomorrow's Cultures*, 4.
5 Eshun, "Further Considerations of Afrofuturism," 290–91.
6 Eshun, "Further Considerations of Afrofuturism," 292. See also Keeling, *Queer Times, Black Futures*, 204–5.
7 Cole, "The White-Savior Industrial Complex."

8   Mbembe, *On the Postcolony*, 2.
9   Towns, "Black 'Matter' Lives."
10 Thomas, *The Dark Fantastic*, 4–7.
11 Gunn, "Black Feminist Futurity." See also Asante, "'Queerly Ambivalent,'" 159.
12 For more about how African epistemologies are often excised from aid, see Hanchey, "Reframing the Present."
13 Okorafor, *Broken Places, Outer Spaces*, 87.
14 Okorafor, "Africanfuturism Defined."
15 Eshun, "Further Considerations of Afrofuturism," 292.
16 Carrillo Rowe, *Power Lines*.
17 See Alcoff, "Problem of Speaking for Others," 157–58.
18 Keeling, *Queer Times, Black Futures*, 211.
19 According to Enck-Wanzer, "Race, Coloniality, and Geo-body Politics," 365, before one can decolonize, one must first define and understand coloniality.
20 In chapter 6 we saw how liquid organizing questions neoliberal Western rationalities in similar ways to anarchist organizing principles. See, for example, Jensen, "'People Can't Believe We Exist!'"

BIBLIOGRAPHY

Ahmed, Sara. *The Cultural Politics of Emotion.* New York: Routledge, 2004.
Ahmed, Sara. *Living a Feminist Life.* Durham, NC: Duke University Press, 2017.
Ahmed, Sara. "The Nonperformativity of Antiracism." *Meridians: Feminism, Race, Transnationalism* 7, no. 1 (2006): 104–26.
Alcoff, Linda. "The Problem of Speaking for Others." *Cultural Critique* 20, no. 1 (1991): 5–32.
Aminzade, Ronald. "The Dialectic of Nation Building in Postcolonial Tanzania." *Sociological Quarterly* 54, no. 3 (2013): 335–66.
Asante, Godfried. "Glocalized Whiteness: Sustaining and Reproducing Whiteness through 'Skin Toning' in Post-colonial Ghana." *Journal of International and Intercultural Communication* 9, no. 2 (2016): 87–103.
Asante, Godfried. "'Queerly Ambivalent': Navigating Global and Local Normativities in Postcolonial Ghana." In *Queer Intercultural Communication: The Intersectional Politics of Belonging in and across Difference,* edited by Shinsuke Eguchi and Bernadette Marie Calafell, 157–76. Lanham, MD: Rowman and Littlefield, 2020.
Asante, Godfried A., and Jenna N. Hanchey. "African Communication Studies: A Provocation and Invitation." *Review of Communication* 21, no. 4 (2021): 271–92.
Asen, Robert, and Daniel C. Brouwer, eds. *Counterpublics and the State.* Albany: State University of New York Press, 2001.
Ashcraft, Karen Lee, and Lisa A. Flores. "'Slaves with White Collars': Persistent Performances of Masculinity in Crisis." *Text and Performance Quarterly* 23, no. 1 (2003): 1–29.
Baaz, Maria Eriksson. *The Paternalism of Partnership: A Postcolonial Reading of Identity in Development Aid.* New York: Zed Books, 2005.
Baldwin, James. *Nobody Knows My Name: More Notes of a Native Son.* New York: Vintage International, 2017.
Bandini, Julia, Christine Mitchell, Zachary D. Epstein-Peterson, Ada Amobi, Jonathan Cahill, John Peteet, Tracy A. Balboni, and Michael Balboni. "Student and Faculty Reflections on the Hidden Curriculum: How Does the Hidden Curriculum Shape Students' Medical Training and Professionalization?" *American Journal of Hospice and Palliative Medicine* 34, no. 1 (2017): 57–63.

Barbie Savior. Instagram page. Accessed December 24, 2019. https://www.instagram.com/barbiesavior.

Barnett, Joshua Trey, and Kevin Michael DeLuca. "The Conditions That Form Us: Media, Affect, Social Change." *Culture, Theory and Critique* 60, no. 2 (2019): 99–106.

Bébien, Arnaud. "Education—Tanzania: Pregnant Teens Forced Out of School." *Inter Press Service*, March 10, 2010. http://www.ipsnews.net/2010/03/education-tanzania-pregnant-teens-forced-out-of-school.

Beck, Erin. *How Development Projects Persist: Everyday Negotiations with Guatemalan NGOs*. Durham, NC: Duke University Press, 2017.

Behar, Ruth. "Believing in Anthropology as Literature," in *Anthropology off the Shelf: Anthropologists on Writing*, edited by Alisse Waterston and Maria D. Vesperi, 106–16. Malden, MA: Wiley-Blackwell, 2011.

Behar, Ruth. "Ethnography and the Book That Was Lost." *Ethnography* 4, no. 1 (2003): 15–39.

Behar, Ruth. *The Vulnerable Observer: Anthropology That Breaks Your Heart*. Boston: Beacon Press, 1996.

Beliso-De Jesús, Aisha M., and Jemima Pierre. "Introduction, Special Section: Anthropology of White Supremacy." *American Anthropologist* 122, no. 1 (2020): 65–75.

Bell, Katherine. "'A Delicious Way to Help Save Lives': Race, Commodification, and Celebrity in Product (RED)." *Journal of International and Intercultural Communication* 4, no. 3 (2011): 163–80.

Bell, Katherine M. "Raising Africa? Celebrity and the Rhetoric of the White Savior." *Portal: Journal of Multidisciplinary International Studies* 10, no. 1 (2013): 1–24.

Bell, Katherine M. "'Wildest Dreams': The Racial Aura of Celebrity Safari." *Communication and Critical/Cultural Studies* 14, no. 4 (2017): 369–84.

Bergland, Renée L. *The National Uncanny: Indian Ghosts and American Subjects*. Hanover, NH: Dartmouth College Press, 2000.

Berry, Maya J., Claudia Chávez Argüelles, Shanya Cordis, Sarah Ihmoud, and Elizabeth Velásquez Estrada. "Toward a Fugitive Anthropology: Gender, Race, and Violence in the Field." *Cultural Anthropology* 32, no. 4 (2017): 537–65.

Biehl, João, Byron Good, and Arthur Kleinman. "Introduction: Rethinking Subjectivity." In *Subjectivity: Ethnographic Investigations*, edited by João Biehl, Byron Good, and Arthur Kleinman, 1–23. Berkeley: University of California Press, 2007.

Biruk, Crystal. *Cooking Data: Culture & Politics in an African Research World*. Durham, NC: Duke University Press, 2018.

Bourgois, Philippe. "Confronting the Ethics of Ethnography: Lessons from Fieldwork in Central America." In *Decolonizing Anthropology: Moving Further toward an Anthropology for Liberation*, 3rd. ed, edited by Faye V. Harrison, 111–27. Arlington, VA: American Anthropological Association, 2010.

Broadfoot, Kirsten J., and Debashish Munshi. "Diverse Voices and Alternative Rationalities: Imagining Forms of Postcolonial Organizational Communication." *Management Communication Quarterly* 21, no. 2 (2007): 249–67.

Brouwer, Daniel C., and Robert Asen, eds. *Public Modalities: Rhetoric, Culture, Media, and the Shape of Public Life*. Tuscaloosa: University of Alabama Press, 2010.

Brouwer, Daniel C., and Marie-Louise Paulesc. "Counterpublic Theory Goes Global: A Chronicle of a Concept's Emergences and Mobilities." In *What Democracy Looks Like: The Rhetoric of Social Movements and Counterpublics*, edited by Christina R. Foust, Amy Pason, and Kate Zittlow Rogness, 75–104. Tuscaloosa: University of Alabama Press, 2017.

Butler, Judith. "Changing the Subject: Judith Butler's Politics of Radical Resignification." In *The Judith Butler Reader*, edited by Sara Salih with Judith Butler, 325–56. Malden, MA: Wiley Blackwell, 2004.

Butler, Judith. "Gender Is Burning: Questions of Appropriation and Subversion." In *Dangerous Liasons: Gender, Nation, & Postcolonial Perspectives*, edited by Anne McClintock, Aamir Mufti, and Ella Shohat, 381–95. Minneapolis: University of Minnesota Press, 1997.

Cacho, Lisa Marie. "The Presumption of White Innocence." *American Quarterly* 66, no. 4 (2014): 1085–90.

Calafell, Bernadette Marie. "Monstrous Femininity: Constructions of Women of Color in the Academy." *Journal of Communication Inquiry* 36, no. 2 (2012): 111–30.

Carrillo Rowe, Aimee. *Power Lines: On the Subject of Feminist Alliances*. Durham, NC: Duke University Press, 2008.

Caruth, Cathy. "Trauma and Experience: Introduction." In *Trauma: Explorations in Memory*, edited by Cathy Caruth, 1–12. Baltimore: Johns Hopkins University Press, 1995.

Caruth, Cathy. *Unclaimed Experience: Trauma, Narrative, and History*. Baltimore: Johns Hopkins University Press, 1996.

Castillo, Debra A., and Shalini Puri. "Introduction: Conjectures on Undisciplined Research." In *Theorizing Fieldwork in the Humanities: Methods, Reflections, and Approaches to the Global South*, edited by Shalini Puri and Debra A. Castillo, 1–25. New York: Palgrave Macmillan, 2016.

Chari, Sharad. "Detritus in Durban: Polluted Environs and the Biopolitics of Refusal." In *Imperial Debris: On Ruins and Ruination*, edited by Ann Laura Stoler, 131–61. Durham, NC: Duke University Press, 2013.

Chávez, Karma R. "Beyond Inclusion: Rethinking Rhetoric's Historical Narrative." *Quarterly Journal of Speech* 101, no. 1 (2015): 162–72.

Chávez, Karma R. *Queer Migration Politics: Activist Rhetoric and Coalitional Possibilities*. Urbana: University of Illinois Press, 2013.

Chevrette, Roberta. "Assembling Global (Non)belongings: Settler Colonial Memoryscapes and the Rhetorical Frontiers of Whiteness in the US Southwest, Christians United for Israel, and FEMEN." PhD diss., Arizona State University, 2016.

Cho, Grace M. *Haunting the Korean Diaspora: Shame, Secrecy, and the Forgotten War*. Minneapolis: University of Minnesota Press, 2008.

Cloud, Dana L. "The Irony Bribe and Reality Television: Investment and Detachment in *The Bachelor*." *Critical Studies in Media Communication* 27, no. 5 (2010): 413–37.

Cloud, Dana L. "'To Veil the Threat of Terror': Afghan Women and the <Clash of Civilizations> in the Imagery of the U.S. War on Terrorism." *Quarterly Journal of Speech* 90, no. 3 (2004): 285–306.

Cloud, Dana L. *We Are the Union: Democratic Unionism and Dissent at Boeing.* Urbana: University of Illinois Press, 2011.

Cole, Teju. "The White-Savior Industrial Complex." *Atlantic,* March 21, 2012. http://www.theatlantic.com/international/archive/2012/03/the-white-savior-industrial-complex/254843/.

Collins, Samuel Gerald. *All Tomorrow's Cultures: Anthropological Engagements with the Future.* New York: Berghahn Books, 2008.

Colpean, Michelle, and Rebecca Dingo. "Beyond Drive-by Race Scholarship: The Importance of Engaging Geopolitical Contexts." *Communication and Critical/Cultural Studies* 15, no. 4 (2018): 306–11.

Colpean, Michelle, and Meg Tully. "Not Just a Joke: Tina Fey, Amy Schumer, and the Weak Reflexivity of White Feminist Comedy." *Women's Studies in Communication* 42, no. 2 (2019): 161–80.

Corrigan, Lisa M. "Decolonizing Philosophy and Rhetoric: Dispatches from the Undercommons." *Philosophy and Rhetoric* 52, no. 2 (2019): 163–88.

Corrigan, Lisa M. *Prison Power: How Prison Influenced the Movement for Black Liberation.* Jackson: University Press of Mississippi, 2016.

Cram, E. *Violent Inheritance: Sexuality, Land, and Energy in Making the North American West.* Berkeley: University of California Press, 2022.

Cruz, Joëlle M. "Africa as Negative Space of Organization." Unpublished manuscript, April 16, 2020.

Cruz, Joëlle M. "Introduction: African Feminist and Queer Coalitions." *Women's Studies in Communication* 43, no. 2 (2020): 101–5.

Cruz, Joëlle M. "Reimagining Feminist Organizing in Global Times: Lessons from African Feminist Communication." *Women and Language* 38, no. 1 (2015): 23–41.

Cruz, Joëlle M., and Chigozirim Utah Sodeke. "Debunking Eurocentrism in Organizational Communication Theory: Marginality and Liquidities in Postcolonial Contexts." *Communication Theory* 31, no. 3 (2021): 528–48.

D'Amico-Samuels, Deborah. "Undoing Fieldwork: Personal, Political, Theoretical and Methodological Implications." In *Decolonizing Anthropology: Moving Further toward an Anthropology for Liberation,* 3rd ed., edited by Faye V. Harrison, 68–87. Arlington, VA: American Anthropological Association, 2010.

Das, Veena. "The Act of Witnessing: Violence, Poisonous Knowledge, and Subjectivity." In *Violence and Subjectivity,* edited by Veena Das, Arthur Kleinman, Mamphela Ramphele, and Pamela Reynolds, 205–25. Berkeley: University of California Press, 2000.

Das, Veena, and Arthur Kleinman. "Introduction." In *Violence and Subjectivity,* edited by Veena Das, Arthur Kleinman, Mamphela Ramphele, and Pamela Reynolds, 1–18. Berkeley: University of California Press, 2000.

Das, Veena, Arthur Kleinman, Margaret Lock, Mamphela Ramphele, and Pamela Reynolds, eds. *Remaking a World: Violence, Social Suffering, and Recovery.* Berkeley: University of California Press, 2001.

Das, Veena, Arthur Kleinman, Mamphela Ramphele, and Pamela Reynolds, eds. *Violence and Subjectivity.* Berkeley: University of California Press, 2000.

Davis, Diane. *Inessential Solidarity: Rhetoric and Foreigner Relations.* Pittsburgh: University of Pittsburgh Press, 2010.

Davis, Diane, and Michelle Baliff, eds. "Extrahuman Rhetorical Relations: Addressing the Animal, the Object, the Dead, and the Divine." Special issue, *Philosophy and Rhetoric* 47, no. 4 (2014).

De Onís, Catalina. *Energy Islands: Metaphors of Power, Extractivism, and Justice in Puerto Rico.* Berkeley: University of California Press, 2021.

Dempsey, Sarah E. "Negotiating Accountability within International Contexts: The Role of Bounded Voice." *Communication Monographs* 74, no. 3 (2007): 311–32.

Dempsey, Sarah E. "NGOs, Communicative Labor, and the Work of Grassroots Representation." *Communication and Critical/Cultural Studies* 6, no. 4 (2009): 328–45.

Derrida, Jacques. "'Eating Well,' or the Calculation of the Subject: An Interview with Jacques Derrida," translated by Peter Connor and Avital Ronell. In *Who Comes after the Subject?*, edited by Eduardo Cadava, Peter Connor, and Jean-Luc Nancy, 96–119. New York: Routledge, 1991.

Derrida, Jacques. "Signature Event Context," translated by Samuel Weber and Jeffrey Mehiman. In *Limited Inc*, edited by Gerald Graff, 1–24. Evanston, IL: Northwestern University Press, 1988.

Derrida, Jacques. *Specters of Marx: The State of the Debt, the Work of Mourning, and the New International.* Translated by Peggy Kamuf. New York: Routledge, 2006.

DiAngelo, Robin. "White Fragility." *International Journal of Critical Pedagogy* 3, no. 3 (2011): 54–70.

Dichter, Thomas W. *Despite Good Intentions: Why Development Assistance to the Third World Has Failed.* Amherst: University of Massachusetts Press, 2003.

Dutta, Mohan J. "Hunger as Health: Culture-Centered Interrogations of Alternative Rationalities of Health." *Communication Monographs* 79, no. 3 (2012): 366–84.

Dutta, Mohan J., and Ambar Basu, "Meanings of Health: Interrogating Structure and Culture." *Health Communication* 23, no. 6 (2008): 560–72.

Easterly, William. *The White Man's Burden: Why the West's Efforts to Aid the Rest Have Done So Much Ill and So Little Good.* New York: Penguin, 2007.

Enck-Wanzer, Darrel. "Race, Coloniality, and Geo-body Politics: *The Garden* as Latin@ Vernacular Discourse." *Environmental Communication* 5, no. 3 (2011): 363–71.

Endres, Danielle, and Mary Gould. "'I Am Also in the Position to Use My Whiteness to Help Them Out': The Communication of Whiteness in Service Learning." *Western Journal of Communication* 73, no. 4 (2009): 418–36.

Eshun, Kodwo. "Further Considerations of Afrofuturism." *New Centennial Review* 3, no. 2 (2003): 287–302.

Fellows, Mary Louise, and Sherene Razack. "The Race to Innocence: Confronting Hierarchical Relations among Women." *Journal of Gender, Race, and Justice* 1, no. 4 (1998): 335–52.

Ferguson, James. *Global Shadows: Africa in the Neoliberal World Order.* Durham, NC: Duke University Press, 2006.

Freud, Sigmund. "The Uncanny." In *The Uncanny*, translated by David McLintock, 121–62. New York: Penguin, 2003.

Ganesh, Shiv. "Organizational Narcissism: Technology, Legitimacy, and Identity in an Indian NGO." *Management Communication Quarterly* 16, no. 4 (2003): 558–94.

Gardner, Benjamin. *Selling the Serengeti: The Cultural Politics of Safari Tourism*. Athens: University of Georgia Press, 2016.

Garrett, Mary. "Tied to a Tree: Culture and Self-Reflexivity." *Rhetoric Society Quarterly* 43, no. 3 (2013): 243–55.

Gill, Rebecca, and Celeste C. Wells. "Welcome to the Hunger Games: An Exploration of the Rhetorical Construction of Legitimacy for One U.S.-Based Nonprofit Organization." *Management Communication Quarterly* 28, no. 1 (2014): 26–55.

Gilliam, Angela. "Militarism and Accumulation as Cargo Cult." In *Decolonizing Anthropology: Moving Further toward an Anthropology for Liberation*, 3rd ed., edited by Faye V. Harrison, 170–91. Arlington, VA: American Anthropological Association, 2010.

Glicken, Anita Duhl, and Gerald B. Merenstein. "Addressing the Hidden Curriculum: Understanding Educator Professionalism." *Medical Teacher* 29, no. 1 (2007): 54–57.

Goeman, Mishuana. *Mark My Words: Native Women Mapping Our Nations*. Minneapolis: University of Minnesota Press, 2013.

Goldstein, Daniel M. "Laying the Body on the Line: Activist Anthropology and the Deportation of the Undocumented." *American Anthropologist* 116, no. 4 (2014): 839–42.

Gordon, Avery. *Ghostly Matters: Haunting and the Sociological Imagination*. Minneapolis: University of Minnesota Press, 2008.

Gordon, Jeremy G., Katherine D. Lind, and Saul Kutnicki, eds. "A Rhetorical Bestiary." Special issue, *Rhetoric Society Quarterly* 47, no. 3 (2017).

Goltz, Dustin Bradley. "It Gets Better: Queer Futures, Critical Frustrations, and Radical Potentials." *Critical Studies in Media Communication* 30, no. 2 (2013): 135–51.

Grandin, Greg. "Empire's Ruins: Detroit to the Amazon." In *Imperial Debris: On Ruins and Ruination*, edited by Ann Laura Stoler, 115–30. Durham, NC: Duke University Press, 2013.

Grosfoguel, Ramón. "The Epistemic Decolonial Turn: Beyond Political-Economy Paradigms." *Cultural Studies* 21, nos. 2–3 (2007): 211–23.

Gumbs, Alexis Pauline. *M Archive: After the End of the World*. Durham, NC: Duke University Press, 2018.

Gumbs, Alexis Pauline. *Spill: Scenes of Black Feminist Fugitivity*. Durham, NC: Duke University Press, 2016.

Gunn, Caitlin. "Black Feminist Futurity: From Survival Rhetoric to Radical Speculation." *Feral Feminisms*, no. 9 (2019). https://feralfeminisms.com/black-feminist-futurity-from-survival-rhetoric-to-radical-speculation/.

Gunn, Joshua. "Father Trouble: Staging Sovereignty in Spielberg's War of the Worlds." *Critical Studies in Media Communication* 25, no. 1 (2008): 1–27.

Gunn, Joshua. "Refitting Fantasy: Psychoanalysis, Subjectivity, and Talking to the Dead." *Quarterly Journal of Speech* 90, no. 1 (2004): 1–23.

Gunnarsdottir, Elsa, and Kathryn Mathers. "'Doing Good' in an Age of Parody." *Africa Is a Country*, January 11, 2017. http://africasacountry.com/2017/01/doing-good-in-an-age-of-parody/.

Gyekye, Kwame. *An Essay on African Philosophical Thought: The Akan Conceptual Scheme.* Rev. ed. Philadelphia: Temple University Press, 1995.

Hale, Charles R. "Introduction." In *Engaging Contradictions: Theory, Politics, and Method of Activist Scholarship*, edited by Charles R. Hale, 1–28. Berkeley: University of California Press, 2008.

Hall, Stuart. "The Whites of Their Eyes: Racist Ideologies and the Media." In *Gender, Race, and Class in Media: A Text Reader*, edited by Gail Dines and Jean M. Humez, 89–93. Thousand Oaks, CA: Sage, 2003.

Hanchey, Jenna N. "Agency beyond Agents: Aid Campaigns in Sub-Saharan Africa and Collective Representations of Agency." *Communication, Culture and Critique* 9, no. 1 (2016): 11–29.

Hanchey, Jenna N. "Catastrophe Colonialism: Global Disaster Films and the White Right to Migrate." *Journal of International and Intercultural Communication* (2022). https://doi.org/10.1080/17513057.2022.2093392.

Hanchey, Jenna N. "Constructing 'American Exceptionalism': Peace Corps Volunteer Discourses of Race, Gender, and Empowerment." In *Volunteering and Communication*, vol. 2, *Studies in International and Intercultural Contexts*, edited by Michael W. Kramer, Laurie K. Lewis, and Loril M. Gossett, 233–50. New York: Peter Lang, 2015.

Hanchey, Jenna N. "A Postcolonial Analysis of Peace Corps Volunteer Narratives: The Political Construction of the Volunteer, Her Work, and Her Relationship to 'The Host Country National.'" Master's thesis, University of Colorado–Boulder, 2012.

Hanchey, Jenna N. "Reframing the Present: Mock Aid Videos and the Foreclosure of African Epistemologies." *Women and Language* 42, no. 2 (2019): 119–47.

Hanchey, Jenna N. "Reworking Resistance: A Postcolonial Perspective on International NGOs." In *Transformative Practice and Research in Organizational Communication*, edited by Phillip J. Salem and Erik Timmerman, 274–91. Hershey, PA: IGI Global, 2018.

Hanchey, Jenna N. "Toward a Relational Politics of Representation." *Review of Communication* 18, no. 4 (2018): 265–83.

Hanchey, Jenna N., and Godfried Asante. "'How to Save the World from Aliens, Yet Keep Their Infrastructure': Repurposing the 'Master's House' in *The Wormwood Trilogy*." *Feminist Africa* 2, no. 2 (2021): 11–28.

Hanchey, Jenna N., and Brenda L. Berkelaar. "Context Matters: Examining Discourses of Career Success in Tanzania." *Management Communication Quarterly* 29, no. 3 (2015): 411–39.

Harney, Stefano, and Fred Moten. *The Undercommons: Fugitive Planning & Black Study.* New York: Minor Compositions, 2013.

Harris, Cheryl I. "Whiteness as Property." *Harvard Law Review* 106, no. 8 (1993): 1707–91.

Harris, Kate Lockwood, and Jenna N. Hanchey. "(De)stabilizing Sexual Violence Discourse: Masculinization of Victimhood, Organizational Blame, and Labile Imperialism." *Communication and Critical/Cultural Studies* 11, no. 4 (2014): 322–41.

Harrison, Faye V. "Anthropology as an Agent of Transformation: Introductory Comments and Queries." In *Decolonizing Anthropology: Moving Further toward an Anthropology for Liberation*, 3rd ed., edited by Faye V. Harrison, 1–15. Arlington, VA: American Anthropological Association, 2010.

Harrison, Faye V. *Outsider Within: Reworking Anthropology in the Global Age*. Urbana: University of Illinois Press, 2008.

Hartman, Saidiya. *Lose Your Mother: A Journey along the Atlantic Slave Route*. New York: Farrar, Straus and Giroux, 2007.

Hegde, Radha. "Fragments and Interruptions: Sensory Regimes of Violence and the Limits of Feminist Ethnography." *Qualitative Inquiry* 15, no. 2 (2009): 276–96.

Hoerl, Kristin. *The Bad Sixties: Hollywood Memories of the Counterculture, Antiwar, and Black Power Movements*. Jackson: University Press of Mississippi, 2018.

Holsey, Bayo. *Routes of Remembrance: Refashioning the Slave Trade in Ghana*. Chicago: University of Chicago Press, 2008.

Houdek, Matthew. "Racial Sedimentation and the Common Sense of Racialized Violence: The Case of Black Church Burnings." *Quarterly Journal of Speech* 104, no. 3 (2018): 279–306.

Humanitarians of Tinder. Website. Accessed December 24, 2019. http://humanitariansoftinder.com.

Hunt, Nancy Rose. "An Acoustic Register: Rape and Repetition in Congo." In *Imperial Debris: On Ruins and Ruination*, edited by Ann Laura Stoler, 220–53. Durham, NC: Duke University Press, 2013.

Hunt, Nancy Rose. *A Colonial Lexicon: Of Birth Ritual, Medicalization, and Mobility in the Congo*. Durham, NC: Duke University Press, 1999.

Hunt, Nancy Rose. *A Nervous State: Violence, Remedies, and Reverie in Colonial Congo*. Durham, NC: Duke University Press, 2016.

Imas, Miguel, Nick Wilson, and Alia Weston. "Barefoot Entrepreneurs." *Organization* 19, no. 5 (2012): 563–85.

"Incredible Mbuji Rock & Tourism Attraction in Mbinga Tanzania." *Sixtz Blog*, July 4, 2016. https://sixtz.blogspot.com/2016/07/incredible-mbuji-rock-tourism.html.

Inui, Thomas S. *A Flag in the Wind: Educating for Professionalism in Medicine*. Washington, DC: Association of American Medical Colleges, 2003.

Jensen, Peter R. "'People Can't Believe We Exist!': Social Sustainability and Alternative Nonprofit Organizing." *Critical Sociology* 44, no. 2 (2018): 375–88.

Jensen, Peter R. "'We Help Who HUD Tells Us to Help': Epistemology and Agency at Two Nonprofit Organizations." *Western Journal of Communication* (2022). https://doi.org/10.1080/10570314.2022.2118551.

Jensen, Peter R., Joëlle M. Cruz, Elizabeth K. Eger, Jenna N. Hanchey, Angela N. Gist-Mackey, Kristina Ruiz-Mesa, and Astrid Villamil. "Pushing beyond Positionalities and through 'Failures' in Qualitative Organizational Communication: Experiences and Lessons on Identities in Ethnographic Praxis." *Management Communication Quarterly* 34, no. 1 (2020): 121–51.

Johnson, Ann. "The Subtleties of Blatant Sexism." *Communication and Critical/Cultural Studies* 4, no. 2 (2007): 166–83.

Johnson, Paul E. "The Art of Masculine Victimhood: Donald Trump's Demagoguery." *Women's Studies in Communication* 40, no. 3 (2017): 229–50.

Johnson, Paul E. "Walter White(ness) Lashes Out: *Breaking Bad* and Male Victimage." *Critical Studies in Media Communication* 34, no. 1 (2017): 14–28.

Jones, Delmos J. "Epilogue." In *Decolonizing Anthropology: Moving Further toward an Anthropology for Liberation*, 3rd ed., edited by Faye V. Harrison, 192–98. Arlington, VA: American Anthropological Association, 2010.

Jones, Marshall B. "The Multiple Sources of Mission Drift." *Nonprofit and Voluntary Sector Quarterly* 36, no. 2 (2007): 299–307.

"JPM Closes Debate on Teen Mothers." *Citizen* (Tanzania), June 23, 2017. https://www.thecitizen.co.tz/news/JPM-closes-debate-on-teen-mothers/1840340-3983644-6nleokz/index.html.

Karikari, Eric, José Castro-Sotomayor, and Godfried Asante. "Illegal Mining, Identity, and the Politics of Ecocultural Voice in Ghana." In *Routledge Handbook of Ecocultural Identity*, edited by Tema Millstein and José Castro-Sotomayor, 240–59. New York: Routledge, 2020.

Keeling, Diane Marie. "Of Turning and Tropes." *Review of Communication* 16, no. 4 (2016): 317–33.

Keeling, Kara. *Queer Times, Black Futures*. New York: New York University Press, 2019.

Kelly, Casey Ryan. *Food Television and Otherness in the Age of Globalization*. Lanham, MD: Lexington Books, 2017.

Kelly, Casey Ryan. "The Man-pocalypse: *Doomsday Preppers* and the Rituals of Apocalyptic Manhood." *Text and Performance Quarterly* 36, nos. 2–3 (2016): 95–114.

Kelly, Casey Ryan. "Neocolonialism and the Global Prison in National Geographic's *Locked Up Abroad*." *Critical Studies in Media Communication* 29, no. 4 (2012): 331–47.

Kelly, Casey Ryan. "Women's Rhetorical Agency in the American West: *The New Penelope*." *Women's Studies in Communication* 32, no. 2 (2009): 203–31.

Kelly, Casey Ryan. "The Wounded Man: *Foxcatcher* and the Incoherence of White Masculine Victimhood." *Communication and Critical/Cultural Studies* 15, no. 2 (2018): 161–78.

King, Claire Sisco. "It Cuts Both Ways: *Fight Club*, Masculinity, and Abject Hegemony." *Communication and Critical/Cultural Studies* 6, no. 4 (2009): 366–85.

King, Claire Sisco. "The Man Inside: Trauma, Gender, and the Nation in *The Brave One*." *Critical Studies in Media Communication* 27, no. 2 (2010): 111–30.

Kleinman, Arthur. "The Violence of Everyday Life: Multiple Forms and Dynamics of Social Violence." In *Violence and Subjectivity*, edited by Veena Das, Arthur Kleinman, Mamphela Ramphele, and Pamela Reynolds, 226–41. Berkeley: University of California Press, 2000.

Kleinman, Arthur, and Erin Fitz-Henry. "The Experiential Basis of Subjectivity: How Individuals Change in the Context of Societal Transformation." In *Subjectivity: Ethnographic Investigations*, edited by João Biehl, Byron Good, and Arthur Kleinman, 52–65. Berkeley: University of California Press, 2007.

Komba, Neema. "The Search for Magical Mbuji." In *Safe House: Explorations in Creative Nonfiction*, edited by Ellah Wakatama Allfrey, 233–48. Toronto: Dundurn, 2016.

Lacan, Jacques. "The Subversion of the Subject and the Dialectic of Desire in the Freudian Unconscious." In *Ecrits: The First Complete Edition in English*, translated by Bruce Fink, 671–702. New York: W. W. Norton, 2006.

Lavelle, Kristen M. *Whitewashing the South: White Memories of Segregation and Civil Rights*. Lanham, MD: Rowman and Littlefield, 2015.

Lechuga, Michael. "An Anticolonial Future: Reassembling the Way We Do Rhetoric." *Communication and Critical/Cultural Studies* 17, no. 4 (2020): 378–85.

Loperena, Christopher Anthony. "A Divided Community: The Ethics and Politics of Activist Research." *Current Anthropology* 57, no. 3 (2016): 332–40.

Lowe, Lisa. *The Intimacies of Four Continents.* Durham, NC: Duke University Press, 2015.

Lugones, María. *Pilgrimages/Peregrinajes: Theorizing Coalition against Multiple Oppressions.* Lanham, MD: Rowman and Littlefield, 2003.

Macharia, Keguro. "On Being Area Studied: A Litany of Complaint." *GLQ: A Journal of Lesbian and Gay Studies* 22, no. 2 (2016): 183–90.

Mack, Noel Ashley, and Tiara Na'puti. "'Our Bodies Are Not Terra Nullius': Building a Decolonial Feminist Resistance to Gendered Violence." *Women's Studies in Communication* 42, no. 3 (2019): 347–70.

Madison, D. Soyini. "The Labor of Reflexivity." *Cultural Studies ↔ Critical Methodologies* 11, no. 2 (2011): 129–38.

Maldonado-Torres, Nelson. "On the Coloniality of Being: Contributions to the Development of a Concept." *Cultural Studies* 21, nos. 2–3 (2007): 240–70.

Malkki, Liisa H. *The Need to Help: The Domestic Arts of International Humanitarianism.* Durham, NC: Duke University Press, 2015.

Mama, Amina. *Beyond the Masks: Race, Gender and Subjectivity.* New York: Routledge, 1995.

Mamdani, Mahmood. *Citizen and Subject: Contemporary Africa and the Legacy of Late Colonialism.* Princeton, NJ: Princeton University Press, 1996.

Martineau, Jarrett, and Eric Ritskes. "Fugitive Indigeneity: Reclaiming the Terrain of Decolonial Struggle through Indigenous Art." *Decolonization: Indigeneity, Education and Society* 3, no. 4 (2014): i–xii.

May, Matthew S. "The Orator-Machine: Autonomist Marxism and William D. 'Big Bill' Haywood's Cooper Union Address." *Philosophy and Rhetoric* 45, no. 4 (2012): 429–51.

Mbembe, Achille. *Critique of Black Reason.* Durham, NC: Duke University Press, 2017.

Mbembe, Achille. *On the Postcolony.* Berkeley: University of California Press, 2001.

McCann, Bryan J. *The Mark of Criminality: Rhetoric, Race, and Gangsta Rap in the War-on-Crime Era.* Tuscaloosa: University of Alabama Press, 2017.

McClintock, Anne. *Imperial Leather: Race, Gender and Sexuality in the Colonial Contest.* New York: Routledge, 1995.

McKinnon, Sara, Robert Asen, Karma R. Chávez, and Robert Glenn Howard, eds. *Text + Field: Innovations in Rhetorical Method.* University Park: Pennsylvania State University Press, 2016.

Middleton, Michael, Aaron Hess, Danielle Endres, and Samantha Senda-Cook. *Participatory Critical Rhetoric: Theoretical and Methodological Foundations for Studying Rhetoric in Situ.* Lanham, MD: Lexington Books, 2015.

Mignolo, Walter D. "Delinking: The Rhetoric of Modernity, the Logic of Coloniality and the Grammar of De-coloniality." *Cultural Studies* 21, nos. 2–3 (2007): 449–514.

Molina, Natalia. *How Race Is Made in America.* Berkeley: University of California Press, 2014.

Morris, Charles E., III. "(Self-)Portrait of Prof. R.C.: A Retrospective." *Western Journal of Communication* 74, no. 1 (2010): 4–42.

Moyo, Dambisa. *Dead Aid: Why Aid Is Not Working and How There Is a Better Way for Africa*. New York: Farrar, Straus and Giroux, 2009.
Mumby, Dennis K., and Cynthia Stohl. "Disciplining Organizational Communication Studies." *Management Communication Quarterly* 10, no. 1 (1996): 50–72.
Muñoz, José Esteban. *Cruising Utopia: The Then and There of Queer Futurity*. New York: New York University Press, 2009.
Muvika Online. "Magic Stone in Tanzania and You Do Not Need to Want to Work!!" Steemit, June 6, 2018. https://steemit.com/magic/@muvikaonline/magic-stone-in-tanzania-and-you-do-not-need-to-want-to-work.
Na'puti, Tiara R. "Archipelagic Rhetoric: Remapping the Marianas and Challenging Militarization from 'A Stirring Place.'" *Communication and Critical/Cultural Studies* 16, no. 1 (2019): 4–25.
Na'puti, Tiara R. "From Guåhan and Back: Navigating a 'Both/Neither' Analytic for Rhetorical Field Methods." In *Text + Field: Innovations in Rhetorical Method*, edited by Sara L. McKinnon, Robert Asen, Karma R. Chávez, and Robert Glenn Howard, 56–71. University Park: Pennsylvania State University Press, 2016.
Na'puti, Tiara R. "Speaking of Indigeneity: Navigating Genealogies against Erasure and #RhetoricSoWhite." *Quarterly Journal of Speech* 105, no. 4 (2019): 495–501.
National Communication Association. "Distinguished Scholars." Accessed June 6, 2021. https://www.natcom.org/distinguished-scholars.
National Communication Association. "2019 NCA Organizational Communication Division Top Paper Panel Account." Memorandum. Accessed June 6, 2021. https://docs.google.com/document/d/1SmrkYHByhyiyLZlg8kY1gCOrFGtnyE795pY89fLkcHw/edit.
Ndlovu-Gatsheni, Sabelo J. *Epistemic Freedom in Africa: Deprovincialization and Decolonization*. New York: Routledge, 2018.
Ngũgĩ wa Thiong'o. *Decolonising the Mind: The Politics of Language in African Literature*. Portsmouth, NH: Heinemann, 1986.
Ngũgĩ wa Thiong'o. *Globalectics: Theory and the Politics of Knowing*. New York: Columbia University Press, 2012.
Nyerere, Julius K. *Ujamaa: Essays on Socialism*. Dar es Salaam: Oxford University Press, 1968.
Ogone, James Odhiambo. "Epistemic Injustice: African Knowledge and Scholarship in the Global Context." In *Postcolonial Justice*, edited by Nicole Waller, Anke Bartels, Dirk Wiemann, and Lars Eckstein, 17–36. Leiden, Netherlands: Koninklijke Brill NV, 2017.
Okorafor, Nnedi. "Africanfuturism Defined." *Nnedi's Wahala Zone Blog*, October 19, 2019. https://nnedi.blogspot.com/2019/10/africanfuturism-defined.html.
Okorafor, Nnedi. *Broken Places, Outer Spaces: Finding Creativity in the Unexpected*. New York: Simon and Schuster, 2019.
Oliver, Kelly. *Witnessing: Beyond Recognition*. Minneapolis: University of Minnesota Press, 2001.
Ono, Kent A. *Contemporary Media Culture and the Remnants of a Colonial Past*. New York: Peter Lang, 2009.

Peck, Raoul, dir. *I Am Not Your Negro.* New York: Vintage International, 2017. Companion book to the documentary film, based on texts by James Baldwin.

Petray, Theresa L. "A Walk in the Park: Political Emotions and Ethnographic Vacillation in Activist Research." *Qualitative Research* 12, no. 5 (2012): 554–64.

Pezzullo, Phaedra. *Toxic Tourism: Rhetorics of Pollution, Travel, and Environmental Justice.* Tuscaloosa: University of Alabama Press, 2007.

Pierre, Jemima. "Activist Groundings or Groundings for Activism? The Study of Racialization as a Site of Political Engagement." In *Engaging Contradictions: Theory, Politics, and Method of Activist Scholarship*, edited by Charles R. Hale, 115–35. Berkeley: University of California Press, 2008.

Pindi, Gloria Nziba. "Promoting African Knowledge in Communication Studies: African Feminisms as Critical Decolonial Praxis." *Review of Communication* 21, no. 4 (2021): 327–44.

Pratt, Mary Louise. *Imperial Eyes: Travel Writing and Transculturation.* New York: Routledge, 2008.

Puri, Shalini. "Finding the Field: Notes on Caribbean Cultural Criticism, Area Studies, and the Forms of Engagement." In *Theorizing Fieldwork in the Humanities: Methods, Reflections, and Approaches to the Global South*, edited by Shalini Puri and Debra A. Castillo, 29–50. New York: Palgrave Macmillan, 2016.

Richey, Lisa Ann, and Stefano Ponte. *Brand Aid: Shopping Well to Save the World.* Minneapolis: University of Minnesota Press, 2011.

Ritchie, Marnie. "Feeling for the State: Affective Labor and Anti-Terrorism Training in US Hotels." *Communication and Critical/Cultural Studies* 12, no. 2 (2015): 179–97.

Ritchie, Michelle. "An Autoethnography on the Geography of PTSD." *Journal of Loss and Trauma: International Perspectives on Stress and Coping* 24, no.1 (2019): 69–83.

Rodney, Walter. *How Europe Underdeveloped Africa.* Baltimore: Black Classic Press, 2011.

Rosaldo, Renato. *The Day of Shelly's Death: The Poetry and Ethnography of Grief.* Durham, NC: Duke University Press, 2014.

Rosaldo, Renato. "Ilongot Visiting: Social Grace and the Rhythms of Everyday Life." In *Creativity/Anthropology*, edited by Smadar Lavie, Kirin Narayan, and Renato Rosaldo, 253–69. Ithaca, NY: Cornell University Press, 1993.

Rosaldo, Renato. "Imperialist Nostalgia." *Representations*, no. 26 (1989): 107–22.

Rosas, Gilberto. "Fugitive Work: On the Criminal Possibilities of Anthropology." Society for Cultural Anthropology, September 26, 2018. https://culanth.org/fieldsights/fugitive-work-on-the-criminal-possibilities-of-anthropology.

Rushdie, Salman. *The Satanic Verses: A Novel.* New York: Random House, 2018.

Rwegasira, Abdon. *Land as a Human Right: A History of Land Law and Practice in Tanzania.* Dar es Salaam: Mkuki na Nyota Press, 2012.

SAIH Norway. "Africa for Norway—New Charity Single Out Now!" Video, 3:44. YouTube, November 16, 2012. https://www.youtube.com/watch?v=oJLqyuxm96k.

Saks, Elyn R. *The Center Cannot Hold: My Journey through Madness.* New York: Hyperion, 2008.

Sandoval, Chela. *Methodology of the Oppressed.* Minneapolis: University of Minnesota Press, 2000.

Scheper-Hughes, Nancy. *Death without Weeping: The Violence of Everyday Life in Brazil.* Berkeley: University of California Press, 1992.

Scheper-Hughes, Nancy. "A Talent for Life: Reflections on Human Vulnerability and Resilience." *Ethnos* 73, no. 1 (2008): 25–56.

Schieffelin, Edward L. "Performance and the Cultural Construction of Everyday Reality: A New Guinea Example." In *Creativity/Anthropology*, edited by Smadar Lavie, Kirin Narayan, and Renato Rosaldo, 270–95. Ithaca, NY: Cornell University Press, 1993.

Schwartz-DuPre, Rae Lyn. "Portraying the Political: *National Geographic*'s 1985 Afghan Girl and a US Alibi for Imperialism." *Critical Studies in Media Communication* 27, no. 4 (2010): 336–56.

Shaw, Carolyn Martin. *Colonial Inscriptions: Race, Sex, and Class in Kenya.* Minneapolis: University of Minnesota Press, 1995.

Shivji, Issa G., Saida Yahya-Othman, and Ng'wanza Kamata. *Development as Rebellion: A Biography of Julius Nyerere.* 3 vols. Dar es Salaam: Mkuki na Nyota, 2020.

Smith, James Howard. *Bewitching Development: Witchcraft and the Reinvention of Development in Neoliberal Kenya.* Chicago: University of Chicago Press, 2008.

Speed, Shannon. *Rights in Rebellion: Indigenous Struggle and Human Rights in Chiapas.* Stanford, CA: Stanford University Press, 2007.

Spivak, Gayatri Chakravorty. *A Critique of Postcolonial Reason: Toward a History of the Vanishing Present.* Cambridge: Harvard University Press, 1999.

Steeves, H. Leslie. "Commodifying Africa on U.S. Network Reality Television." *Communication, Culture and Critique* 1, no. 4 (2008): 416–46.

Stoler, Ann Laura. "Introduction: 'The Rot Remains'; From Ruins to Ruination." In *Imperial Debris: On Ruins and Ruination*, edited by Ann Laura Stoler, 1–35. Durham, NC: Duke University Press, 2013.

Stoler, Ann Laura. "Preface." In *Imperial Debris: On Ruins and Ruination*, edited by Ann Laura Stoler, ix–xi. Durham, NC: Duke University Press, 2013.

Sullivan, Noelle. "International Clinical Volunteering in Tanzania: A Postcolonial Analysis of a Global Health Business." *Global Public Health* 13, no. 3 (2018): 310–24.

Talley, Heather Laine. "White Women Doing White Supremacy in Nonprofit Culture." *Woke@Work* blog, Equity in the Center, October 2, 2019. https://equityinthecenter.org/white-women-doing-white-supremacy-in-nonprofit-culture/.

Talton, Benjamin, and Quincy T. Mills. "Race and Gender in Research and Writing in Africa and Its Diasporas: An Introduction." In *Black Subjects in Africa and Its Diasporas: Race and Gender in Research and Writing*, edited by Benjamin Talton and Quincy T. Mills, 1–14. New York: Palgrave Macmillan, 2011.

Thomas, Ebony Elizabeth. *The Dark Fantastic: Race and the Imagination from Harry Potter to the Hunger Games.* New York: New York University Press, 2019.

Ticktin, Miriam. *Casualties of Care: Immigration and the Politics of Humanitarianism in France.* Berkeley: University of California Press, 2011.

Timberg, Craig, and Daniel Halperin. *Tinderbox: How the West Sparked the AIDS Epidemic and How the World Can Finally Overcome It.* New York: Penguin, 2013.

Towns, Armond R. "Black 'Matter' Lives." *Women's Studies in Communication* 41, no. 4 (2018): 349–58.

Tuck, Eve, and K. Wayne Yang. "Decolonization Is Not a Metaphor." *Decolonization: Indigeneity, Education and Society* 1, no. 1 (2012): 1–40.

Underman, Kelly, and Laura Hirschfield. "Detached Concern? Emotional Socialization in Twenty-First Century Medical Education." *Social Science and Medicine*, no. 160 (2016): 94–101.

Valencia, Sayak. *Gore Capitalism.* Translated by John Pluecker. Cambridge: MIT Press, 2018.

Visweswaran, Kamala. *Fictions of Feminist Ethnography.* Minneapolis: University of Minnesota Press, 1994.

Wanzer, Darrel Allan. "Delinking Rhetoric, or Revisiting McGee's Fragmentation Thesis through Decoloniality." *Rhetoric and Public Affairs* 15, no. 2 (2012): 647–58.

Wanzer-Serrano, Darrel. *The New York Young Lords and the Struggle for Liberation.* Philadelphia: Temple University Press, 2015.

Weheliye, Alexander G. *Habeas Viscus: Racializing Assemblages, Biopolitics, and Black Feminist Theories of the Human.* Durham, NC: Duke University Press, 2014.

Weisbrod, Burton A. "The Pitfalls of Profits." *Stanford Social Innovation Review* 2, no. 3 (2004): 40–47.

World Wide Opportunities on Organic Farms International. "Welcome to WWOOF." Accessed March 8, 2016. http://wwoofinternational.org.

Wynter, Sylvia. "Unsettling the Coloniality of Being/Power/Truth/Freedom: Towards the Human, After Man, Its Overrepresentation—An Argument." CR: *The New Centennial Review* 3, no. 3 (2003): 257–337.

Young, Allan. "America's Transient Mental Illness: A Brief History of the Self-Traumatized Perpetrator." In *Subjectivity: Ethnographic Investigations*, edited by João Biehl, Byron Good, and Arthur Kleinman, 155–78. Berkeley: University of California Press, 2007.

INDEX

Achebe, Chinua, 1
activist anthropology, 15, 199n59, 199n61, 205n1
activist research/scholarship, 12–15, 89, 99, 198n46, 205n42, 208n38
affective economy, 63
African Americans, 76–77
African epistemologies, 10–11, 17, 119, 139, 146, 189–90, 215n12
Africanfuturism, 184, 190, 214n37
African organizing, 10–11, 119–24, 139, 213n16. *See also* liquid organizing
agency. *See* liquid agency
Ahmed, Sara, 87–88, 95, 163, 202n24, 205n2, 206n15, 207n25
American exceptionalism, 12, 61–62, 78, 98, 113
Aminzade, Ronald, 14
anthropology, 94, 99, 196n18, 198nn47–48; activist, 15, 199n59, 199n61, 205n1; decolonial, 5, 208n38; fear of good writing, 89, 197n33, 198n46; focus on "the other," 9; fugitive, 4, 15; and methodology of book, 4, 9, 12–13. *See also* ethnography
anti-Blackness, 14–15, 119
anxiety, 27–28, 41–43, 163
Asante, Godfried, 14
Asian Americans, 107
Austria, 102

Baldwin, James, 58, 197n31, 206n18
Beck, Erin, 4, 7
Behar, Ruth, 89, 99, 198n47
Belgium, 165
Beliso-De Jesús, Aisha, 12
Berkelaar, Brenda, 120

Berry, Maya, 13, 15, 99, 184, 199n59, 199n61, 205n1, 205n42
Black volunteers, 65, 74–77, 80–84
Bourgois, Philippe, 199n59, 199n61
Broadfoot, Kirsten, 121
Butler, Judith, 30, 61, 63, 197n29

Cacho, Lisa Marie, 96
Canada, 60, 69, 139, 157, 159
capitalism, 4, 15, 18–19, 151, 169, 188, 202n14; techno-, 213n27. *See also* neoliberalism
Carrillo Rowe, Aimee, 18, 56, 62–63, 93, 107
Caruth, Cathy, 97–98, 109
Chamoru People, 146
Chávez Argüelles, Claudia, 13, 99, 184
China, 107
class, 15, 36, 198n47
Cloud, Dana, 63–64, 73
coalition of knowledges, 16
Cole, Teju, 30, 62, 80, 188
collectivity, 17, 21, 129, 172, 174–77, 189
Collins, Samuel Gerald, 183, 187
colonial amnesia, 20–21, 93–95, 102
colonialism, definition, 10
coloniality, definition, 9–10
Colpean, Michelle, 89, 205n1
communal responsibility, 144, 154–59, 161, 168, 174
communication studies, 97, 207n30
community hall, 7, 38, 48, 117–19, 139, 141–43, 164–65, 182
contact zones, 5–6, 18, 162, 196n19, 197n33
Cordis, Shanya, 13, 99, 184
Court of Appeal, 211n2

critical development studies, 4–5
Cruz, Joëlle, 10–11, 17, 120–21, 131–32, 145, 147, 195n3, 213n16
customary use, 142, 144, 147, 151–52, 154, 211n2

Dar es Salaam, 25, 44, 77, 103
Das, Veena, 207n20
death, 118, 124, 139, 153, 200n70, 204n30, 207n20; and haunted reflexivity, 92–93, 96, 99, 102–13; and HIV/AIDS care, 16; of Joe, 2, 91, 99, 102–13; in "making a difference" discourse, 65–66
decolonial anthropology, 5, 208n38
decolonial coconspirators, 3, 6, 20, 95
decolonial dreamwork, 4, 19–20, 22, 189–90, 192–93
decolonial justice, 6, 20, 86, 95, 100–101
decontextualization, 67, 71–73, 109
Democratic Republic of the Congo, 168
denial, 20, 63–64, 66–67, 80–81, 172; of fragility, 31, 34; through decontextualization, 71–73; through rewording, 69–71, 76; through slippage, 67–69
Derrida, Jacques, 101, 105, 113, 209nn57–58
development, 4–6, 12, 14–16, 19–20, 29, 54, 144, 184; development goals, 7
displacement, 18, 51, 67, 74–77, 109
donors, 4, 7, 19, 58, 69, 127, 175–78, 187; donor control, 132–40, 192; and land, 142–48, 154–61; and liquid vs. solid logics, 14, 17, 21, 119–23, 132–40, 155, 189; and NGO collapse, 165–74, 179, 181, 183; of technology, 118–19

efficiency, 27–28, 37, 40–41, 52, 55
empathy, 27–28, 177
English language, 32, 53, 65, 79, 124, 129, 155, 179, 212n20, 212n24
entrepreneurship, 120, 187, 214n1
environmental justice, 18
epistemic freedom, 9, 19, 197n35, 201n86
epistemic injustice, 10–11, 21, 27, 40, 111–12, 122, 137, 143, 145–47, 210n2; and donor control, 139–40; material effects of, 159–61
epistemic justice, 17, 122, 147, 172, 197n35
epistemological injustice, 3, 21, 143–47, 189
Eshun, Kodwo, 195n6, 213n27
ethics, 6, 56, 105, 166, 177, 209nn57–58; anthropological, 199n61; ethical debt, 31; medical, 26, 47, 51, 54, 84

ethnocentrism, 15
ethnography, 2, 5, 12, 99, 198n47, 205n35, 205n41
Eurocentrism, 209n43
exceptionalism, 35, 74, 77, 204n33; American, 12, 61–62, 78, 98, 113; and irony, 77–80

Facebook, 132
fantasy, 97, 99, 179, 197n31; and haunted reflexivity, 101, 108–9; of neocolonialism, 26–27, 28–34, 39, 56, 59–87; and subject formation, 8, 18, 61; of white masculinity, 28–34, 39, 56; of white saviorism, 2, 15, 59–87, 98, 188
Fellows, Mary Louise, 207n23
femininity, 29–30, 57
feminism, 205n1, 207n23, 213n11; African, 11, 200n64, 213n16; Black, 15, 200n64; Women of Color, 4–5, 18
Finland, 60
fluid epistemologies, 10–11, 16, 57, 164, 171, 173, 189, 198n44
fluidity, definition, 145
fluid organizing, 120–23, 128, 130–32, 167
fluid (re)mapping, 21, 141–62, 189, 212n13
foreclosure, 9, 17, 119, 183–84, 195n8; and subjectivity, 20, 60–63, 87, 197n29; and white saviorism, 20, 60, 64, 84–85
fragility, 156, 163–64; embracing, 51–55; of white masculinity, 20, 30–31, 34, 36, 41–45
Freud, Sigmund, 109
frontier, 29, 31, 57, 202n24
fugitivity, 14, 99, 171–73, 183, 200n64, 208n40; fugitive anthropology, 4, 15

Gardner, Benjamin, 211n9
gender. *See* femininity; feminism; masculinity; patriarchy
Ghana, 14, 77
ghosts, 3, 27, 56, 85, 164, 190, 209n57; and haunted reflexivity, 20–21, 64, 90–98, 102–6, 109–14. *See also* haunted reflexivity
Global North, 62, 195n8
Global South, 10, 28–29, 99, 120, 195n8
Goeman, Mishuana, 144–46, 212n13
Goldstein, Daniel M., 199n61
Gordon, Avery, 105, 110
Great Britain, 62, 132, 139, 179; British colonialism, 2, 7, 69, 150, 191–92. *See also* United Kingdom

Grosfoguel, Ramón, 10
Guardian Department, 125
Gumbs, Alexis Pauline, 184–85, 187
Gunn, Joshua, 29–30
Gunnarsdottir, Elsa, 63
Gyekye, Kwame, 213n14

Hagati Valley, 1, 90, 164
Hairston, Andrea, 213n11
Hale, Charles R., 198n46
Hall, Stuart, 29
Harrison, Faye, 16, 197n32, 198n46
haunted reflexivity, 3, 13, 19, 20, 26–27, 31, 57, 60, 88–91, 197n31; and death, 92–93, 96, 99, 102–13; and fantasy, 101, 108–9; and innocence, 21, 92–114, 189–90; and liquid agency, 6, 16–17, 100; and trauma, 56, 64, 90, 93–99, 109
Health and Medicine Department, 130, 157
heteronormativity, 18, 94, 98
heteropatriarchy, 13
hidden curriculum, 27, 33, 55
Hirschfield, Laura, 28
HIV/AIDS, 32, 46, 49–50, 53, 58, 71, 128, 181; and home-based care, 7, 16
HIV/AIDS Care and Treatment Center (CTC), 58–59, 181
Home-Based Care program, 7, 16, 129, 134–35, 181
humanitarianism, 61
human supremacy, 18

ideology, 4–6, 8, 15, 35, 62, 64, 105, 144, 189, 205n11
Ihmoud, Sarah, 13
imperial nostalgia, 15
Indigenous peoples, 14
innocence, 207n28; and haunted reflexivity, 21, 92–114, 189–90; and neocolonialism, 81, 86, 92; race to, 101, 207n23
interculturality, 12–13, 18, 86, 88, 143, 198n48
interdisciplinarity, 11–16, 201n76
International Monetary Fund, 144
intersubjective care, 20
irony, 21, 81–82, 85–87, 108, 139, 182; and exceptionalism, 77–80; irony bribe, 64; and white saviorism, 20, 63–64, 66–67, 73–80
ivory tower saviorism, 59, 83, 85

Japan, 107
Jensen, Peter, 121–22, 132

Keeling, Kara, 201n76
Kelly, Casey Ryan, 28
Kenya, 65, 77
Kleinman, Arthur, 206n16

Lacan, Jacques, 61, 197n29, 207n20
Lake Nyasa, 2
land, 10, 21, 108, 111–12, 119, 173, 177, 180, 189, 192, 202n14; and donor control, 142–48, 154–61; and NGO funding, 34, 143–44, 147–54, 160–61, 165, 167–70, 178, 186; as property, 141–54, 157–62, 167–71, 174–75, 211n2, 211n9; racially gendered, 29–30, 66; as separable, 145, 147–48, 154–57, 159
Land Act (1999), 144
Lavelle, Kristen, 67
law, 8, 26, 29–30, 35, 96, 121, 203n32; land law, 141–54, 211n2, 211n9. *See also* customary use; property
liberalism, 11, 13, 100, 145, 184
Liberia, 10, 120
liquid agency, 21–22, 182–84, 187; definition, 3–4; and haunted reflexivity, 6, 16–17, 100; and NGO collapse, 146–47, 162, 164, 171–79, 189
liquid organizing, 3, 10, 17, 21, 119–32, 137, 139, 174, 191, 198n44, 215n20; definition, 11; and (re)mapping, 145–46, 161–62, 189
Lowe, Lisa, 17, 201n85
Lugones, María, 205n1

Madison, D. Soyini, 93, 100
madness, 14
"making a difference" discourse, 62, 65–66, 68, 73–74
Mama, Amina, 62, 70
Man, 12–13, 197n35
masculinity, 98–99, 202n14; and fantasy, 28–34, 39, 56; fragility of, 20, 30–31, 34, 36, 41–45; and paternalism, 26, 35–36, 43; and sovereignty, 29–31, 34–39, 41–43, 55; white, 13, 15, 20, 26–31, 34–57, 188, 202n24
Mathers, Kathryn, 63
Mbembe, Achille, 188, 200n65, 208n36
Mbuji, 2, 111–112, 163
medical missions, 20, 28–32, 55–57, 202n24
melancholia, 94, 206n19
methodology of book, 2, 4, 9, 12–13. *See also* ethnography

Mignolo, Walter, 9–10
Mills, Quincy, 86
mission drift, 121
modernity/coloniality, 9
Molina, Natalia, 29, 201n85
Morris, Charles, III, 89
Mumby, Dennis, 121
Munshi, Debashish, 121
Mwanza, 181

Na'puti, Tiara, 13, 117, 146
National Communication Association, 97, 207n30
nation-state, 12, 198
Ndlovu-Gatsheni, Sabelo, 56, 111, 119, 141, 200n65; on epistemic freedom and justice, 10, 17, 122, 143, 197n35; on "native informants," 210n2
(neo)colonialism, definition, 10
neoliberalism, 4, 11, 15, 98, 144, 169, 177, 211n9, 214n1, 215n20. *See also* capitalism
Ngũgĩ wa Thiong'o, 10, 25, 146, 163, 184, 214n31
Nigeria, 10, 77, 120, 213n27
non-racialism, 14–15, 200n70
Nyerere, Julius, 15, 144, 200n70

Okafor, Nnedi, 185
Oliver, Kelly, 106

participation (Swahili meaning), 129
paternalism, 6, 31, 56, 60, 68, 79, 99, 186, 208n36; and white masculinity, 26, 35–36, 43
patient-centered care, 28
patriarchy, 5, 184; hetero-, 13
Peace Corps, 2, 7, 88, 90, 102–3, 163, 168, 212n2
Pierre, Jemima, 12
Pindi, Gloria Nziba, 200n64
politics of care, 13
politics of relation, 18, 177, 208n36
postcolonialism, definition, 10
Pratt, Mary Louise, 196n19
praxis, 13, 15, 86, 122
precarity, 21, 106–7, 120, 123, 139, 147
property, 186; land as, 141–54, 157–62, 167–71, 174–75, 211n2, 211n9; whiteness as, 96
psychoanalysis, 8, 20, 61

qualifications, 62, 78–79
queerness, 14, 99

racial-colonial systems, 19, 81, 85, 105, 184, 192, 208n36
racialization: and anthropology, 12, 15, 99, 196n18, 205n11; and colonialism, 5, 15, 90, 94, 177, 189, 196n13, 201n85; of volunteers, 60, 62
racial privilege, 13, 62, 74, 77–78, 86, 98, 199n59
racial scripts, 29
racial violence, 56, 84–85, 90, 92
racism, 31, 94, 97, 113, 192; anti-Black, 14–15, 119; and white saviorism, 80–86. *See also* white supremacy
rationality, 9–10, 77, 101, 120–21, 145, 197n35, 215n20
Razack, Sherene, 207n23
redirection, 16, 139, 168, 171, 172–74, 182
relationality, 11, 17–18, 31, 34, 45, 48, 84, 122, 177
research travel, 86
rhetoric (scholarly field), 4, 198nn46–48, 199n53, 206n9; and methodology of book, 4–5; and reflexivity, 89; and relationality, 18; and white saviorism, 5, 12–13
Rosaldo, Renato, 86–87, 203n33
ruination, 3, 162, 172, 187–88; and liquid agency, 177–79, 182; productive, 6–9
Rushdie, Salman, 88
Ruvuma Region, 1

Saks, Elyn, 8, 98, 99
Sandoval, Chela, 107
Schieffelin, Edward L., 205n41
schizophrenia, 8, 98
service and leadership trips, 65, 78
Seventh Day Adventists, 34
sexuality, 10, 13, 15, 29, 89, 94, 99. *See also* heteronormativity
Shell Oil, 213n27
slavery, 4, 14, 196n19, 210n71
Smith, James Howard, 196n26
socialism, 14–15, 144
social justice, 7
social media, 63. *See also* Facebook
Sodeke, Chigozirim Utah, 10–11, 17, 120–21, 131–32, 145, 147
solidarity, 120
South Africa, 15
sovereignty, 57, 100, 107; challenging, 45–48; masculine, 29–31, 34–39, 41–43, 55
Speed, Shannon, 208n38

Spivak, Gayatri Chakravorty, 61, 195n8, 197n29, 209n43
Stohl, Cynthia, 121
Stoler, Ann Laura, 6, 206n19
study abroad, 64–65
Swahili language, 32–33, 37, 42, 48, 52, 65, 129, 155, 211n20
Sweden, 60

Talton, Benjamin, 86
theory, 9–10, 13, 15, 61, 90–91, 109, 206n19; decolonial, 18; feminist, 200n64
Ticktin, Miriam, 13
time management, 27–28, 37
tourism, 86, 111, 144, 148; voluntourism, 60, 64, 69, 78, 86
translators, 181; medical students' treatment of, 20, 26–27, 32–49, 53–56, 188
trauma, 63, 192, 207n23; and haunted reflexivity, 56, 64, 90, 93–99, 109; self-traumatized perpetrator, 95, 206n19
trust-based organizing, 11, 120, 124
Tuck, Eve, 207n23
Tully, Meg, 89, 205n1

Uganda, 179
uncertainty, 31, 48–51
underdevelopment, 30, 44
Underman, Kelly, 28
United Kingdom, 60. *See also* Great Britain
United States, 2, 52, 62, 65–66, 68, 77–80, 85, 92, 139, 149, 156, 168; aid from, 60–61; and colonial amnesia, 94; enabled by death, 113; medicine in, 26, 33, 43–45, 51; race in, 107, 197n31; and rhetoric, 12; and white masculinity, 20, 28
University of Nairobi, 214n31
US Medical Licensing Examination, 33

Velásquez Estrada, Elizabeth, 13, 99, 184
Village Land Act (1999), 144

villagization, 14
Viongozi Wa Shirika, 2–3, 14, 67, 149, 155, 181; and liquid agency, 16, 172, 174–76; and liquid organizing, 21, 122, 126–33, 137–38; and liquid (re)mapping, 157–59
Visweswaran, Kamala, 101, 108
voluntourism, 60, 64, 69, 78, 86

Walcott, Derek, 6
Wanzer, Darrel, 9, 198n46
weak reflexivity, 89, 205n1
white masculinity, 13, 20, 26–31, 34–57, 188, 202n24
whiteness and colonialism, 2, 5, 86, 95–97, 112–13, 197n31; and epistemic injustice, 17; and irony, 80–81; and methodology of book, 13–14, 92
whiteness as property, 96
white saviorism, 5–6, 45, 190, 208n36; and denial, 20, 67–73, 80; and fantasy, 2, 15, 59–87, 98, 188; and irony, 20, 63–64, 66–67, 73–80; and ivory tower saviorism, 59, 83; and methodology of book, 15, 20; and nostalgia, 84–87; in rhetoric, 12–13; white savior industrial complex, 30, 188–89
white supremacy, 73, 77–78, 90, 196n18
The Wild Thornberrys, 66
WisCon, 213n11
witnessing, 21, 102–13, 158, 207n20
World Wide Opportunities on Organic Farms (WWOOF), 102, 209n50
Wynter, Sylvia, 13

Yang, K. Wayne, 207n23
Yeats, W. B., 1, 193
Young, Allan, 94, 206n19
Youth Leaders Tanzania, 182, 186–87, 192–93

Zimbabwe, 45
Žižek, Slavoj, 63

www.ingramcontent.com/pod-product-compliance
Lightning Source LLC
Chambersburg PA
CBHW020835160426
43192CB00007B/664